THE GREATEST SHOWS ON EARTH

A History of the Circus

LINDA SIMON

REAKTION BOOKS

Published by Reaktion Books Ltd
33 Great Sutton Street
London EC1V 0DX, UK

www.reaktionbooks.co.uk

First published 2014
Copyright © Linda Simon 2014

Printed and bound in China by Toppan Printing Co. Ltd

A catalogue record for this book is available from the British Library

ISBN 978 1 78023 358 1

CONTENTS

Dancing Girl, Egyptian, 1292–1186 BCE, painted limestone.

INTRODUCTION

And if you ever came home, you came home in a gilded chariot . . .
William Dean Howells

Wherever the circus came from, it started like this: someone captivated attention by doing what others could not do. This was a display of startling agility: walking on one's hands. Springing from hands to feet, over and over. Juggling balls, or knives. Bending so far that one's head jutted from under the genitals, with legs wrapped around the neck. In short, making a spectacle of oneself. The body as spectacle is the origin of the circus.

In the Museo Egizio, in Turin, a wall fragment from 1300 to 1200 BCE depicts a figure of a dancing girl, an acrobat, her long, black hair skimming the ground, her back arched, balancing on hands and feet. At the Los Angeles Museum of Art, a Mexican ceramic statuette of a contortionist dates from 200 BCE to 500 CE, and a painted ceramic statuette, even older, shows a man doing the splits. His hands are raised triumphantly above his head; he is grinning broadly, exultant. A statuette from Hellenic Greece depicts a young, nude African acrobat, his body raised upward from his hands. If acrobatics began in play – the simple joy of doing a somersault – these performers honed that sense of play into theatrics, evoking admiration, wonder, envy, fear – responses shared by artists who, from ancient times, captured these fleeting exhibitions.

In ancient Rome, during interludes between chariot races, gladiator contests and animal baiting, jugglers and acrobats trotted into the vast arena to offer light diversion. Some such performers displayed their

Ceramic acrobat,
from Xochipala,
Mexico,
900–500 BCE.

Slip-painted ceramic
acrobat, Mexican,
200 BCE–500 CE.

Netsuke of an
acrobat, Japanese,
18th century,
wood with inlay.

talents at religious rites or court gatherings. Some took to the road. In ancient Greece and China, tumblers and dancers travelled to village harvest festivals; throughout medieval Europe, such showmen were popular attractions at the many local fairs: Bartholomew, St Giles and Scarborough in England and Saint-Germain and Saint-Laurent in France, to name just a few. Itinerant performers, who arrived from somewhere else and disappeared, were news in themselves, different, exotic, even a bit dangerous. Some travelled with musicians, jesters, fortune tellers and dancers, living together in caravans.

Some strung taut ropes above the commerce of the fair and walked from one side to the other, pretending to waver and lose their footing; they drew crowds eager to see foolish people risk their lives. Viewers were at once astonished and terrified. Funambulists, after all, did fall from great heights, and they died. When they succeeded, rumours flew: they were in league with the Devil, they were sorcerers who could work miracles, they were something more than human. There seemed a blurred line between the miraculous and the sham.

In fifth-century France, mountebanks, who occasionally walked on slack ropes, were forbidden by a series of councils of bishops to perform at religious festivals, and in the ninth century rope dancers, in particular, were outlawed. Animosity might have been generated by their defiling sanctified property by stringing ropes between steeples; or because they charged for their performance, and took money that should be going to the Church; or simply because they flaunted themselves. In the fourteenth century, when a noted rope dancer lost his footing and fell, shattering his bones, King Charles v gave voice to what others were thinking: 'Surely,' said the king when he learned of it, 'bad luck must befall the man who presumes so much of his senses, his strength, his lightness or any other thing.'[1]

The girl who walked barefoot on hot coals, the woman who drank boiling oil, the strong man who could balance eight other men on a plank across his chest, the man who swallowed fire – these acts stretched, but did not break, the credulity of the audience. They made some wonder: what could humans do? What should they do?

Some performers brought animals they had trained to do tricks: dogs paraded on their hind legs and one, at least, could answer questions about history; monkeys in costumes climbed ropes; turkeys danced; and cats, even, were taught to play the dulcimer. Some acrobats dressed as fierce animals – lions or tigers – and terrorized the audience. Some travelled with trained bears, others wore bear costumes. Some entertained with puppets. All wore gaudy costumes, spangled, tasselled, piped with silver or flesh-coloured, the better to evoke nakedness. Memoirs of fairs often remark on buttocks and breasts and shapely legs.

Some travelled with their own booths and a makeshift stage, platform or bench, from which they hawked potions to cure this or that ailment. Of course, they performed: handsprings, contortions, somersaults, cartwheels. They became known as mountebanks or, if they entertained by leaping, saltimbanques, terms that came to be applied, often disparagingly, to any wandering troupes. Merchants encouraged the performers, whatever they wanted to do. Crowds of spectators meant potential customers. Petty thieves, especially pickpockets, were fond of them, too.

William Hogarth,
Southwark Fair,
1734.

When they were not performing at fairs, mountebanks and saltimbanques entertained on the outskirts of cities and towns. To some artists they seemed romantic figures, gathering in their own small communities, outsiders to bourgeois society. Honoré Daumier's saltimbanques look sad and discouraged and poor. Questing for recognition and affirmation, they gaze longingly at the bustling commercial world whose attention they covet. In one drawing, a performer holds his head in his hands, as if overcome with dejection. Picasso's saltimbanques, a suite of paintings made shortly after he arrived in Paris early in the twentieth century, also portray nomadic performers, sometimes in groups that look like families. Like Daumier's, Picasso's gaunt

'The Mysteries of the Life of the Saltimbanque', from *L'Illustration Européenne*, 1872.

saltimbanques gather at the margins of a world that cares little for them after they entertain. But these depictions of entertainers, captured in repose, contrast with the vibrant, stirring energy that drew viewers to their performances.

Some mountebanks staged short playlets or pantomimes, comic or tragic, with music or dancing. These troupes competed at fairs or festivals with professional players, who might have honed their performances for aristocratic audiences at court. Beginning in the sixteenth century, travelling acting companies with a distinctive cast of characters drew audiences in Milan, Florence and Venice, and soon after in Paris, Madrid and London. Their comedies featured a pair or two of lovers, typically Harlequin and Columbine, and a cast of bawdy characters who thwarted the lovers' happiness: the devious servant Arlechino, for example; the miserly merchant Pantalone; the lecher, often a hunchback, Pulcinella; and the hapless, clumsy zannis. Sometimes masked, always flamboyantly costumed, these characters were precursors to clowns. Early in the eighteenth century, some 200 years after this improvised, itinerant theatre appeared in Europe, the Italian dramatist Carlo Goldoni dubbed it *commèdia dell'arte* – theatre that informed music halls, vaudeville and most certainly the circus.

The feats and antics of individual performers, however, do not define the event completely. The circus requires an assembly, an audience, to acknowledge the spectacle and experience it together. In 1838, when Nathaniel Hawthorne saw a travelling menagerie during a trip to the Berkshires in Massachusetts, he marvelled not so much at the animals as at the viewers' response: 'A man put his arm and his head into the lion's mouth, all the spectators looking on so attentively that a breath could not be heard. That was impressive, its effect on a thousand persons, more so than the thing itself.'[2] That common experience required a distinct space rather than the distracting marketplace of the fair, 'swarming', as one spectator put it, 'with prostitutes, buffoons and all manner of rabble'.[3] The circus, wrote the poet E. E. Cummings, 'may be described as a gigantic spectacle; *which is surrounded by an audience*, in contrast to our modern theatres, where an audience and a spectacle merely confront each other'.[4]

The circus, therefore, has links to the ancient Roman arena where thousands upon thousands gathered to witness public games. Central to these games were two-horse chariot races, fraught with danger. Friezes and sarcophagi depicted the victorious charioteer, trailed by the fallen and the injured, often with twisted or broken limbs. On children's tombs, circus scenes were one of the most popular decorations, with the winged Erotes or cupids in place of human charioteers. The Roman circus celebrated human superiority: of one man over another, of man over beast. Hundreds of lions, tigers, elephants and bears were slaughtered during weeks of festivals. Sometimes men were themselves victims: army deserters, for example, who

The actor Paul Legrand as Pierrot, by Charles-Michel Geoffroy, 1855.

Edgar Degas, *Harlequin and Columbine, c.* 1884, pastel.

were sacrificed for the games. Sometimes animals were forced into the arena to tear each other apart. Bloody, dangerous, cruel: huge audiences – the Circus Maximus held nearly 4,000 – watched mortal combat, and they cheered.

During the Renaissance, at the same time that the *commèdia dell'arte* gained popularity, interest in the ancient Roman games revived in Italy, inspiring artists' paintings and sketches, architectural and garden designs, and even the casting of circus images on coins. The strenuous and perilous circus games evoked a sense of national solidarity and civic glory. As circuses developed, performers' distinct talents were often associated with particular national character. 'The French were graceful and daring on the trapeze', noted the circus historian George Speaight; 'the Germans were clever and methodical in the Icarian games; the Anglo-Saxons were vigorous and full of endurance in carpet acrobatics and on horseback; the Spaniards were supple and light; the Italians impetuous; the Japanese hieratic in balancing; the Arabs fiery, as if the burning wind of the Sahara was animating them.'[5] Some performers took stage names designed to evoke those connotations, and circus managers touted the ethnic diversity of their performers. The nineteenth-century British impresario George Van Hare, for example, summed up his offerings:

> The Brothers Beri, the Gymnastic Marvels of the World. Mdlle Clementine, Mdlle Josephine, the greatest Bare-back Equestrienne in the World, in her extraordinary Courbette, leaping through Forty Baloons [sic], &c. Mr Neville, premier Equestrian of America. Romero, Luigi, Herr Christoff, the Phenomenon, on the Sué le Corde. The great troupe of Bedouin Arabs. Les Freres Daniels, les virtuosos comiques. Clowns: Dan Castello, the great American Clown and Leaper; Harry Croueste, the Queen's Jester; M. Oriel and Mr H. Lupino. Tom Mathews, the Grimaldi of the day, and Burlesque Horse Tamer . . .[6]

Viewers had no way of knowing, nor did they care, if Luigi was Italian or the Bedouin Arabs were men from Liverpool, their skin bronzed with make-up. The circus displayed the world.

Lofty perfection

What the circus has meant for audiences in the past, what it means to us now, has been shaped in part by individuals' experiences at performances and in part by representations of the circus in art and literature. Those perceptions have combined to create the cultural myth of the circus: dazzling and fantastic, a living cabinet of wonders, a theatre of the improbable and even the impossible, an escape from reality – not only the escape afforded by a few hours of diversion, but escape from the circumscribed reality of one's daily life. To run off and join the circus means to slough off responsibility, to return to childhood, to leave the confines of one's community and set out for parts unknown. To become part of circus magic, to find yourself in the spotlight of a darkened ring, the center of attention; to don a mask or a costume and transform your identity; to fly through the air; to sit atop an elephant, riding into town at the head of a resplendent parade; to crack a whip in a cage of ferocious lions; even to squirt water from a toy gun and make thousands of people laugh.

The circus entices us with the possibility of reinvention, especially of reinventing and perfecting one's body. Aerial and acrobatic acts, central to the circus experience, present us with bodies magnificently strong and controlled, performing feats ever more daring and death-defying. Like viewers at the grisly Roman games, we are lured by the spectacle of terrifying risks. Our empathy for the performers' peril reflects, at the same time, our desire to inhabit those amazing bodies, and to achieve the performers' transcendence: 'the elevating of players – clowns, fools, mimes, jesters, musicians, puppets, dwarves, aerialists – above the status of ordinary mortals', as the art historian Naomi Ritter puts it. 'The acrobat's lofty perfection translates readily into a divine grace . . . the soaring aerialist embodies that image of freedom'.[7] Acrobats and aerialists have inspired artists and writers to consider their own vulnerability to failure, and to muster the courage that they perceive in circus performers.[8]

To assume shared motivations for artists' fascination with the circus, though, is to ignore some significant differences. While some artists identified with the marginality of circus performers, others

'Male and Female Trapeze Performers', American poster, 1875.

Mâle and Female Trapeze Performers.

Entered according to Act of Congress, in the year 1879, by Currier &Ives, in the Office of the Librarian of Congress at Washington.   Currier Company, Buffalo, N.Y.

celebrated their visibility, their being the object of the audience's rapt gaze. Some artists saw circus performers as wilfully subversive, defiant of conventions; others, as victims of social constrictions. Some saw circus performers as wild beings, revealing humans' visceral animal instincts; others, as superhuman, defying material forces. These artists, notes the circus historian Joanne Joys, interpret circus performers 'as if they were the last manifestations of the angelic spirit on earth since they are compelled to overcome the limitations of the world and its gravity by an almost religious asceticism and by their cheerful familiarity with death and what lies beyond'.[9] Among many artists who drew and painted aerialists, Paul Klee was enchanted with their vibrancy and energy. The tightrope represented for him a visual metaphor for earth and the aerialist a figure who defies gravity; but we need to be careful, I think, about how we understand this defiance – in the dark Nietzschean sense of a rope dancer over an abyss? Or as an expression of joy and freedom? As a performer despising the force that draws him to earth? Or, as Klee suggested, one who learns to balance the forces that act upon him? The complexity of artists' attraction to the circus reveals itself in their works, and those works contribute to our own understanding of the cultural meaning of the circus.

A gaudy dream

The circus has given us the myth of a world within the world. From the time of travelling mountebanks and saltimbanques, we have thought of the archetypal circus as a tight-knit community, of performers living together, sharing a special language, not connected – and refusing to be connected – to the mundane lives of their audiences. 'The lure of the circus is for the Outside World to feel', equestrienne Josephine Robinson wrote in a memoir. 'They see the flashing spangles gleam in the light as the bareback rider flies by, her whole body poised to meet her horse's motion. They are fascinated by the spangle shimmer, and the circus becomes to them a thing of whirling magic.' But even though performers know the hard work and training that produce that magical effect, Robinson admitted that the circus offers a special, embracing community: 'For us, the lure of the circus is the laugh of comrades, the helping hand in need, the sympathy at a fall, the little big things that make life possible and lovely.'[10]

Anthropologist Kenneth Little, travelling with a contemporary European circus, confirmed that circus artists rarely venture into the towns or cities where they perform. They prefer socializing with other performers, feeling out of place if they are on their own. When Little suggested to a performer to whom he was teaching English that they stroll around the city and practice the language by talking about what they saw, the artist refused. 'He was dead set against such a suggestion,' Little recalled, complaining that he would never be able to concentrate on the lesson. Asked why this would be the case, he said he never felt safe away from his camping trailer.[11] The image of the circus community offering safety, sympathy, and understanding has become part of the circus myth.

'What every boy expected to do, some time or other,' William Dean Howells wrote early in the twentieth century, 'was to run off. He expected to do this because the scheme offered an unlimited field to the imagination, and because its fulfillment would give him the highest distinction among the other fellows.' And 'the true way of running off', Howells proclaimed, was joining the circus.

> Then, if you were ever seen away from home, you were seen tumbling through a hoop and alighting on the crupper of a bare-backed piebald, and if you ever came home you came home in a gilded chariot, and you flashed upon the domestic circle in flesh-colored tights and spangled breech-cloth.[12]

For Howells and other boys growing up in small Midwestern towns, circuses – and so many toured the country that barn sides were covered with a kaleidoscope of alluring posters – intimated the possibility of stardom, glamour and reinvention. The circus offered the 'true way of running off' from the constraints of whatever reality lay before you.

In 1839, the New York *Knickerbocker* reported a conversation overheard between two villagers who had just seen the circus in their town: one tells the other that the circus manager offered him a job: 'to go along with him, and see a little of the world, what I've always a great hankerin' for, and the great folks of the world, and a sight of things that I and you never dreamed of, and wont never dream of, if we stay here from now to never.' Seriously considering the offer, the villager asks his friend to join him:

> We should pull together han'somely, and make our fortunes . . . What takes my eye, these circus-actors live like gentlemen. They crack their jokes, they do, drink their wine, and live on the fat o' the land . . . It must be mighty agreeable to be dressed in such fine clothes, and to ride on such flashy horses, and to have nothing' to do but to be looked at, and to be laughed at, and to go a-larkin' and a travellin', and seein' all the world, and to be admired by all the girls in the country.[13]

Seeing the world dressed in finery, coming home a hero, having no other occupation than putting yourself on display: these were the glorious images of circus life.

'Wouldn't it be great?,' one writer confessed in an essay in the popular American magazine *McClure's*:

> No more splitting kindling and carrying in coal; no more 'Hurry up, now, or you'll be late for school,' no more poking along in a humdrum existence never going anyplace or see-ing anything but the glad free, untrammeled life, the life of a circus boy . . . And then . . . Travel all around, and be in a new town every day! And see things! . . . And when the show came back to your own hometown next year, people would wonder whose was that slim and gracile figure . . . They'd screw up their eyes to look hard, and they'd say: 'Yes, sir. It is. It's him. It's Willie Bigelow. Well, of all things!' And they'd clap their hands, and be so proud of you. And they'd wonder how it was that they could have been so blind to your many merits when they had you with them.[14]

Surely actors and dancers had the chance to be seen and applauded, but the circus offered something more: the chance to reveal the extraordinary person you knew you were, a person of 'many merits' and undiscovered talents.

'The circus comes as close to being the world in microcosm as anything I know,' wrote the essayist E. B. White:

> in a way, it puts all the rest of show business in the shade. Its magic is universal and complex. Out of its wild disorder comes order; from its rank smell rises the good aroma of courage and daring; out of its preliminary shabbiness comes the final splendor . . . For me the circus is at its best before it has been put together. It is at its best at certain moments when it comes to a point, as through a burning glass, in the activity and destiny of a single performer out of so many. One ring is always bigger than three. One rider, one aerialist, is always greater than six. In short, a man has to catch the circus unawares to experience its full impact and share its gaudy dream.

Miss Rose Meers, the 'Greatest Living Lady Rider', poster for the Barnum & Bailey Greatest Show on Earth, 1897.

White managed to catch sight of a girl rehearsing her riding act, swinging on and off the horse, dropping to her knees and rising again, then just standing as the horse went around the ring. 'The richness of the scene was in its plainness, its natural condition – of horse, of ring, of girl, even to the girl's bare feet that gripped the bare back of her proud and ridiculous mount', he reflected. 'The enchantment grew not out of anything that happened or was performed but out of something that seemed to go round and around and around with the girl, attending her, a steady gleam in the shape of a circle – a ring of ambition, of happiness, of youth . . .'. He could see that the young rider was fully aware of

> the delicious satisfaction of having a perfectly behaved body and the fun of using it to do a trick most people can't do, but she was too young to know that time does not really move in a circle at all . . . Everything in her movements, her expression, told you that for her the ring of time was perfectly formed, changeless, predictable, without beginning or end, like the ring in which she was travelling at this moment with the horse that wallowed under her.

The impromptu performance generated nostalgia, never far from White's sensibilities, and a reminder of the inexorable passage of time. If the circus ring seduced through its image of an endless, repeated present, of the illusion of forever, White was starkly aware that the linear progression of life ends only in death. Despite the lyricism of his description, White thought he failed, ultimately, in conveying the impact of what he observed that day: 'a writer, like an acrobat,' he said, 'must occasionally try a stunt that is too much for him.'[15]

Writers and artists have taken on the challenge of that stunt: of freezing a transcendent moment, of capturing fragility, of escorting us into another world. 'Go to the circus!' artist Fernand Léger once exclaimed. 'You leave behind your rectangles, your geometrical windows, and enter the land of circles in action . . . The ring is freedom; it has neither beginning nor end.'[16]

The romance of outlawry

It is no wonder that a diversion so powerfully exciting generated fearful opposition. Watching circus bodies seemed, to some people, wicked; spending money on an hour of pleasure seemed sinful. 'Circuses flouted convention as part of their pitch – flaunted and cashed in on the romance of outlawry, like Old World Gypsies', wrote Edward Hoagland, who had worked in the circus as a teenager in the 1950s. 'If there hadn't been a crime wave when the show was in town, everybody had sure expected one. And the exotic physiognomies, strangely cut clothes, and oddly focused, disciplined bodies were almost as disturbing.'[17] Despite the display of Stars and Stripes, despite rousing marching music, the circus, Hoagland noted, 'wasn't quite *American*'.[18]

Proponents of 'muscular Christianity', as it became known in 1857, held that a sound and strong body was commensurate with spiritual strength and enlightenment. Still, the strong bodies of circus performers were threatening; maybe it was the costumes, or the music. In the mid-nineteenth century, clergymen exhorted their congregations to resist the illicit lure of the circus, and educators warned parents to stand firm, keeping their children away from the bawdy, gaudy, potentially corrupting spectacle. Those reactions were given voice in newspaper editorials, intoned from pulpits and published in several cautionary pamphlets by the American Sunday School Union. One of these, *The Circus*, for example, relates the story of two young boys, Silas and Alfred, who notice an advance man putting up circus posters. He tells them not to say anything to their father, but to bring money for tickets and come back after school. But the children, bursting with excitement, do tell their father, who decides it is time they knew the truth.

The men who work at the circus, he says, 'are generally idle and worthless people, who go about from place to place, and get their living by taking money of many persons who cannot afford to spend it so foolishly'. Once little boys are enticed to join the circus, with its promiscuous drinking and gambling, 'there is no hope', he assures them, 'of their making useful men'. Furthermore, he claims, there is

Elizabeth Shippen Green Elliott, 'Boy Peering through a Wall Chink at a Clown', drawing from *Harper's New Monthly Magazine*, 1907.

much cruelty: how else would horses be trained to do tricks unless they were whipped very hard? He promises, as consolation, to take the children to see wild beasts caged in a menagerie.[19]

A more maudlin tale was *Slim Jack*, whose theme is the suffering and pain endured by child performers – a concern among social reformers that was second only to animal welfare. Sally, a child enchanted by the circus, learns from her aunt that illusion masks a hard reality: 'Do not think they are happy or well used because they jump so readily, or because their dress is grand and glittering. Underneath, there is often a sad heart in that little body.' She tells Sally about poor Jack, orphaned after his father and mother, hard-working English immigrants, die. When Jack is eight, a circus comes to town and the manager notes that Jack's agility would serve him well as a tightrope walker. He is more than willing to join the circus, and the manager makes a financial deal with Jack's foster father to take Jack away and train him. Jack returns several years later, spangled and aglitter, but he soon suffers a terrible fall and can never walk again, much less pursue his career as a circus star. Jack confesses that he was seduced by the applause, but came to be ashamed to be known as a circus performer. Predictably, he dies, but not before testifying to his faith in God.[20]

Moral opposition dogged the circus throughout its history, but did not detract from its enduring allure and metaphorical power. The

American poster for *The Circus Girl*, 1897.

nineteenth-century conceit of running away to join the circus retained its vitality as a personal myth of glamour and reinvention well into the twentieth century. In the 1940s, for example, one young girl who had ridden horses throughout her childhood, and who often wore a crown as part of her riding costume, announced that she was going to run away to become Queen of the Circus. When she was fourteen, she wrote a prediction of her future that reiterated that desire to become a circus queen and, not surprisingly, to marry the man on the flying trapeze. The young girl grew up to be Jacqueline Bouvier Kennedy Onassis.[21]

The myth of the circus as a site of freedom, power and enchantment contradicts the hard reality of circus life. Although artists and writers imagine the circus as a challenge to bourgeois values, a rejection of the commodification of culture, in fact the circus is a business, always precarious, subject to financial pressures and its audience's fickle desires. Since the eighteenth century, when the modern circus began, hundreds of circuses have been established, and most have failed. Performing requires years of rigorous training, much like ballet or competitive gymnastics: training that consumes the performer's entire life. And even the most proficient and well-rehearsed performer faces risks. Clowns tumble from stilts or the tops of ladders. Aerialists suffer breaks, tears, bruises and fractures; even a fall to the net – and in early circuses there was no net – can cause a broken neck; and yet aerialists return to the trapeze and the wire, determined to devise ever more dangerous feats. Animal trainers, stabbed, mauled and bitten, stride back into the cage, stitched and scarred, determined to exert their will against their wild adversaries.

This determination is sometimes incredible and nearly inexplicable: performers are obsessed with controlling their bodies, and by extension their minds. They know that the power of concentration is as crucial to their success as exhausting rehearsals. Their ability to rise above pain, even to deny it, is part of that expression of control. They perform when their wrists are bleeding from abrasion with the rope, when their torn tendons have not healed, when their wounds are still raw. 'The weary hours of exercising, of straining tired muscles one long inch farther, of traveling day after day, with always another stand ahead, the peril of injury or death always with us – all these, were my inheritance,' the rider Josephine Robinson recalled.[22] But then there is also the spotlight, the audience's anticipation, their attention so complete that not a breath can be heard. That glorious feeling of accomplishment. And that coveted, addictive, irresistible burst of applause.

ONE

TRICK RIDERS

When he was eight years old, Philip Astley became his father's apprentice as a veneer cutter and cabinetmaker in the Staffordshire market town of Newcastle-under-Lyme; but after nine years of apprenticeship, he knew that he neither wanted to work alongside his domineering father nor spend his days in the confines of the woodshop. In 1759, in an act of defiance and rebellion, seventeen-year-old Philip left his parents' home to pursue a grand, if not grandiose, idea of his future: he would become a horseman. In eighteenth-century Britain, men on horseback were quite simply heroes. Courageous feats required horses: knights rode them, gentlemen owned them, soldiers took them into battle. For the young Astley, horses offered an escape from his class, his circumscribed prospects and the future his father had laid out for him.

Although horse trainers were notably fit and strong, their manliness lay not only in physical power but in their exertion of will over a beast prized for its muscularity; they boasted of their unique ability to win their animals' loyalty and obedience. Horse trainers had the reputation not as cruel subjugators of their powerful animals, but as humane and skilful masters who relied little on their whips. As the equestrian manager Charles Montague put it,

Thomas Rowlandson and Augustus Pugin, drawing of Astley's Amphitheatre for Rudolph Ackermann's *Microcosm of London*, 1808–11.

Much might be said as to the best method of training horses; but after all, it resolves itself into this: The horse must first be brought to feel that you are his master – his superior; not through fear of your power; but on the contrary, through his experience that though you have the power, it is always accompanied by kindness and by firmness, but *never* with cruelty.[1]

The young Astley was certain that he possessed this unique aptitude. Over six feet tall, boisterous and by all accounts a daredevil, he joined a cavalry regiment of the newly formed Dragoons, where he first was assigned the job of breaking in new horses, and where he first proved his talents. Within a short time he became a soldier, and, surprisingly for a young man resistant to authority, distinguished himself for discipline and bravery in the Seven Years War. When he was discharged in 1766, at the rank of sergeant-major, his general bestowed upon him a stately white steed with which Astley decided to seek his fortune. Among the skills he had honed as a soldier were swordsmanship and trick riding, both of which he put to use in his new career.

At first he travelled around the provinces, performing at the many local fairs, passing his hat for pence and learning new feats from fellow equestrians. Trick riding was a popular entertainment but, like all itinerant performance, financially unpredictable. Tired from the vagaries of the performance circuit, in 1768 Astley opened a riding school near Westminster Bridge in London. In the mornings he offered lessons to aspiring horsemen and women, often children of the aristocracy; in

Astley's Amphitheatre, 1777, drawing by William Capon.

the afternoons he performed. Soon he constructed a rudimentary amphitheatre: a circular arena surrounded by seats for his audience. Astride his mount, wearing his military uniform and brandishing a sword, Astley rounded the vicinity giving out publicity handbills, and began to draw the viewers he coveted.

Contemporary accounts depict him as astounding. His height alone made him a spectacle on horseback, but his tricks reflected physical prowess and daring that to some viewers suggested supernatural, perhaps diabolical, powers. He did not regret such rumours, even as he denied them. In fact, he did have a certain trick: he discovered that by galloping in his small circular arena, centrifugal force would allow him to stand and perform acrobatics, including headstands, on his horse's back. He soon added a menu of balancing tricks and a second, smaller horse, Billy, whose feats included counting, mind reading and playing dead. Sometime before 1769 Astley was joined by an equestrienne, his wife Patty, and several years later by their son, John.

Successful though he was in his afternoon horse shows, Astley was frustrated when wet weather made performances impossible. Gradually, he improved his arena, first with a canvas cover, then with a partial shed and, in 1780, with a roofed building holding two tiers of boxes, a pit and a gallery. He kept admission fees low enough – tickets ranged from two shillings and sixpence for boxes to sixpence for the gallery – to attract viewers from all classes: theatregoers who might otherwise see Shakespeare at Drury Lane, opera lovers who might go to Covent Garden, governesses who might otherwise spend sixpence on ale at a nearby pub.

Astley was not the first to offer equestrian performances, nor was his the first theatre in the round, but his horsemanship was notable and his determination to earn acclaim was insatiable. Realizing that an ever-changing programme would ensure return visits, he soon added a cast of jugglers, clowns, tumblers, magicians and rope dancers. Rope dancing, familiar to fairgoers, was a rather tame performance of acrobatics on a rope strung about six feet from the ground. Magical acts included mechanical automatons and exhibitions of the wonder of magnets. These acts were mere interludes between the more daring equestrian feats, although to generate glamour some performers took exotic names or pedigrees. A strongman styled himself Signor Colpi; his equestrian clown was Fortunelly; a woman who paraded with hair so long it trailed behind her for several feet was advertised as French. In 1780, the first act on his playbill was 'The *Ombres Chinoises* [shadow puppets], or Lilliputian World.' Somehow he found a zebra: 'The Beautiful Zebra will walk round the Riding School for the inspection of the nobility, gentry, and others.' But horse riding was the centre of the show, and Astley or his impressive son, John, was the star attraction: 'the greatest performer that ever appeared in any age, and as horseman stands unparalleled by all nations', boasted his handbill.[2] A handbill of 1786 advertised John Astley's ability to display 'various curious Attitudes, dancing, ballancing [sic], and flying over the Garter and Stick, at the same Instant jumping at least twelve Feet perpendicular from the Ground, and sixteen Feet horizontally . . . The Equestrian Exercises of Young Astley, are peculiar to himself, and his Abilities so well known, that they need no Encomiums.'[3] Astley did not call his entertainments 'circus'. Astley's Amphitheatre Riding-House was a performing arts destination featuring a varied roster of entertainers, similar to a fair or what would one day be called vaudeville. The special designation of 'circus' was invented by one of Astley's chief competitors, the horseman Charles Hughes.

Like Astley, Hughes was a former soldier with equestrian skills and notable bearing: 'a fine stalwart fellow, who could have carried an ox away on his shoulders, and afterwards eaten him for supper', as Charles Dickens later described him.[4] His British Horse Academy, located near Astley's, was the first step in his entry into show business. In 1782, with his partner Charles Dibdin, Hughes built a stone amphitheatre at a well-travelled crossing, St George's Circus. If Astley's Amphitheatre advertised its founder and star, Hughes and Dibdin wanted to evoke a more elite connotation: their amphitheatre was called the Royal Circus, Equestrian and Philharmonic Academy – a name that indicated a new kind of hybrid theatre, and the first time 'circus' was associated with the performing arts. Besides a circular ring for equestrian acts, the Royal Circus had a full stage that could be combined with the ring for extravagant spectacles or used alone for pantomimes and musical acts.

Thomas Rowlandson
and Augustus Pugin,
'The Royal Circus',
drawing for Rudolph
Ackermann's
*Microcosm of
London,* 1808–11.

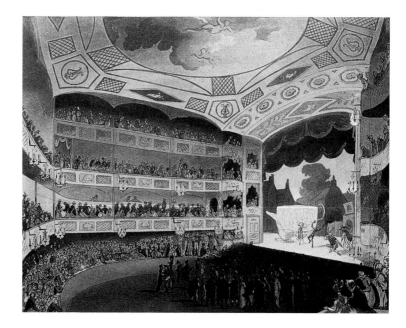

An ample panoply of entertainment filled the shows – clowns, magicians, musicians, trained dogs – but as on Astley's bill, horse riding was the prominent attraction:

Hughes, with the celebrated Sobieska Clementina, the famous Miss Huntley, and an astonishing Young Gentleman (son of a Person of Quality) will exhibit at Blackfriars-road more Extraordinary things than ever yet witnessed, such as leaping over a horse forty times without stopping between springs. Leaps the Bar standing on the saddle with his Back to the Horse's Tail, and Vice Versa, Rides at full speed with his right foot on the saddle, and his left two in his Mouth. Two surprising *feet*. Mrs Hughes takes a fly and fires a Pistol – rides at full speed standing on Pint Pots – mounts pot by pot, higher still, to the terror of all who see her. H. carries a lady at full speed over his head – surprising! The young gentleman will recite verses of his own making, and act Marc Antony between the leaps![5]

Circus performer leaping through a ring of fire, *c.* 1870s.

Mirth, astonishment, admiration – and now terror – were the reactions Hughes, and circus men who followed, aspired to generate.

In eighteenth-century London, founding any theatre was legally risky. Only two theatres, Drury Lane and Covent Garden, were sanctioned under the strict Licensing Act of 1737, while other venues fell under the rubric of public entertainment, needing permission from the Lord Chamberlain. The Disorderly Houses Act of 1752 attempted to control gambling as well as the dissolute classes and petty thieves who gathered around gaming halls. Theatres offering music, dancing and even horsemanship could obtain special licences, but Hughes's stage – which Astley soon copied – seemed too close to legitimate theatre, defined as offering drama or, in fact, any performance involving prose. Legislators, especially worried about prose in the form of political satire, required that scripts be submitted for approval. Spurred by noisy protest from the licenced theatres' management, first Hughes – enforcers read The Riot Act from his stage – and then Astley were clapped in jail. Fortunately for Astley, one of his former riding students was the daughter of the Lord Chancellor, Edward Thurlow, who came to his rescue and helped him to procure a licence, limited to the summer and provided that he feature equestrian acts. When Hughes, too, managed to obtain a licence, the two venues became energetic competitors. Not to be outdone by the Royal Circus, Astley decorated the interior of his theatre to look like verdant foliage and renamed it 'The Royal Grove'.

Circus amphitheatres competed in their programmes, decor and size. When Drury Lane expanded from 2,000 seats to more than 3,000 in 1791, patrons complained that they could no longer hear the actors or feel connected to the action on stage. Size, though, was no impediment to the enjoyment of circus spectacles, and with seats all around the ring, viewers had a privileged sightline no matter where they sat. The experience of the circus, then, became enhanced by the number of patrons sharing it. Unlike noisy, rowdy, and often vice-ridden fairgrounds, the circus theatre advertised its comfort and safety. Fairgoers became theatregoers, certainly a rise in status; for less than a shilling, they experienced a diversion that had not previously been available to them.

As a circus impresario, Astley was hardly satisfied with the success of a single venue; as one nineteenth-century writer put it, he was 'Napoleonic' in his determination to create a circus empire at home and abroad.[6] Certainly he was Napoleonic towards his workers: 'a very despot in his theatre. He had the reputation of applying his whip indiscriminately to his biped and quadruped players.'[7] Astley also boasted that he disciplined performers by withholding food until he was satisfied with their work. If they quit in protest, he claimed that he could replace them quickly and easily. Neither was he to be daunted by British law.

When legal harassment continued over his enterprise in London, he built an amphitheatre in Dublin before bringing his show to Paris in the 1780s. In this city horsemanship was widely admired and horse racing had been newly encouraged by Louis XVI. Races near the Bois de Boulogne, at Vincennes and at Fontainebleau drew an aristocratic crowd; Astley's amphitheatre, as it did in London, attracted viewers of all classes who were keen on seeing equestrian prowess. In Paris, though, legitimate theatre felt no less threatened by Astley's offerings: there were even stricter laws against theatrical upstarts. When he could obtain a licence limiting his offerings only to performances on horseback, Astley circumvented the law neatly by designing a platform to be carried by eight horses, on which acrobats, clowns and jugglers performed.

At a time when the established theatres – the Comédie Française and Opéra, for example – were floundering financially, Astley drew audiences consisting of both upper-class Parisians and those of the lower classes, who usually took their entertainment at fairs. Acrobats, tumblers, rope dancers, contortionists, strong men and strong women – all these performers made their way to Astley's. Despite restrictions, Astley's amphitheatre on the Faubourg du Temple thrived, and was visited even by the Court of Versailles. Legend has it that Marie Antoinette was so entranced by John Astley's performance that she presented him with a gold medal encrusted with diamonds and nicknamed him the English Rose. But his success in Paris was cut short by the Revolution: the amphitheatre was converted into barracks and his royal fans were executed. After the Revolution his building was restored to him when he petitioned to Napoleon. Undaunted even when two of his theatres burned to the ground – all relied on candles, oil lamps or gaslight – Astley established a total of nineteen throughout England and France. He inspired many imitators: by 1803 England had eight independent circuses; by 1843 twenty-one.

It took one of Charles Hughes's performers to bring the circus across the Atlantic. John Bill Ricketts, like Astley and Hughes, was trained in the cavalry and went on to establish the Circus Royal in Edinburgh, touring in Scotland and Ireland before sailing to America in 1792. The new nation had yet to establish a circus, although several years before Thomas Pool had billed himself as the first American to perform equestrian feats, with a clown in his entourage to entertain between the acts. Among Pool's several feats was riding at half speed, standing on the saddle, tossing an orange and catching it on the tine of a fork. He also had taught two horses to play dead.

Ricketts planned more ambitious offerings. While an arena was being built, he opened a riding school in Philadelphia, at the time the nation's capital; soon a small troupe of British performers joined him: several equestrians, a few acrobats, a rope dancer and a clown. The first American circus had its debut on 3 April 1793 in an uncovered wooden structure seating about 800 in boxes and a pit, with a ring 42 feet in diameter. Ambitious and intrepid on horseback, the young, handsome Ricketts – he was apparently in his early twenties – was clearly the main attraction. George Washington, an accomplished horseman himself, first attended a performance on 22 April 1793 and came often afterwards. Contemporary reviews noted particularly Ricketts's grace and good taste: he rejected as 'both unfashionable and vulgar' tricks that evoked fear and tension in his viewers. 'Indeed,' commented a reviewer in the *Federal Gazette and Philadelphia Daily Advertiser*, 'his selection of exercises are chosen with infinite taste.'[8] Aiming to provide a wholesome, amusing and diverting programme, Ricketts urged parents to bring their children – unusual for eighteenth-century audiences. Newspaper reports remarked on the attendance of young boys and girls among the audience as early as May 1793.

To attract return patrons, Ricketts offered both a changing roster of performers and new equestrian feats: he strode multiple horses; juggled fruit, bottles, glasses of wine and hoops; stood on a horse with a nine-year-old boy on his shoulders, an act he called Two Flying Mercuries; and performed a signature dance that came to be known as 'the Ricketts hornpipe'. He also introduced the equestrian pantomime:

Saxby, Dunbar & Co.'s circus, American poster, 1872.

WILL BE SEEN IN SAXBY, DUNBAR & CO'S INTERNATIONAL CIRCUS.

early productions featured a simple narrative plot, dialogue and music connecting comic scenes. Eventually, these stage productions became more elaborate and complex and featured shipwrecks or battles, such as *The Siege of Oxtrace; or, Alexander the Great*. When Ricketts left the city in July, possibly along with tens of thousands of other Philadelphians fleeing a yellow fever epidemic, the city took over his amphitheatre as a makeshift hospital for the destitute ill. He and his troupe began a fourteen-month tour, travelling through the south during the winter of 1793–4 and establishing themselves in New York City the next winter in a permanent theatre.

Hugely popular in New York, Ricketts threatened the livelihood of stage theatres, which tried, but failed, to limit him through legislation. He built a permanent structure in Philadelphia, nearly twice as large as his first, with a ring and stage; in Boston he erected his Equestrian Pantheon in the city centre; and in 1797 he sent a travelling company to Canada, where he established circuses in Montreal and Quebec City. Despite his success, maintaining large troupes and many theatres was financially draining, and when the dome of his Philadelphia structure collapsed in 1798, and both the Philadelphia and New York theatres burned down in 1799, Ricketts found himself bankrupt. After selling his horses in the West Indies, he decided to return to England; in 1800 he was lost at sea.

If Ricketts embraced children as an appropriate audience for the circus, still he – and his contemporaries in Britain and France – stressed the demonstration of equestrian skill as central to the circus experience. At the time, horses were believed to have a unique psychological and emotional relationship to humans, and horsemanship represented a particularly genteel accomplishment. 'Horsemen had long served as emblems of conquest – of nurture over nature, of reason over passion – and indeed of civilization itself', notes historian Marius Kwint. 'Horses themselves enjoyed a privileged status as fetish-objects of the British ruling classes . . . They were, moreover, proving their quotidian value as the chief muscular force in the growth of commerce and industry.'[9] Not only in Britain, but throughout Europe, horses were perceived as intelligent and loyal to humans, with prodigious memories and even moral sense. Hippodramas were not merely *about* men on horseback, but featured horses as actors who felt and displayed thought, insight and emotion.

The master of the hippodrama in Britain was Andrew Ducrow, born in Southwark in 1793 into a circus family; his father was a strong-man known as the Flemish Hercules. First performing as a mime, he soon discovered his talent as an equestrian and gained considerable acclaim in France and Holland before being hired at Astley's. As ambitious as Astley – and with the same fiery temper – Ducrow leaped at the chance to take over the Astley empire after Philip's death in 1814 and John's in 1821.

Ducrow was famous for costume changes on horseback and for a skit known as 'The Peasant's Frolic' or 'Flying Wardrobe', in which Ducrow, pretending to be a drunk from the audience, insisted on mounting a horse. As he teetered precariously on horseback, he removed his coat, waistcoat, trousers and shirt until he was left wearing his ele-gant riding outfit. The act proved so popular that it was copied by many other performers for generations to come. Ducrow's agility earned him acclaim, as this description from *Blackwood's Magazine* conveys:

Why the horse is but the air, as it were, on which he flies! What godlike grace in that Volant motion, fresh from Olympus . . . What seems to 'feathered Mercury' to care for the horse, whose side his toe but touches, as if it were a cloud in the ether? As the flight accelerates, the animal absolutely disap-pears, if not from the sight of our bodily eye, certainly from that of our imagination, and we behold but the messenger of Jove.[10]

Besides his horsemanship, Ducrow brought his theatrical experi-ence to his staging and directing of spectacles. Nothing less than perfection pleased him, and, like Astley before him, he never held back from lashing out at his performers. Difficult as he was to work for, the results were overwhelmingly successful. For 30 years, until his theatre succumbed to fire in 1842 – he died shortly afterwards – Ducrow's hippodramas were so popular in London that legitimate theatres, such as Covent Garden, began to offer them. At Astley's, Ducrow's successor William Batty carried on the tradition by staging such typical fare as 'The White Maiden of California', in which slain Indians, rising from the dead, emerge from traps on stage astride cream-coloured horses – an awe-inspiring special effect. Perhaps the most famous hippo-drama was the rhapsodic 'Mazeppa', based on a poem by Byron. The plot was alluringly Romantic: a captive Tartar prince, Mazeppa, is punished for his forbidden love of a Polish woman by being stripped naked and bound to a wild steed. Galloping through a treacherous mountain range, the horse and its prisoner battle storms and predators and cross a raging river before arriving on the Steppes of Tartary. There, the exhausted horse and nearly dead Mazeppa are discovered by the Abder Khan, who identifies Mazeppa as none other than his long-lost son. Revived, Mazeppa engages in a fierce battle against his father's enemies; he is victorious, of course, and proceeds to vanquish the Poles who impris-oned him and, in the end, wins the hand of his love.

First performed in 1831, 'Mazeppa' proved enormously popu-lar for its heart-stopping tension, even though a dummy was substituted for the star equestrian during the chase. It was simply too dangerous a feat for a man. But the hippodrama became even more popular when it was performed by the American actress Adah Isaacs Menken in 1861, first in Albany, New York, and soon after in cities throughout America and Europe, including New York, New Orleans, San Francisco, London, Paris and Vienna. Horsemen wearing flesh-coloured tights had long had a sexual allure for circus viewers, but a voluptuous woman portraying a man, whose pink silk body suit made her appear nude – this was scandalous, and audiences flocked to see her. Menken per-formed to sold-out houses, earning more than $500 a night. Publicity over her reputation helped to fuel interest. A former ballet dancer and artists' model, Menken was reported to have married several wealthy husbands; had been left a small, or large, fortune; and despite her impressive equestrian skills, she wanted most to be recognized as a poet.

Clearly, Menken was a new type of horsewoman. Equestriennes had been featured by Astley, Hughes, Ducrow and others, but less prominently than the main acts: men on horseback. With Menken, the potential attraction of women on horseback was undeniable

Adah Menken,
c. 1860.

and circus impresarios saw its money-making potential. Among these was Antonio Franconi, an Italian bird trainer and equestrian who took over Astley's Paris theatre in 1793. Forced to leave Paris at times and tour with his circus because of political problems, he took over permanently after Astley's death and named his theatre the Cirque Olympique. It remained a circus, with a ring, until 1847, when the ring was filled in with seats and performances took place on a stage. Antonio's sons Henri, Laurent and Victor also became impresarios, establishing circuses and hippodromes in major European cities, and in May 1853 Henri's circus opened in New York. The new entertainment was an immediate and huge critical and financial success, but one review in the *New York Daily Times* voiced a complaint that would recur as circus performances became increasingly terrifying and sexualized: Franconi, the reporter noted,

has introduced an entertainment new to this country. Females, dressed in distinctive jockey colors, race round the course, cheered on by the assembled multitude. Monkies, strapped to the back of frisky ponies, are sent careering over hurdles in a brutal manner. Thorough-breds – so called – are whipped into madness and let loose that they may reach some hoped-for goal. Gymnasts balance each other on poles, or try how near they may venture to destruction without an actual catastrophe ensuing. In short, everything which can *excite*, rather than delight, is prepared for the patrons of the Hippodrome, and offered to them as an entertainment worthy of their support.

The paper advised Franconi to make the venue more respectable: 'Mr Franconi should abolish all the groggeries; prohibit better; have

Ada Castello, also
known as 'The Great
Zazell', riding
'Jupiter', c. 1899.

an available and watchful police; deny the privilege of admission to
known immoral characters, and certainly refuse it to all females unat-
tended by a gentleman. In short, make the Hippodrome more like a
place of innocent recreation and less like a gambling booth.'[11]

Equestriennes signalled a new direction for circus performance.
Circus illustrations pictured them as dainty and demure: typically, a
young woman shown galloping bareback on a black horse, standing on
pointe, dressed in a knee-length tutu. In some performances, however,
scanty costumes, 'mad' riding and blatant exhibitionism conveyed a
different message. As the art historian Nicola Haxell notes, many painters
depicted these new horsewomen as dominatrices: 'Her dominance

Miss Louise Hilton
at Gentry Brothers
Circus, c. 1920.

42

GENTRY BROS. CIRCUS

MISS LOUISE HILTON
THE GREATEST RIDER THE WORLD HAS EVER KNOWN

over the horse (or horses) in her charge extended to the men in the audience: she returned their gaze – not as a reciprocal statement of desire, but as an acknowledgement that she, too, had power.'[12] A woman on horseback – and more titillating, a daring woman on horseback – proved to be an undeniable attraction.

Equestrian directors looked for talent – grace, posture and perseverance – among the circus's young performers, usually acrobats in a family troupe. In the late 1840s, the American equestrian Spencer Q. Stokes discovered a comely child, Omar Kingsley, who was eight or nine at the time, and began to train him as a trick rider. The young Omar had joined the circus at the age of six. He was possibly a runaway, but could have been apprenticed by his parents or even, as historian Shauna Vey speculates, 'rented' for a fee. Stokes saw his potential as a performer and, more significantly, as a girl.[13] Dressed in frilly white, with a cinch-waisted bouffant skirt and crinoline, Omar posed for a publicity photograph emerging demurely from behind a theatre curtain, brandishing a whip. In 1851 Kingsley made his debut in Europe, where Stokes billed him as Mlle Ella, Ella Stokes or Ella Zoyara. Thomas Frost recalled that in London, Mlle Ella was a singular sensation: 'the young artiste's charms of face and form were a never-ending theme of conversation and meditation' by admiring viewers who looked upon the graceful rider 'with enraptured eyes'.[14] Stokes and his protégé toured Europe for eight years, earning rave reviews and inspiring copycats. Performers calling themselves some form of 'Ella' appeared in other European and American circuses. Kingsley sometimes dressed as a woman even out of the arena, and rebuffed some romantic advances. As he grew into manhood, however, cross-dressing became problematic, and his identity as a woman not completely convincing. After his New York debut in 1860, two New York newspapers reported the shocking disclosure that Zoyara was really a man. If some potential viewers felt insulted by the deceit, Stokes used the revelation in his advertisements to fuel curiosity. In fact, audiences were not deterred, but rushed to see Kingsley's performance as a trick rider, a cross-dresser – and a strong, powerful woman.

The appeal of equestriennes was underscored by the romantic tale of Ella Bradna, trained as a child in her circus family, who was

Frederick Glasier, *Circus Girl*, c. 1908.

Banner act, *c.* 1875.

performing in Paris at the Nouveau Cirque in 1900 when a fan threw a bouquet of flowers, causing her horse to buck and Ella, standing en pointe, to fall into the audience. She landed on the lap of a young cavalry lieutenant, one Frederick Ferbere, the heir to a German brewing fortune. Two months later they were married, with Ferbere giving up his surname and family inheritance to become Fred Bradna and join his wife as a circus performer. The couple had a long, successful career, Ella as a bareback rider and Fred, eventually, as one of the most famous circus ringmasters.

By 1919, when the artist Marsden Hartley went to the circus, a woman's demonstration of power on horseback was not surprising. For his part, he insisted that the athleticism and daring of equestriennes detracted nothing from their attractiveness, and he was captivated by 25-year-old May Wirth, who had been adopted into an Australian circus family who nurtured her talent as a rider. 'Five handsome sidewheels round the ring, and a flying jump on the horse, then several complete somersaults on the horse's back, while he is in movement round the ring, is not to be slighted for consideration,' Hartley noted, 'and if, as I have said, you have a love or even a fancy for this sort of entertainment, you all but worship the little lady for the thrill she gives you through this consummate mastery of hers.' The 'little lady', as he put it, accentuated her youth and femininity by wearing a huge bow in her hair, and she displayed her mastery of two extremely difficult tricks: a backward somersault on a forward-moving horse, and a forward somersault feet to feet. Wirth, he said, was 'powerfully built, and her muscles are master of coordination, such as would be the envy of multitudes of men, and with all this power, she is as simple in her manner and appearance as is the young debutante at her coming out function'. She admitted to him that riding was 'terrifically hard labour' that combined skills in wire walking, handsprings, somersaults and ballet, all of which she began learning as a child of three. Challenging as it was, though, Wirth could imagine no other life. 'I always wanted to do what the boys could do,' she told Hartley, 'and I was never satisfied until I had accomplished it.'[15]

The writer Nellie Revell dedicated her novel *Spangles* (1926) to Wirth. The romance centers on a young bareback rider with the stage name of Spangles, who is taken from the circus to live with her aunt and uncle in Paris. The selfish couple want nothing more than to take advantage of her inheritance, and they insist that she conform to their upper-class, effete world, which is characterized by greed and hypocrisy. The American circus, on the other hand, is portrayed as kinder, more authentic and morally sound, and Spangles is relieved when finally she returns to the circus community.[16]

In Britain, by the late nineteenth century, trick riders had fallen out of favour, and the British circus, insisting on riding as the central attraction, declined. Tent circuses vied for audiences throughout the countryside, and London could support only one circus at any time, as the increasingly popular music hall drew away audiences. In 1879 the theatre historian Henry Barton Baker published a sentimental eulogy for Philip Astley, remembering his own visits to Astley's Amphitheatre as a child. 'Those amongst us who are old enough may recall our own sensations of delight at the deliciously mixed perfume of sawdust, gas, and stale orange-peel which greeted us upon our entrance into that temple of enchantment,' Baker wrote.

Poster showing Don Quixote and Sancho Panza, Nouveau Cirque, Paris, 1892.

> Our raptures at the looking-glass and gilding, and the brilliant lights; our trembling expectancy of the wonders hidden behind that mystic curtain; our roars of laughter at the antics of the clowns, whom we regarded as beings of superhuman wit; our open-mouthed wonder at the 'highly-trained' horses; our rapturous admiration of the lovely riders in muslin skirts, who jumped through hoops and vaulted over ribbons.[17]

That experience of circus – rapturous, enchanting, magical – was not yet dead: the intimate one-ring circus thrived and proliferated in Paris.

TWO

CIRQUES INTIMES

The circus is a tiny closed off area of forgetfulness.
Henry Miller

In February 1899, in a brothel, 35-year-old Henri de Toulouse-Lautrec collapsed. Long an alcoholic, probably syphilitic, he had been frighteningly erratic for months – incoherent, violent, paranoid, hallucinating – and continuously drunk. His condition was so dire that two close friends appealed to his mother to commit him to a mental hospital. Vacillating, afraid of public scandal about her prominent son, she instead hired a male nurse to care for him, but soon she realized that she had no choice. In early March, Lautrec became a patient at Dr René Semelaigne's clinic in Neuilly, near the Bois de Boulogne. A small palace set on the grounds of a huge park, the clinic seemed to Lautrec like nothing less than prison. After five days, he stabilized enough to be lucid; after two weeks, he declared himself cured. He needed no medical help, he protested noisily to his many visitors; what he needed was freedom. And a drink. Finally, he and his loyal friend Maurice Joyant conceived a plan to convince his doctors that he was well enough for release. Since one symptom of his illness was loss of memory, he had to prove that he could remember vividly. He would create an album of drawings of the circus, he decided, recalling details of the bareback riders, clowns and acrobats that he had seen 25 years before, attending Paris circuses as a child, and in the 1880s with friends. With all the intensity he could muster, in the next weeks he produced more than 50 crayon, chalk and charcoal sketches.

Henri de Toulouse-Lautrec, *At the Circus: The Spanish Walk*, 1899, drawing.

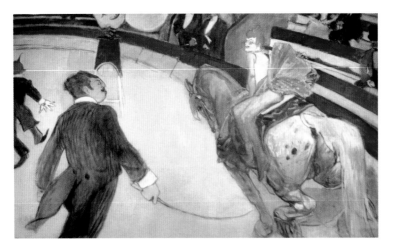

Henri de Toulouse-Lautrec, *Equestrienne at the Cirque Fernando*, 1888, oil on canvas.

Besides attesting to his memory, the project gave Lautrec a chance to celebrate the performers he so admired. When he saw his first circus, at the age of ten, he was impressed, he wrote to a cousin, by the elephants and lions. But his attention later fixed on the spectacular human performers whose bodies were so dramatically different from his own. Suffering from what some physicians believe was a rare form of dwarfism that caused fragile bones, Lautrec had broken both legs by the time he was fifteen. He grew to be just under five feet tall, with shortened legs and a disproportionately long torso; he needed always to support himself with a cane. Drink made him even more unstable, but drink he did. Weak and incarcerated, it is no wonder that he envied agility, strength and camaraderie. The energy and wildness of his lines can be read as reflections of his debilitating mental symptoms or, and I think more accurately, of his desperate desire to feel the freedom and prowess of the performers he chose to depict: to inhabit their bodies.

The central image of his *Acrobats in the Circus*, for example, is a male performer whose back and leg muscles bulge as he balances a smaller figure, possibly a child, on his broad shoulders and with apparent ease lifts another acrobat, a woman, on his outstretched left arm. Two fellow performers look on appreciatively. In none of the drawings did Lautrec indicate an audience; they were irrelevant, in his view, to what happened in the ring. Horses, his recurring subject as a young artist, appear in many sketches: an insouciant jockey sits backwards

Henri de Toulouse-Lautrec, *Acrobats in the Circus*, c. 1880s, pastel.

on a horse's rump as they round the ring; the famous black clown Chocolat, a favourite of Lautrec's at the Nouveau Cirque, clings desperately, and comically, to his galloping steed. While most of the drawings evoke joy and play, some intimate an ominous sense of risk: a magnificent horse rears on his hind legs, towering over a rider crouched beneath; three women aerialists perch on a trapeze, one dangling by her knees. 'Perhaps,' writes art historian Anne Roquebert, 'he felt, remembering how any act performed under the big top without a safety net spells danger, that this bravura aspect of individual turns echoed his own situation . . . one false move could be fatal'.[1]

With the album as evidence, Lautrec submitted to an interview with his doctors; at end of March, they allowed him supervised outings from the clinic; in mid-May, they at last released him. 'I bought my freedom with my drawings,' he boasted to friends.[2] That freedom was short-lived. He drank. He suffered a stroke. Two years later, he was dead.

Like many artists in turn-of-the-century Paris, Toulouse-Lautrec loved the spectacle of the circus. 'Lautrec advocates a taste for and a sense of perfection,' wrote his friend the journalist and art collector Thadée Natanson. 'Perfection of muscles, nerves, skill and technique. No endeavor towards perfection failed to satisfy him.'[3] But it was not only admiration of skill that attracted him and other artists, including Cézanne and Degas, Picasso, Renoir, Pierre Bonnard, Georges Seurat, Fernand Léger, Suzanne Valadon and Jean-Louis Forain: all these artists interpreted – and often romanticized or idealized – circus performances. They focused most often on performers themselves, rarely depicting the spectacle as a whole, but rather an intimate and close portrait of equestriennes, clowns and acrobats: their muscularity

Georges Seurat,
The Circus, c. 1891,
oil on canvas.

and daring; the risks they took; the awe or laughter or joy they so powerfully evoked. The circus, as they saw it, represented a place that exalted and encouraged self-expression.

Their paintings, drawings and sculptures contributed to the myth of the circus as transformative and transgressive: 'The circus is a tiny closed off area of forgetfulness', Henry Miller wrote.

For a space it enables us to lose ourselves, to dissolve in wonder and bliss, to be transported by mystery. We come out of it in

Pierre-Auguste
Renoir, *Acrobats at
the Cirque Fernando,*
1879, oil on canvas.

a daze, saddened and horrified by the everyday face of the world. But the old everyday world, the world with which we imagine ourselves to be only too familiar, is the only world and it is a world of magic, of magic inexhaustible.[4]

For Miller, the circus served as an antidote to the pressures of everyday life, infusing with mystery what seems too familiar. This power of the circus, Miller wrote, attracted such artists as Rouault, Miró, Chagall, Seurat and Léger.

Some theorists argue that besides the aesthetic potential of the circus to re-enchant the mundane, artists saw in the circus an expression of creativity that defied the materialism of the marketplace. 'Artists were often dropouts from society because of their antibourgeois stance and bohemian demeanor', writes the art historian Phillip Dennis Cate.[5] Modernists, especially, were trying to wrest themselves from the commercialization of art. For artists scorned – or fearful of being scorned – for blazing new aesthetic paths, the dazzling skill demonstrated by aerialists and acrobats contested the distinction between 'high' art and 'low'. Visceral, muscular circus performances served as an antidote to over-intellectualization by traditional artists and conservative critics. Certainly artists understood that circus performers, expressing their art through their bodies, were vulnerable always to viewers' capricious tastes. 'We see them, these men and women, risking their bones in the air to receive a few bravos . . . Historians, philosophers . . . and poets, we, too, jump around for the stupid public,' wrote the brothers Goncourt in their journals; artists included themselves in that company.

As British and especially American circuses expanded to huge spectacles, Paris circuses emerged as iconic, a nostalgic version of what the true circus was supposed to be. Artists went there often, sometimes to see the acts, sometimes to socialize with one another or with the performers, with whom they felt a special affinity. As a gathering place, the circus was like a local bistro. 'When everyone went out,' Picasso's mistress Fernande Olivier recalled,

> it was generally to the Médrano Circus . . . Picasso would
> go to the bar, which was filled with the hot, rather sickly

smell rising from the stables, and he and Braque would spend the whole evening there, chatting with the clowns. He enjoyed their awkwardness, their accents and their jokes . . . Picasso esteemed them and felt real sympathy for them . . . No one ever left the Médrano before the performance was over, and some people would go three or even four times a week.[6]

Picasso may have had a special attraction to the circus because his first lover, Rosa Ortiz, was a trick rider, and his first art dealer, Clovis Sagot, a former clown.

Certainly Picasso's love for the circus was deeply personal: with his face lathered for shaving, he sometimes pretended to be a whiteface clown. 'I liked the clowns best of all,' he told his friend Brassaï. 'Sometimes we stayed out in the wings at the bar and talked to them through the whole performance.' It was at the Médrano, he recalled, that clowns gave up the classic *commèdia* costumes for 'the burlesque type'. 'It was a real revolution,' Picasso said. 'They could invent their own costumes, their own characters, do anything they fancied.'[7] This bold reinvention of public personae delighted him. To be masked and costumed represented for modernists like Picasso a slippery, protean identity: a carefully honed image that might mask an estranged and isolated private self. As the writer Wallace Fowlie put it, reflecting on Picasso's studies of acrobats: 'Picasso's energy . . . upsets the world and what remains on the finished picture is a delirious kind of joy, so intense that it ends by becoming the artist's personality.' Picasso's acrobats, Fowlie wrote, epitomized a 'spiritual hope' for transformation.[8]

The Médrano in Montmartre was one of four major circuses in late nineteenth-century Paris. Astley's amphitheatre, which had opened in Paris in 1783, was followed in 1843 by the Cirque des Champs-Élysées, later called the Cirque d'Été, which offered performances from May through to October; soon the Cirque Napoléon – in 1870 renamed the Cirque d'Hiver – opened near the Bastille, where the circus was held from 1 November to the end of April. A parade of performers marched through the city from the Cirque d'Été to the Cirque d'Hiver at the end of October, signalling the end of one season and the start of another.

Pablo Picasso,
At the Circus,
1905–6, etching.

Architecturally, the Cirque d'Hiver was striking: a twenty-sided polygon 42 metres in diameter, rising to a peak of 27.5 metres, with a capacity of nearly 4,000. Two equestrian statues flanked the entrance, and stables for more than 50 horses were at the back. Both the summer and winter circuses focused on equestrian feats, with interludes by clowns and acrobats. By the second half of the century, though, audiences were no longer so impressed by the aristocratic connotations of horses. Members of the Jockey Club preferred betting on horse races or frequenting the ballet, where they could pick up courtesans among the dancers. Several hippodromes did exist, notably the Hippodrome du Pont de l'Alma, with a capacity of 10,000; when it was torn down in 1897, its replacement was half the size – and in 1907 this hippodrome became a cinema. With horse-riding feats

Le Cirque Napoléon.

The original Cirque Napoléon, renamed Cirque d'Hiver in 1870, in an engraving from 1853.

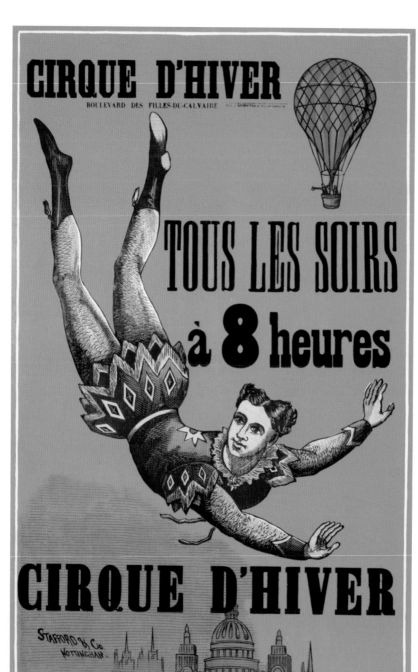

diminishing in popularity, aerialists, acrobats and clowns took an increasingly central place in the circuses of Paris. Audiences followed their favourite performers and each season were introduced to new acts as well, the better to generate repeat visits from ticket buyers.

With the cost of seats ranging from half a franc to two francs, the circus was affordable for the working class and families. On Thursdays, when schoolchildren had a day off, and on Sundays, circuses offered matinees with lowered ticket prices. Yet there was nothing tawdry about the venues: seats upholstered in red velvet, balustrades edged in gilt, glittering gas-lit chandeliers and sculptures, fountains and friezes made circuses elegant and glamorous destinations.

The success of the summer and winter circuses inspired others. In 1886 Joseph Oller founded the Nouveau Cirque, notable for its hydraulically powered movable floor that could sink slowly, fill with water and become transformed into a swimming pool deep enough for diving. With arc lights illuminating the artificial lake, acrobats performed an aquatic burlesque. The Cirque Fernando, opened on 25 June 1875, was a sixteen-sided polygon a little smaller than the Cirque d'Hiver, about 34 metres (111 feet) in diameter, with a central ring of 14 metres (46 feet). A ceiling more than 21 metres (69 feet) high was supported by sixteen columns. Several chandeliers glittered from the roof. The building could accommodate about 2,000, with seats arranged in tiers. The Cirque Fernando changed its name in 1897 when its ownership passed from the equestrian Ferdinand Beert to the clown Geronimo Médrano, known as Boum-Boum, who had been the Cirque Fernando's featured act.

Many attested to the easy camaraderie among audience members and performers at the Médrano. 'You could stroll past the photographs of famous performers, which lined the walls of the circular corridor under

Adolphe Léon Willette, poster for the Nouveau Cirque, Paris, *c.* 1890.

61

the seating, and come to the bar at the back of the ring curtains,' recalled Antony Coxe.

> Here there was always a clown or an auguste ready to pass the time of day, his prosaic small talk and matter-of-fact gestures contrasting strangely with the magnificence of his sequined dress or the grotesque pattern of his make-up. You could chat with a trainer, watch a troupe of acrobats limbering up, or pass on to the stables to inspect the horses . . . Here the public and the performers met on an equal footing, for there is no backstage in a circus.[9]

Physical culture

A firm line between public and performers did, of course, exist: performers possessed skills that the public could only admire, unless that admiration developed into aspiration, and aspiration to achievement. In 1880 the dream of joining the circus became reality for 36-year-old aristocrat Ernest Molier. An accomplished rider, Molier decided to become a circus impresario, an unusual career choice for the wealthy son of a treasurer and magistrate. Growing up in Le Mans, Molier had been a desultory student with no goal for his life. At the age of twenty, he arrived in Paris and developed a passion for horses. Treated like a dilettante by conventional Haute École riding masters, he schooled himself in equestrian science by reading and riding in the Bois de Boulogne. By the time he was 25, Molier had become an incomparable horseman, and he went on to train not only horses, but also monkeys, dogs and camels. As a riding master himself, he counted among his students some of the most acclaimed equestriennes of the day. Rebelling against the dictum that women should ride only sidesaddle, his students sat astride their horses; to preserve their reputations, he cautioned them to ride in the Bois de Boulogne only at night.

Molier drew his performers from friends who prided themselves on their riding skill and who in their spare time, of which they had plenty, engaged in boxing, fencing and gymnastics, which was increasingly popular in the late nineteenth century. Bolstered by their enthusiasm,

James Tissot, *Women of Paris: The Circus Lover*, 1883–5, oil on canvas.

Molier transformed his riding stable to include a ring 13 metres in diameter with seats for several hundred viewers; in 1898 he expanded into an even more spacious arena. There, such prominent members of the leisure class as the Comte de Sainte-Aldegonde and the Comte Hubert de La Rochefoucauld could show off.

The first performance of the Cirque Molier was by invitation only. But news spread quickly and high society clamoured for admission. Soon Molier offered two seatings for a spectacle that he mounted two or three times a year: one for his prominent friends, and another to include their mistresses. The *New York Times* reproduced the coveted invitation:

> Monsieur Ernest Molier
> Will be at home, on foot and on horseback, on June 6 to bachelors, to gentlemen with wrinkles, and to widowers and widows. On June 11 to the married and unmarried of both sexes. Respond S. V. P.

'As to the audiences,' the report continued,

> the masculine portion is made up of well-known clubmen, swells, and that conglomerate class known as 'the boys.' The feminine portion is a combination of women who are indifferent to social prejudices, actresses, and resident members of the foreign nobility. Americans also are never disposed to refuse an invitation. The best society does not go, because the best society in Paris goes nowhere, but all the gay and pleasure-loving people of both sexes are only too glad to go if they are invited.[10]

According to French newspapers, the best society among physicians, magistrates and financiers eagerly attended the Cirque Molier, and stayed for the champagne and dinner that followed each performance.

Besides Molier's friends, the performers included actors, actresses and singers whose usual stage was the Palais Royal or Paris Opera House. Journalists and theatre critics tried their talents at juggling and clowning. When the novelist Pierre Loti was elected to the Académie Francaise in 1891, the *New York Times* noted among his achievements that he had been 'an applauded gymnast at the aristocratic Cirque Molier, and an athlete'.[11] Loti, the pseudonym of Julien Viaud, came to the Cirque Molier with some previous acrobatic experience in the Etruscan Circus, where he had performed masked and costumed. Like many others in Molier's troupe, he saw the circus as an escape from the constraints and false posturing of his social class.

As a man about town, Molier had an eye for attractive young women, and he staged pantomimes in which they appeared nearly naked. Their skimpy costumes were featured alluringly on the Cirque's posters. Apparently Molier hired fifteen-year-old Marie-Clémentine Valadon; when she became famous as the artist Suzanne Valadon, she claimed to have performed on the trapeze for six months before a fall ended her aerial career. The Dutch dancer Margaretha Zelle MacLeod, later known as Mata Hari, hoped to join the circus as an equestrienne but Molier, evaluating her talents, encouraged her to continue as a dancer. His student Blanche Allarty, whom he had trained since she was thirteen, had more promise, he thought; she became one of his star equestriennes – journalists nicknamed her La Centauresse – and his wife.

Molier's circus had its vociferous critics in the press, who deemed it unseemly for the nobility to display themselves as clowns and buffoons. Equally damning, these critics believed, was the flaunting of their muscular bodies in low-cut leotards. The cult of gymnastics, many critics held, was motivated not by a desire to improve health but rather by anxiety over the degeneration of the race, specifically of the wealthy and privileged. It seemed to some contemporary viewers that Molier's circus gave performers more than a chance to exhibit their athletic skills; their bodies attested to their status and power.

Concern over degeneration was much debated at the turn of the century, when industrialization and urbanization threatened to produce weak and flabby bodies, and when the lower classes proliferated with larger families than the elite. Less than a decade before the Cirque Molier opened, France had been defeated in the Franco-Prussian War, and the Paris Commune of 1871 stunned the aristocracy when workers rose up as an armed militia to demand political rights and economic equality. The Comte de La Rochefoucauld, for one, may well have begun gymnastics to emulate the kind of training undergone by his cousin, an army captain, or his brother, a cavalry officer. Only the military gave men a chance to hone and prove their physical strength, but the recent defeat made that strength questionable. Money, social status and military rank no longer defined masculinity and power. The Austrian writer Max Nordau summed up these anxieties in his widely read, inflammatory *Degeneration* (1892), accusing French elite culture of the infectious spread of decadence, immorality and the feminization of men.

In America, too, degeneration loomed as a threat. Popular magazines lamented the prevalence of neuraesthenia, or nerve weakness, a result, physicians believed, of the stresses of fast-paced urban life. Some sufferers sought relief in electrotherapy, infusions of electricity, believed to be the essential life force. Theodore Roosevelt, who claimed to have cured himself of nerve weakness through activity in the outdoors, exhorted men to live the 'strenuous life' by engaging in hunting, boxing and competitive sports. In 1900 the American exercise proselytizer Bernarr Macfadden inaugurated a magazine, *Physical Culture*, that urged men and women to strengthen their bodies or risk no less than the downfall of civilization. 'There can be no doubt', one article writer warned, 'that the conditions of physical and mental decadence that has been the history of many of the great nations of the world, whose civilization has passed and gone, has been brought about by a failure to observe the natural laws of exercise, both for the physical and mental man'.[12] Although this advice was meant to apply to all men and women across class lines, critics of the Cirque Molier accused aristocrats of engaging in bodybuilding to assuage their anxiety about their imperilled social status, and exhibiting the muscular results of their exercises to point to their supremacy over others who were not so well-endowed, physically, morally or socially.

Certainly exhibitionism was an important motivation for the Cirque's performers, as portrayed by the French-born painter James Tissot in his *The Women of Paris: The Circus Lover*, a depiction of the Cirque Molier. Central to the painting are two men on a trapeze: one, facing the viewer, is the bare-chested Comte de La Rochefoucauld, sporting a monocle and with a handkerchief tucked into his red jersey. Behind him we see the bare back of another performer, likely his aerialist partner, the painter Théophile Pierre Wagner. Surely they are on exhibition; but who is watching these half-naked men? Some women seated in the gallery appear attentive, but two women in the forefront of the painting are Tissot's central subjects. These are members of the *demi-monde*, showing off their modish costumes and hats. It was warm in the arena, and one woman holds a fan opened across her breast as she watches the performers; the other is turned towards us, or perhaps towards the man seated behind her. Most of the audience, rather than raptly focusing on the performers, are engaged with one another; this circus is a social event, and the men on trapeze seem to be enjoying themselves merely for the pleasure of display, not yearning for affirmation from viewers.

In America, another wealthy man, one Mr Waterbury, established his own private circus in 1889 at the cost of $50,000. 'Fashionable and elegant gentleman of leisure were the performers,' noted the *Washington Post*, 'and the well bred daughters of rich men sold peanuts to the guests.' Scornful of the pretension, the newspaper conceded that rich people might do what they wished with their money, apparently finding little satisfaction in 'the fashionable life'. Yet the article questioned why young men would undergo weeks of rigorous training 'at enormous expense of time and money, to imitate a class of artists they affect to scorn'.[13] More than imitating these performers, though, the amateurs longed to possess their strength, to master their own bodies and to discover within themselves wildness and courage.

Many artists and writers who were drawn to circus images and themes empathized with, and perhaps envied, performers' control. As the fiction writer Jules-Amédée Barbey d'Aurevilly admitted,

> I have always been a great frequenter of circuses, an amateur of those physical spectacles which not only give me a pleasure of the senses . . . but an intellectual pleasure far more deep and refined. If only we writers could write as these people move, if only we had in our style the inexhaustible resources of their

Peter Newell, 'The
Amateur Circus
at Nutley', from
Harper's Weekly,
1894.

vigour, their almost fluid suppleness, their undulating grace,
their mathematical precision, if only we had the control of
words that they have of their movement we should be great
writers.[14]

Artists, too, appear obsessed with the strength and daring of
exhilarating feats. Edgar Degas, for example, was fascinated by Olga
Kaira, known as Miss Lala, all the rage in Paris in 1879 for her iron jaw
act. Gripping an iron and leather bit by her teeth, suspended from the
rafters of the Cirque Fernando, she lifted weights – including three men
– and even fired a cannon held between her legs. Reporters dubbed
her 'The Venus of the Tropics' and 'Black Venus'; posters billed her
as 'La Femme Canon', 'the cannon-woman'. Degas was in the audience for four performances in late January 1879, sketching quickly in
his notebook, then using those sketches for more detailed drawings and
pastels. In all he produced about twenty studies, straining to get the
effect he was after: an accurate sense of the architecture of the Cirque

Edgar Degas, *Miss
Lala at the Cirque
Fernando*, 1879,
oil on canvas.

Fernando, the slant of the roof, the arch of the performer's back, the
colour of her skin, her astounding muscularity. He sketched her from
the front and from the side, again and again; he invited her to his
studio for a closer look. Finally, in his oil painting *Miss Lala at the
Cirque Fernando*, Degas portrayed her as a solitary figure dangling
above the arena; he does not show her face, although he knew it well,
only her illuminated body, demonstrating what appears to be superhuman skill. The audience is irrelevant; only two individuals matter
in this painting: a voyeur and an exhibitionist.

A mad little universe

At the turn of the twentieth century, the Barnum & Bailey Circus, already featuring three rings and two platforms, already colossal, undertook a European tour. In Germany, the parade itself was so immense that people watching it thought it was the entire event. They saw no reason to buy tickets for anything more. In Paris, once the initial excitement waned, the three-ring circus failed as entertainment. The pace was too fast, the multiple acts too distracting, the whole atmosphere too noisy. Audiences wanted to be able to concentrate on one central attraction. Moreover, they wanted to see particular performers – clowns, acrobats, trapeze artists – whose careers they followed and whose acts they favoured. Barnum & Bailey was an assault on the senses.

The Cirque Molier responded with a parody, the 'Barnum Express', in which an American impresario, held up by a train delay, asks Molier to present French circus acts in the American style – as rapidly as possible. Molier agrees, and there follows a frantically paced performance accompanied by blaring music. To the American, the performance is a huge success, and he buys the circus from Molier, leading the performers away as if he were the Pied Piper. But the intimate one-ring circus was the only model that endured in Europe, and the most intimate of these was fashioned by an American artist, the as yet unknown Alexander Calder.

Calder, the son and grandson of artists, graduated from the Stevens Institute of Technology in Hoboken, New Jersey, in 1919 with a degree in mechanical engineering and set out to find a job. He lasted two weeks as an automobile engineer, then worked as a draftsman for the Edison Company, an insurance claims adjuster and a salesman before deciding to study art. In 1923 he enrolled in the Arts Students League of New York, where his teachers included John Sloan, Thomas Hart Benton and George Luks, painters who took as their subjects the gritty reality of urban life. Eking out a living as a freelance illustrator, Calder spent two weeks sketching at the Ringling Bros Barnum & Bailey Circus in Madison Square Garden, submitting his work to the *National Police Gazette*. His editor balked at publishing his drawings, not because of their quality but because the circus was so stingy in handing out free tickets to the press.

Nevertheless, a few were printed but more relevant to Calder's artistic career were his two oil paintings *The Flying Trapeze* and *Circus*, and the many whimsical drawings he made of animals in the circus's menagerie, where he spent several hours each evening. Calder's affection for the circus had begun, his biographers agree, in childhood, when he was given the popular Humpty Dumpty Circus, a set of articulated wooden figures and animals. He was so fond of the toys that he later set himself the task of constructing his own set, miniature circus performers made of wood, movable at the joints, surely not the engineering feat for which he had been trained.

After a few years studying art in New York, Calder followed many of his compatriots and moved to Paris, with his toys packed in his baggage. Soon he became a frequent visitor to the Cirque Médrano. At the same time, he took a new direction in art, making wire sculptures – a portrait of the dancer Josephine Baker, a star at the Folies Bergère, for example – and resumed his circus construction, this time using bent and twisted wire, wine bottle corks and cloth scraps. His tiny troupe grew to more than 50 human and animal performers, each about six inches tall, that he manipulated to perform acrobatics, bareback riding, aerial acts and clowning. His circus included a sword swallower, a man on stilts, a strong man, a pair of seals that tossed a ball between them and a lion tamer whose thickly maned lion roared from a painted cage. He even created a ringmaster complete with top hat and rhinestone-studded pin. Calder had become an impresario, producing and directing what the Paris press called 'The Smallest Circus in the World'.

In 1926 Calder gave a circus performance for a few friends who crowded into his small Left Bank studio; they were delighted, and he was encouraged. For the next five years, Calder sailed back and forth between Paris and New York, always carrying his circus, first in two suitcases and eventually in five, and giving performances in hotel rooms, friends' apartments and occasionally in a gallery that was showing the wire and wood sculptures for which he was becoming known. Although he would often pass around a hat after performing, and sometimes sold tickets for a few dollars each, the circus was not a way to earn a living. In 1927 in New York, he took a paying job as supervisor of the manufacture of action toys for the Gould Manufacturing Company's Toddler Toys division.

Once again in Paris, Calder entertained at various venues, including the Galerie Billiet, where he had his first Paris one-man show. Calder's *Circus* was brief at first – fifteen minutes, performed by a small troupe of figures – but eventually expanded to two hours. When he performed in his own studio, Calder placed planks over workbenches to build bleachers, and guests ate peanuts. A big man and burly, Calder sat on the floor or knelt on basketball kneepads, manipulating his toys and giving voice to the performers, while a record player provided appropriately lively music. 'Ramona', a popular song at the time, was a favourite choice. Word spread among the Paris art world; a few prominent critics published exuberant reviews. Viewers returned with friends, who brought other friends, including Joan Miró, Edward Steichen, Jean Cocteau, Piet Mondrian, Fernand Léger and, at one performance, the eminent circus clown Paul Fratellini, who was amused by Calder's tiny toy dachshund and asked Calder to create a larger one for his brother Albert to incorporate into his act. Mondrian invited Calder back to his studio, where he was astonished by Mondrian's geometrical paintings. 'I thought at the time', Calder said, 'how fine it would be if everything there moved; though Mondrian did not approve of this idea at all'.[15] Nevertheless, movable planes of colour became part of Calder's signature style.

Although his circus was unscripted, Calder deliberately included acts that seemed perilous for his tiny figures – the trapeze artist might lose her grip, the tightrope walker might plummet – the better to evoke fear and thrills in his viewers. Calder, art historian L. Joy Sperling noted, 'was the agent of ultimate control in the destiny of his own mad little universe'. Spontaneous, irreverent and responsive to his audience's reactions, it seemed to some modernist artists that Calder was creating the kind of surreal, magical theatricality they aspired to in their own works. He had miniaturized and distilled the essence of the circus experience. Like many of his contemporaries, Sperling wrote, Calder 'believed that our most profound emotions are hidden deep in the unconscious, that the object of the creative process is to release that unconscious and thus expand the conscious mind'.[16] Calder, though, expressed his interest simply: 'I love the mechanics of the thing', he said, 'and the vast space – and the spotlight.'[17]

That single beam of light, fixing attention on a singular performance, defined the exhilarating, ethereal spectacle of the *cirque intime*.

THREE

THE BIGGEST TENTS

Within 'the big top', as nowhere else on earth, is to be
found Actuality. Living players play with living.

E. E. Cummings

By the time Phineas Taylor Barnum became a circus impresario,
he had earned and lost fortunes as a merchant, bank president,
publisher and land developer. His American Museum, Menagerie
and Aquarium, a gigantic emporium of the natural and unnatural,
had been a fixture of lower Manhattan for more than 25 years until
it burned down in 1868, news of which reached Barnum as he was
delivering a speech as a Connecticut state assemblyman. There was
hardly an American as well known as the self-proclaimed 'Prince of
Humbug', who had taken Jenny Lind, the Swedish Nightingale, on
a spectacularly successful tour; promoted a blind, aged black woman
as 160-year-old Joice Heth, George Washington's nurse; and escorted
Charles Sherwood Stratton, a dwarf Barnum made famous as General
Tom Thumb, around the world. Boisterous, enthusiastic and undaunted in his optimism, he was certain that whatever he did, he would
succeed: 'If he was shipwrecked and thrown on a desert island,' a
friend once commented, 'he would try to sell maps of the islands to its
inhabitants.'[1] And, Barnum believed, he would undoubtedly make a
handy profit on those maps.

In 1870, at 60 years old, Barnum was travelling the country, rest-
lessly retired and eager, he said, to 'go it once more', when William
Cameron Coup, who had managed a sideshow and the Yankee Robinson
Circus, came to him with a business proposition. The 33-year-old Coup

Phineas T. Barnum,
c. 1855–65.

THE FIRST BARNUM'S MUSEUM, New York.

'The First Barnum's Museum, New York', 1853.

and his partner Dan Castello wanted to expand their own circus, which was just completing its first season. What they needed from Barnum was his incomparable expertise at publicity, his showmanship and his name. And, of course, his money. As senior partner he would own two-thirds of the show; Coup and Castello would be the managers, Barnum the publicist. Part of his duties – and no small part – was to put in appearances at the show, preferably greeting the audience from the ring.

Barnum jumped at the new opportunity to display himself and put his talents to use. Immediately, he placed orders for animals and published hundreds of thousands of copies of *Barnum's Advance Courier*, a publicity pamphlet containing advertisements, reviews (many written by his own staff) and testimonials from famous men, which inundated towns on the planned tour. In April 1871 the P. T. Barnum Museum, Menagerie and Circus, International Zoological Garden, Polytechnic Institute and Hippodrome played for a week in Brooklyn, and then proceeded on through New York state and New England. For the price of a single ticket, viewers made their way through several tents containing a menagerie and the kind of exhibitions that

Barnum had featured at his American Museum: automata; magicians; extraordinary humans, such as a giant, dwarf, bearded woman and 'armless wonder'; and various individuals promoted as anthropological specimens. At the end of the series of tents, the audience took their seats under the big top for a performance of equestrians, clowns and acrobats. Everywhere it opened, the show was a huge success, turning away scores of potential viewers, and Barnum returned bursting with ideas for expanding and improving. He would buy many more animals for the menagerie; increase the number of horses by hundreds; expand the size of the tent to hold more seats; and take the circus on tour by rail.

Any wagon show was vulnerable to weather, and the slow pace of travel meant that the circus needed to stop frequently in small towns, unloading, setting up tents and taking everything down every evening. It was expensive and often gruelling. The entire show bumped along rutted roads night after night, damaging wagons and keeping performers awake. Lewis B. Lent, whose New York Circus had a permanent home at the Hippotheatron in Manhattan from 1866 to 1874, had already put his show on twelve rail cars for its national tour. Barnum's idea was grander: he would have cars built especially for circus equipment, staff and animals. The show could travel hundreds of miles each

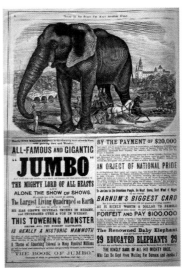

The cover and a page from the *Barnum Courier*, 1883.

night, arrive in cities in the morning, parade down the main street as the tent was set up and accommodate the larger audiences that a city location would draw. In its first season on rails, travelling on 65 cars as far as Topeka, Kansas, the show opened in 145 different cities and offered three performances a day.

Even with extra performances, the circus could not accommodate everyone who wanted a ticket. Enlarging the ring, Barnum quickly learned, was not the answer: viewers complained of being too far from the performers to see them. So in the 1872 season, Barnum added another ring, and P. T. Barnum's Great Traveling Exposition and World's Fair, Menagerie, Caravan, Hippodrome, Polytechnic Institute, National Portrait Gallery, Hall of Classic Statuary, Mechanics, and Fine Arts, Garden of Zoology and Ornithology – what he now called 'The Greatest Show on Earth' – became a two-ring circus offering simultaneous acts. Viewers could see everything, and there was more to see in a show that lasted three hours.

It was the two-ring circus that Booth Tarkington remembered as a child in Indianapolis. He recalled the equestrian feats; 'hair-raising exploits' on tightrope, slack rope and trapeze; acrobats' leaping and tumbling; and the 'uproarious jester, the clown' filling intervals with 'hilarities'. But even more indelible than the exciting acts was the quality of light that, for Tarkington, conveyed the magic of the circus: 'The enormous white tent was filled with a hazy yellow light, the warm, dusty, mellow light that thrills the rejoicing heart because it is found nowhere in the world except in the tents of a circus – the canvas-filtered sunshine and sawdust atmosphere of show day.'[2]

Barnum's two-ring extravaganza was not quite the greatest show on earth. In England, circus director George Sanger, as self-aggrandizing as Barnum – he dubbed himself 'Lord' – also believed that bigger was better. A showman who began his career in 1848 as a magician at fairs, he soon set up a circus with two horses and assorted performers, some of whom were his nieces and nephews. Charging a penny for admission and threepence for reserved seats, and passing a hat at intermission, he managed to make a profit, which he invested back into his show. After three years of touring in a tent, he had 60 horses; then he added six lions, and in 1860 experimented with three rings, an innovation that proved unpopular with British audiences, who found competing acts chaotic. Sanger gave up the idea, and by 1871 he again was so successful that he was able to buy Astley's venue in London besides maintaining shows in Manchester, Birmingham, Liverpool, Glasgow, Dundee, Aberdeen, Bath, Bristol, Exeter and Plymouth. The most famous circus man in England, he decided to take his show on tour throughout Europe, with 46 carriages, 160 horses, eleven elephants, twelve camels and a staff of more than 200 people. Sanger had become a major force in the circus world.

In America Barnum had many competitors among about 30 circuses that were travelling the country. There was Fayette Ludovic Robinson, who had been a shoemaker before he decided to try his hand at entertaining. Around 1850, after a few years as an actor and minstrel singer, he founded the Yankee Robinson Quadruple Show, giving viewers four tents for the price of one ticket: a menagerie, museum, minstrel singers and the main ring. After the Civil War, he often produced battle reenactments as part of the circus show.

Adam Forepaugh was a Philadelphia butcher and horse dealer whose customers for both horsemeat and live animals included circuses and the Union Army. After the war, he decided that the circus business might be a profitable enterprise and, indeed, proved himself an able and creative impresario. 'Magnificent', 'startling' and 'mammoth' were recurring accolades as Forepaugh grew in size and stature. By the time Barnum opened his show, Forepaugh reigned as his foremost rival. Their competition was visible in posters: 'Barnum Imitates 4-Paw' blared one poster in 1884; 'A Giant Among the Pigmys' pictured Forepaugh towering above his intimidated rivals, Barnum among them.

The year after Barnum opened, the Sells brothers, Ohio stable owners, put a show on the road. Campbell's Circus was playing to acclaim in Washington, DC. By 1875, when Barnum was touting the greatness of his show, John Robinson's circus called itself the Great World's Exposition, Museum, Menagerie, Aquarium, and Strictly Moral Circus. 'Indorsed by the Press as the Best. Pronounced by the Public the Greatest', boasted its billboard ad. Advertising the strict morality of a circus was one way to fight the image of grift and vulgarity that caused educators and clergymen to warn against attending. Some impresarios offered free tickets to preachers and some cut prices for school groups, but opposition remained firm.

Earl Benson, the son of a Methodist minister, recalled that in 1892, when he was nine years old, he saw posters for the Great London Circus, due to come to his town in two weeks. He wanted so badly to go that he set himself the task of earning enough, somehow, to surprise his father with two tickets, with some money left for peanuts and popcorn. Babysitting helped him towards his goal, but he worried about how to earn the rest when, to his delight and amazement, he was rewarded with two free passes for lugging bucket after bucket of water for the circus elephants. He could hardly contain his excitement when he rushed home to tell his father. 'Look, here are two passes! I earned them!' he shouted. 'Father was sitting with an open Bible in front of him, working on his next sermon,' Benson remembered. 'He looked up at me, grasped the arms of his chair, and swallowed hard, obviously struggling with a strong emotion.' Then, with the passes in his hand, he walked out of his study to the kitchen, picked up the lid of the stove and dropped the passes into the fire. 'My boy,' he said, 'this is the best place for circus tickets.'[3]

Barnum, a teetotaller, proselytizer of temperance and active member of the Universalist church, was adamant about maintaining and promoting his circus as a moral enterprise. 'Of course,' he wrote to theatre reviewer William Winter, 'there will be no bar about the premises . . . and I shall as always before cater to the tastes of the moral, religious, and refined – never permitting a word or gesture that is objectionable to ladies, children, or others who desire to enjoy innocent amusement blended with instruction.'[4] 'The truth is,' Barnum insisted to Schuyler Colfax, a circus fan and former vice president under Ulysses S. Grant, 'I would abandon the show business if *cash* was my only reward. I want to *elevate* traveling exhibitions and reform them altogether, for they are an *important* power for good or evil.'[5] Most of his employees, he boasted, were total abstainers, therefore more reliable and trustworthy than those who drank. Drinking, he said, was an 'unnatural appetite': 'It is all a delusion and a snare. It is an unmitigated evil, causing more misery and crime than all the other evils combined.'[6]

Barnum's goal of mounting a morally upstanding and high-minded circus, though, never interfered with his hunger for profits. Tireless advance publicity, he believed, would 'awaken and electrify the country'; excursion trains would bring those electrified viewers from far distances; and a huge investment would reap huge financial rewards. In August 1872 he explained to Mark Twain that he had had 'an immense tent made, over 800 feet long by 400 broad, and transported it to Boston' where it could seat 11,000. His staff included 'over 1200 men, women, & children . . . 750 horses, including 300 blooded race horses & ponies; camels, elephants, buffaloes, English stag and stag hounds, ostriches, &c, &c.' The cost was more than $50,000; yet after three weeks, with 20,000 people at two performances each day, Barnum had completely repaid his outlay, with what he called 'a handsome surplus'. He planned to have two tents for the next season, 125 railroad cars to transport the show, and he would stop throughout New England, the Midwest and West for one night in each town. 'If I *can* do this,' he said, 'I can *make* half a million.'[7]

By late 1880 Barnum had decided that his partnership with William Coup was no longer advantageous. Coup went out on his own, and Barnum took a new partner, the owner of the esteemed and profitable Great London Circus, James Anthony Bailey. The 33-year-old Bailey was as different from Barnum as anyone could be: slim and slight, quiet and nervous, he preferred working behind the scenes. And work he did, for long days, every day, overseeing all aspects of his circus from managing money to reprimanding performers to loading wagons. A worrier and micro-manager, Bailey seems an odd choice for Barnum. Born James A. McGinniss in Detroit, Michigan, orphaned when he was eight, he had lived with his sister and guardian for three years until he ran away from home and joined up with a circus. At thirteen he became a bill poster for Robinson & Lake's one-ring circus, where he took on the surname of one of the advance men. For twenty years, circus was the only life he knew, and he knew it intimately. His management of the Great London Circus, which he shared with James Cooper and, after Cooper's retirement, with James L. Hutchinson, was ample evidence of Bailey's brilliance as a circus director; Barnum decided it was wiser to have Bailey as a partner than a competitor. The

Ringling Bros and
Barnum & Bailey
circus train in Safety
Harbor, Florida, 1992.

new agreement made Barnum senior partner; he was to provide half
the capital and receive half the profits, with the rest divided between
Bailey and Hutchinson, who were charged with the business and
management of the show. As in his partnership with Coup, Barnum
provided his name and face, which was emblazoned, along with Bailey's,
on posters and advertisements.

Despite the difference in their temperaments – or perhaps because
of it – the partnership thrived, and the Barnum & Bailey Circus,
expanded to three rings, proved incomparable. Throughout their ten
years together, Barnum was effusive in his praise of Bailey: 'I shall never
cease to admire many traits in your character, your manliness & integrity,
nor your marvelous perceptions of how to hit public taste & to do it in
the best way,' Barnum wrote to Bailey in 1885. And in 1891, five days
before he died, Barnum took pains to assure Bailey of his 'unalterable
esteem, affection, and trust'.[8]

Poster for the
Ringling Brothers Big
New Parade, 1899.

In October 1889 the Barnum & Bailey Circus – 1,200 people,
330 horses and scores of animals – sailed for England, fulfilling one

Poster for the Barnum & Bailey Greatest Show on Earth, 1897.

of Barnum's fondest dreams. A few days before opening at the Olympia Theatre on 11 November Barnum was feted at a banquet at the Hotel Victoria, where aristocrats and other notables praised his tireless efforts to provide 'moral' entertainment and, not least, his impressive ability to spring back from misfortune. The opening was breathlessly antici-pated, and the Greatest Show on Earth did not disappoint. 'It is precisely in the immensity, the complexity, the kaleidoscopic variety, and, to use the word in its strict etymological sense, the incomprehensibility of the show that Mr Barnum's genius is displayed,' exulted *The Times*. Although the article suggested that a viewer might feel 'oppressed by the variety of the efforts made for his entertainment', still, the reporter acknowledged, as a business ploy, the three-ring, two-platform circus was a brilliant idea: no one could see everything at once, so Barnum could count on repeated visits.[9]

The show played for three months, with the Olympia expanded from 5,000 to 12,000 seats. Even at low ticket prices, Barnum was making a sizable profit, turning people away at every performance. Audiences were dazzled and overwhelmed not only by the quality of the acts, the variety of animals in the menagerie and the human oddities in the freak show, but also by the final extravaganza, which had a cast of thousands of performers: a historical spectacle called 'Nero; or, The Destruction of Rome', in which the clash of civilizations ended, appropriately enough for Barnum, with the dawn of Christianity.

Josephine Robinson, a star equestrienne in the show, called it 'the most stupendous venture known to the show world. It took both men to make it a success. Mr Barnum was the advertiser, who loved the limelight, who rode around in the ring, and announced who he was. But Mr Bailey was the business man, content to be invisible, demanding it in fact, and interested only in the success of the show.' 'Nero and the Fall of Rome', she said, 'took London by storm. After the opening, it was impossible to get tickets . . . unless you ordered them for weeks ahead.'[10]

Besides the human and animal performers, ballet dancers, choir and orchestra that constituted Barnum & Bailey's circus, there was a huge cast of workers behind the scenes – more, certainly, than most in the audience could imagine. 'It will surprise persons acquainted only with English circuses', commented the historian Thomas Frost, 'to learn that the staff of the combined shows comprises a manager and an assistant manager, advertiser, treasurer, equestrian director, riding-master, band leader, lion performer, elephant man, doorkeeper, and head ostler, besides grooms, tent-men, &c., to the number, all told, of nearly a hundred.'[11] Nearly 100 in 1881, when Frost was writing, doubled and tripled as American circuses grew. As the *New York Times* noted, 'The circuses of Europe are mere side-shows compared with the mammoth affairs that pitch their tents in almost every city of the Union each year.'[12]

During Barnum's twenty years as circus impresario, he and Bailey acquired many smaller circuses and even some mammoth affairs, burgeoning into an ever greater show. In 1852 there were about 30 American circuses; consolidation halved that number by 1884. But one circus had begun which would become Barnum & Bailey's most formidable rival.

Sunday school circus

In 1870 August Rungeling repaired a harness for Andrew Gaffney, a rider with Dan Rice's circus. Because the rider came from McGregor, Iowa, where the Rungeling family was then living, August did not charge him for the work but accepted instead a circus pass for his family: his wife, Salomé, and eight children. It took just one visit to the circus to inspire the oldest brothers to put on their own production in their backyard under a tent made of scraps of canvas, carpets and blankets. Albert, eighteen, took the role of ringmaster and juggler of hats and plates. Charles, six, was the equestrian, riding a pony. Otto, twelve, trained a goat. And John, four years old, imitated clown Dan Rice's song 'Root, Hog, or Die!' Charging a penny for admission, the brothers made enough from their performances to buy muslin for a real tent.[13]

The boys spent the next year practising their acts and making props. In the summer of 1871, after a noisy parade down the main streets of McGregor, Ringling's Big Circus opened under a large tent erected in a vacant lot. Admission this time was five cents and the show, more elaborate and varied than the backyard version, included tumbling, a trapeze act, Charles's equestrian display and considerable clowning. The boys' friends joined in the performance and neighbours eagerly filled the tent. The circus was a success, and the Ringling Brothers had found their life's work.

In the autumn of 1875 the family moved to Baraboo, Wisconsin, where for a few years Alfred and Charles helped out in their father's harness shop. The brothers, though, did not let go of their dream. In June 1882 they once again organized a show, this time the Ringling Brothers Classic and Comic Concert Company, and in November they set out from Baraboo to take it on tour. Throughout the icy winter they played in music halls in the Midwest, hardly making a profit; they spent the spring and most of the summer revamping, and in August set out again as the Ringling Bros. Grand Carnival of Fun.

By the spring of 1884 they had joined with Yankee Robinson, who was eager for a partnership. The once-successful circus had fallen into bankruptcy, but Robinson hoped to revive it: Yankee Robinson's Great Show and the Ringling Brothers Carnival of Comedy soon became the Yankee Robinson and Ringling Bros Great Double Shows, Circus and Caravan. After Robinson died in August 1884, the Ringlings continued to thrive, touring under increasingly grandiose names: the Carnival of Fun became the Ringling Bros Great Double Shows and Congress of Wild and Trained Animals, and later the Ringling Bros United Monster Shows, Great Double Circus, Royal European Menagerie, Museum, Caravan and Congress of Trained Animals. By 1886 the Ringlings had a 90-foot round tent, a 30-foot middle tent and a 75-by-45-foot sideshow tent. They had eighteen wagons and a substantial menagerie. By 1890, like other major circuses, they were moving by rail, with a team of advance men travelling ahead in special cars filled with steam boilers for making paste and carrying tons of bills.

The Ringlings had competitors other than Barnum & Bailey, which was thriving under Bailey's directorship after Barnum died in April 1891. The Sells Brothers' four-ring circus, the Great Wallace Show, John Robinson's Ten Big Shows and the formidable Adam Forepaugh's Big Show were among those receiving ecstatic reviews in the press. In 1891, for example, the *Washington Post* enthused about Forepaugh's circus, which attracted 20,000 people and featured an extraordinary menagerie: 'it would take almost a column of THE POST just to tell the names of all the animals therein.' The lion tamers, Colonel Edgar Daniel Boone and Miss Carlotta, 'put their lions through performances that have only previously been accomplished by the more docile animals, as the horse, dog, and elephant, for instance . . . Pedestals were formed by the tawny beasts, seesaw was played with child-like simplicity and joy, a pistol was fired by one of the lions, and, to crown the entertainment, a lion was shown riding a bicycle.' A Wild West show followed, and then the Hanlon-Volters trapeze artists, Japanese jugglers and acrobats, Miss Allington's wonderful contortion act and trained stallions. On the hippodrome track, which went around the circus rings, there were horse, elephant, camel, chariot and wheelbarrow races, and a race by equestriennes.

Extravagant newspaper reports echoed the claims blaring from circus posters: Forepaugh called itself the Largest Show in the World; Barnum and Bailey, the Greatest; the five Ringlings, whose posters featured headshots of each brother, were Monarchs of the Circus World. And the Ringlings distinguished themselves further as self-made men intent on being the most moral and upright of all circus

Poster for the Sells Brothers Enormous United Shows, 1895.

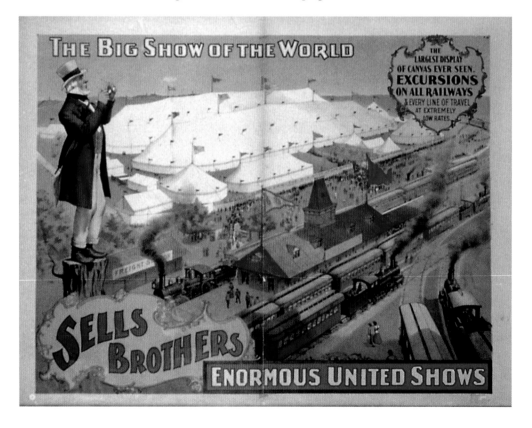

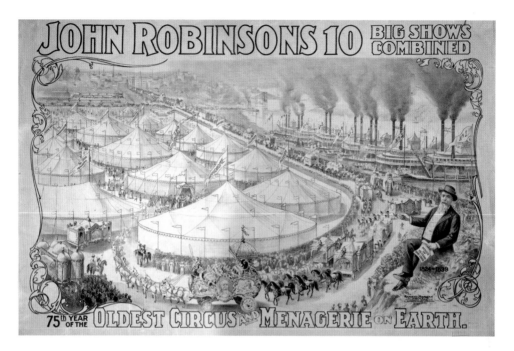

Poster for John Robinson's circus and menagerie, 1899.

impresarios. 'Starting With a Dollar They Have Built Up the Largest Show in the World,' announced one of their posters, illustrating their rise from a backyard circus, through early trials and setbacks, to their eventual grandeur. The brothers created their reputation as gentlemen, allowing no grift, no shortchanging at the ticket booth, no confidence men outside of their sideshow. They cooperated with local police to rid the premises of pickpockets and gambling. They published rules for circus personnel, prohibiting flashy dress and boorish behaviour and warning employees to be neat, modest, quiet and polite. They must behave, said the Ringlings' rule book, like ladies and gentlemen. 'In the profession they used to call us "The Sunday School Boys",' Charles Ringling recalled proudly.[14] No matter that teetotaller Barnum publicized his own efforts at providing moral entertainment; the Ringlings outdid him fivefold.

During Barnum & Bailey's six-year European tour that began in 1897, the Ringlings made their biggest advances: performing in arenas, rather than under tents; lighting with electricity powered by their own generators, making it possible to offer shows at night; and

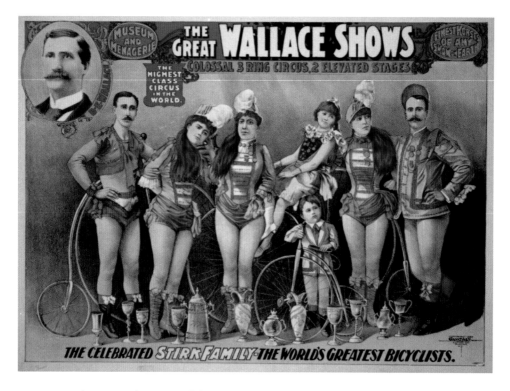

increasing the size and variety of their offerings. They believed their expertise as showmen extended beyond the circus ring. When the Spanish– American War began the brothers sent a telegram to Secretary of War Russell Alger offering 25 elephants for special service in Cuba. 'In the heavy underbrush,' the Ringlings wrote, 'they would be particularly useful, where horses cannot travel freely. They could be armored so heavily as to be utilized as moving forts. We have men competent to handle the animals, who are anxious to enlist, and the value of the elephants in the light artillery has been fully demonstrated in India.' Alger did not take them up on the offer, but the gesture became part of the Ringling legend.[15]

By the time Barnum & Bailey returned from Europe in 1903, the Ringlings had moved themselves into a sure position as 'Kings of the Show World'. Despite economic downturns along the way, despite family bickering and disagreements, they had amassed a fortune, and they used their profits for expansion and acquisition. In 1905

Poster for the Great Wallace Shows featuring the Stirk Family, 1898.

90

Forepaugh, which had previously combined with Sells, was sold at auction. The Ringlings and Bailey bought it in partnership, signing non-competition agreements to perform in different parts of the country. In 1906 Bailey died, and his widow sold his interest in the Forepaugh-Sells show to the Ringlings; the following year, they bought Barnum & Bailey, but still ran the two circuses independently. Only in 1918 did they unite the shows, and Ringling Brothers Barnum & Bailey Combined Show – known as the 'Big One' – rose to dominate the circus world.

The Big One grew exponentially. In 1908 it advertised 60 acrobats, 60 aerialists, 60 riders, 50 clowns and the tallest giraffe in the world. In 1925, according to circus historian Mark St Leon, it had burgeoned into

a moving township of sixteen hundred people that travelled on four special trains of one hundred cars each, many of the cars twenty metres long. The big show carried nearly eight hundred horses and nearly one thousand other animals, including forty-two elephants, giraffes, camels, and all sorts of other beasts rarely seen in America outside a zoo . . . There were three rings and two stages and these were worked almost continuously throughout the two-and-a-half hour program. No act was allowed more than five minutes, save a few centre ring star acts . . . and there was not a second's delay from the time the big parade took place around the hippodrome track that surrounded the three rings until the final chariot race. One hundred clowns worked the hippodrome track continuously while the acts were in progress.[16]

The Ringling circus was eager to feature the most coveted star acts, and, as clown Emmett Kelly recalled, joining the Big One was a high point of a performer's career. 'You can troupe all over the world, and you can listen to applause in far-away places and you can read flattering publicity from hell to breakfast,' Kelly wrote, 'but when you open with Ringling Brothers and Barnum & Bailey in Madison Square Garden, New York City, you have "arrived".'[17] Certainly its programmes listed the most famous names in circus history: animal trainers Alfred Court, Mabel Stark and Clyde Beatty; tightrope walkers Bird Millman and Con Colleano; the daring aerialists the Wallendas, Lillian Leitzel and Alfredo Codona; equestriennes Dorothy Herbert, Josie de Mott Robinson, Ella Bradna and May Wirth; the flying Concellos; equestrian director Fred Bradna; clowns Pat Valdo, Poodles Hanneford and Emmett Kelly. For a few years, missing from that roster had been the Ringling brothers themselves.

By 1926 John was the sole surviving brother, and the most volatile and impetuous. In the spring of 1929 he learned that the American Circus Corporation, owners of the Sells-Floto, Hagenbech-Wallace, John Robinson, Sparks, and Al G. Barnes circuses, had contracted to

A young Theodore Roosevelt III at the circus, 1924.

President Calvin
Coolidge and
Mrs Coolidge at
the circus, 1924.

open at Madison Square Garden for the 1930 season – an event that always had belonged to the Ringlings. Incensed by this effrontery, John decided to buy the American Circus Corporation, financing the purchase with a note for nearly $2 million. He planned to sell shares of his new corporation to repay the note, but in October, with the crash of the New York stock market, that plan was dashed completely.

For the next few years, although the Ringling circus survived dismal economic times, John's debt proved impossible to repay, and, vulnerable to takeover, he succumbed to Samuel W. Gumpertz, a former acrobat who had become a prominent businessman. After John died in 1936, his nephews John Ringling North and his brother Henry worked tirelessly to wrest control back to the family. Finally, in 1938, they succeeded and began anew with what Henry called 'a philosophy of circus showmanship to fit the new age in which we were living'. In the optimistic 1920s, the brothers believed, audiences had 'looked fondly over their shoulders at a seemingly serene past', but the Depression created a mood of 'world-woe. The past was thoroughly discredited by the hardships of the present. In their stagnation, people looked, not too hopefully, to the future.' The Norths thought there was no sense in reprising the 'tinsel glitter' of past circuses. 'The young parents who now brought their children to the circus had been raised on more sophisticated entertainment, and their children were more sophisticated than they. Automobiles and movies, to which color and sound had just been added, had done that.'[18]

News that the Norths were intent on modernizing the circus alarmed some fans who still looked back with nostalgia to the old days of sawdust and tanbark. Even as early as 1904, the *Washington Post* had characterized the circus as 'the one sweet and soothing comfort left us on this calamitous globe. Our eyes have somehow become accustomed in the bewildering array of things going "round and round" . . . and we have come to consider the "Big Show," with its multifarious appurtenances, as one of the chief delights of life's feast.'[19] By 1938 the world was spinning faster and more calamitously, but the Norths saw that their competitors were offering more than sweet and soothing comfort. Charlie Chaplin, Spencer Tracy and Katherine Hepburn, the Ziegfeld Follies, Busby Berkeley: all these entertainers and more were new rivals of the circus.

In 1938, then, the Norths reinvented the circus as spectacle: costumes, lighting, big production numbers and, especially, 'a unity of theme instead of a hodgepodge of unrelated acts . . . Above all', they decided, the circus 'needed an infusion of Barnumesque showmanship tuned to the age of radio'.[20] Focused on glamour and spectacle rather than danger and risk, they designed harmonious costumes for all the performers, featured aerial ballets and, for an Indian-themed production, hired the wild animal collector and actor Frank Buck as the central attraction. Buck entered the ring wearing a pith helmet, riding an elaborately bedecked elephant and trailed by 'native' hunters, 'maharanis', dancers wearing translucent saris, a hippopotamus and a giraffe. Even band members wore Bengal Lancer uniforms.

Ever alert to what they believed viewers wanted, the Norths produced a Mother Goose theme one year – perhaps a gesture towards

Arthur Rothstein, 'Sneaking under the circus tent', 1936.

comfort – and a Kentucky Derby theme just before the war, when, they decided, audiences felt prosperous once again. The Norths were eager to recruit talent from outside the circus world, such as stage designer Norman Bel Geddes and, for a guest appearance, New York mayor Fiorello La Guardia. In late 1941 John North approached George Balanchine about choreographing 'a pachydermal extravangaza' for the spring tour of 1942, whose theme – as the nation faced war – was 'Gayety'. Balanchine accepted, but stipulated that his friend Igor Stravinsky must write the score. Stravinsky, who had written music for the Ballets Russes production of *Pulchinella* in 1920, agreed to write a short piece, provided his commission was large. *The Ballet of the Elephants*, later renamed *Circus Polka*, was first performed at Madison Square Garden on 9 April 1942 with 50 elephants and 50 ballerinas, all costumed in pink tutus. Atop the premier elephant was ballerina Vera Zorina, then Balanchine's wife. Brooks Atkinson, reviewing the performance for the *New York Times*, was not overly impressed by the elephants' pink skirts, but nevertheless found their dancing delightful.

After Japan's attack on Pearl Harbor in December 1941, the Norths considered shutting down the circus for the duration of the war. Besides seeming 'frivolous', as Henry put it, the circus would have been impossible to produce without enough workers. But President Roosevelt assured the Norths that the government would cooperate in deferring needed personnel and material; the circus would help to keep up the country's morale. The Norths' own morale suffered, however, when family animosity flared, causing John to be ousted as president in favour of his cousin Robert Ringling.

In 1943 the Ringling Brothers circus opened at Madison Square Garden to a cheering crowd of more than 14,000. Unlike John, Robert produced nostalgia: thick sawdust, pink lemonade and evocations of the 1890s: 'Girls and boys, garbed in their best velvet finery of the turn of the century, pedaled their tandems with sure foot. Down the street strolled the dandies with their lady friends.' There was no Stravinsky for this show; instead Merle Evans's band played a sentimental waltz, 'After the Ball is Over'. At that moment, looking back to simpler times was more comforting than thinking about the precarious present. If the circus provided a diversion from worries over the war, still 'the patriotic touch of the evening' took the form of a parade into the arena of representations of the United Nations, 'in their picturesque and colorful holiday costumes and trappings, "exultant in the vision of happy tomorrows"', and 'Drums of Victory' – a medley of songs of the various armed forces – was the show's finale.[21]

Chillingly, one of the highlights of the season was the 'Clown Fire House', a slapstick skit in which the clowns' house burst into blaze, a midget fire engine rushed into the ring and clowns ran around scorched. 'It was still the old funny Clown Fire House', reported the *New York Times*, 'with new gales of laughter from the patrons.'[22] In one year that skit would evoke no laughter at all. On 6 July 1944 the circus suffered its most devastating catastrophe.

The show was playing in Hartford, Connecticut. At 2:40 pm, just as the Wallendas were preparing to begin the third act, a small fire in a corner of the grandstands whipped into an uncontrollable blaze. If the tent had been fireproofed, there was no evidence of it in that moment, as it fell, burning, on top of the women and children who made up most of the audience. With their clothes, hair and bodies on fire, some managed to escape. But hundreds did not: more than 160 died and more were injured, many severely. The casualty count mounted daily. 'Hartford had lost fewer lives on the beachheads in France than the circus fire had taken today,' reported the *New York Times*.[23] Robert, in shock, flew to Hartford from Chicago. That evening, five of his associates were arrested, charged with involuntary manslaughter. Within days, the circus was beset with damage suits, and Ringling Brothers promised to meet their obligations. With the five men out on bail, the circus retreated to its winter home in Sarasota, Florida, to regroup. In August it was on the road once again.

On 8 May 1945 the show was playing at Madison Square Garden when VE Day was announced, but jubilation over the war's end did not translate into a successful future for the circus. After a profitable year in 1948, attendance declined as audiences gravitated to other, more dazzling forms of entertainment: Disneyland, for example, which opened in July 1955, and movies and television. Acrobat and circus historian Duncan Wall sees the demise of the huge circus as caused partly by its own decisions to stop promoting individual stars. 'In the gigantic traveling circuses . . . the circus became a business, plain and simple. Success was measured by profit, with performers there to serve the bottom line.' While movie companies publicized actors and actresses, creating demand for their performances, circuses reduced their emphasis on individual stars in favour of promoting the spectacle. Furthermore, selling the circus as family entertainment geared it to children. Clowns became more exaggerated, their skits focused on broad gags. Children, Wall writes, became the target audience because they 'were less demanding, willing to overlook a mangy tiger or an acrobat's frayed costume. Acts could be recycled ad infinitum, since children were always growing into and out of the circus.'[24]

The *New Yorker* complained in 1950 that the circus 'has fallen victim to two contemporary diseases – the Tie-In and the Speedup

. . . Our program featured stories about Cecil B. DeMille (doing a movie about the circus), June Allyson (appearing in a movie with a lion) and Betty Hutton (appearing in a movie as Annie Oakley).' The circus performers 'all seemed to be in a tremendous hurry, as if they feared that their audience, educated to the fast boff, the one-minute commercial, might get bored and tune them out'. Aerial performances seemed unusually short, and the writer,

> surrounded by haste and commercial reference . . . remembered that there used to be plenty of time for Leitzel, Colleano, and Zacchini . . . And we recalled the completely static and wonderful moment at the old circus when the curtains went up on the living statues and everybody held his breath, hoping that the white horse wouldn't spoil the effect with a single twitch of his tail.[25]

The tie-in did, indeed, seem to the Norths a way to revive interest in the circus. With their cooperation, DeMille filmed *The Greatest Show on Earth* in 1952, with major Hollywood stars in leading roles: Betty Hutton (in her role as Annie Oakley), Cornel Wilde, Charlton Heston and Jimmy Stewart, as a mysterious clown hiding behind his circus make-up. The movie, which won an Academy Award, perpetuated the idea of the circus as a place of glamour and allure, risk and danger – and secrets. DeMille's circus, like the archetypal circus of the nineteenth century, was a place to run away to. A few years later, *Trapeze* featured Burt Lancaster, a former trapeze artist, Tony Curtis and Gina Lollobrigida in a steamy tale of love and rivalry. Movie stars, larger than life, drew more interest from audiences than little-known performers far from viewers in the huge three-ring arenas.

If audiences were not filling the big top, they were still hungry for circus myths. Books on the circus proliferated. Nearly 300 appeared between 1950 and 1960 – double the number of just a decade earlier. Most of them were for children and portrayed the happy, magical world of circus life: the kind of warm, moral and embracing circus community that Charles Dickens had created in *Hard Times* (1854). As Mark St Leon notes, 'The fictional world of the circus (like the typical platoon in a war movie) constituted a kind of ideal society, diverse but tolerant, tight-knit, ready to pull together in times of crisis, or the ideals of neighborhood and front-porch friendliness abandoned in the flight to the suburbs.'[26]

FOUR

CAVALCADES

Friday I tasted life. It was a vast morsel. A Circus passed the
house – still I feel the red in my mind though the drums are
out. The Lawn is full of south and the odors tangle, and I hear
to-day for the first time the river in the tree.

Emily Dickinson

Emily Dickinson's rhapsodic response to the circus that came to
Amherst, Massachusetts, in 1866 echoed the experiences of
many adults and children in towns and villages where travelling tent
shows and, later, railroad circuses arrived from spring to early autumn.
Although the circus parade was designed to entice viewers to buy
tickets for the show, it also gave townspeople a chance to be part
of the exhibition, to march alongside performers and even reach out
to touch them. Nowhere was it possible to get as close as when they
paraded through the streets, even past one's own house. Dickinson
was not alone in suddenly feeling 'the red' in her mind when the
circus transformed the lawn of her house into a magical landscape.
Spangled costumes, gilded chariots and shiny brass trumpets: these
incongruous images heightened the difference between the fantasy
of the circus and the viewers' everyday world.

Throughout the nineteenth century and into the twentieth, the
idea that there was one 'circus day' was not the reality: in any season, a
circus might visit up to 200 towns, and audiences had chances to see many
troupes. Those circus days were the culmination of weeks of anticipation, beginning long before the barker lured patrons to step right
up and 'See what the world contains beside yourself – see it all to-day.'[1]

Circus parade around
tents, c. 1874.

Before circuses began travelling by rail, publicity posters announced that the show would play 'on or about' a specific date. 'They never knew how long it would take them to pull the heavy equipment through the muddy roads or ford through creeks and rivers where the bridges weren't strong enough to support the wagons,' recalled Emmett Kelly, who became enraptured with the circus as a child. Barnum's company needed fourteen horses just to pull the hippopotamus cage, and, Kelly said, 'one of the old stories handed down claims that after a particularly rugged night the driver of the first wagon to sight the show's destination would shout "China!," meaning that the show had plowed its way clear through the earth.'[2]

These 'mud shows', as they were known, often came through towns every few days. The Wallace Show, the Frank Robbins Show, the Sautelle Show: all these and more made a circuit of small towns. Large troupes boasted their greatness; smaller troupes made more modest claims: 'Not the Best but as Good as some Who Call Themselves Great' announced an advertisement by J. Ricardo and John L. Fitz, Triple Bar Performers and Acrobats.

> A thousand cries rent the air; the strolling mountebanks and gypsying booth-merchants; the peanut vendors; the boys with palm-leaf fans for sale; the candy sellers; the pop-corn peddlers; the Italian with the toy balloons that float like a cluster of colored bubbles above the heads of the crowd . . . the red-lemonade man, shouting in the shrill voice that reaches everywhere and endures forever: 'Lemo! Lemo! Ice-cole lemo!' . . . all the vociferating harbingers of the circus crying their wares.[3]

Booth Tarkington's description in his novel *The Gentleman from Indiana* captured a nineteenth-century town's palpable anticipation of a circus.

'All we needed to do was see the signs on the fences and in the empty store windows to start going to the dogs and neglecting our education,' William Saroyan wrote, evoking his childhood experiences in California around 1920. 'All we needed to know was that a circus was on its way to town for me and [my pal] Joey to start wanting to know what good a little education ever did anybody anyway.'[4] Weeks, and sometimes months, before the circus arrived, posters appeared everywhere: in drugstores, barbershops, hotel lobbies, tobacco shops and the village luncheonette.

Outside the town centre, huge advertisements – some more than six feet high – appeared on barn sides and fences; if those were not available, a publicity team bought lumber, hastily built a fence around any empty lot and plastered it with colourful and shamelessly exclamatory lithographs. As the advance man Charles Murray recalled, 'The circus bill-poster was a member of the Santa Claus family – coming from nowhere and vanishing into nothing, but leaving the glowing traces of his visit in highly colored pictorial illustrations that covered the dead walls in town and along the country roads.'[5] When he and his team asked farmers for permission to post on their barns, some hesitated, afraid, they said, that the church, or neighbours, might not approve of the circus; but Murray suspected that those farmers only pretended to be reluctant – an offer of free tickets usually ended their worries.

At the end of a season, every surface possible was covered in a palimpsest of posters from one or another troupe. 'Wherever stood a boy, or man, or woman, or gaping child,' Murray claimed, 'a shower of pictorial circus matter fell.'[6] That pictorial matter underscored the sensational: many images showed wild animals, especially a lion and tiger roaring, leaping menacingly at the viewer. Even seals were billed as ferocious sea lions, sea leopards and sea elephants; they were illustrated not balancing balls on their snouts or playfully slapping their tails, but roaring angrily – in one poster, they fiercely intimidate a polar bear cowering in the water. Small circuses that could not afford their own illustrators might buy a stock piece showing an assortment of popular acts – balancers, aerialists, jugglers – with room to add their own name at the top.

'On the posters,' notes circus historian Antony Coxe, 'flamboyant pseudonyms were used in place of the simple word "circus." Shows went out under names such as "Equescurriculum," "Hippolymiad," and "Cirqzooladon"; they were called "Egyptian Caravans" and "Paris

Poster showing 'Great Jumbo's Skeleton', 1888.

Pavilions," and described as "Nickel-Plated."'[7] And their offerings, the posters blared, were Mighty, Overwhelming and Colossal. Turner and Co.'s 'Extensive and Unequalled Circus' toured in 1851; Cooper, Bailey & Co.'s Great International Allied Shows arrived in San Francisco in 1896 before setting out for Asia; John B. Doris's Great Inter-Ocean Circus crossed routes in Indiana with The Great Forepaugh Museum, Menagerie, Triple Circus and Roman Hippodrome, spiking a feud between the two enterprises. Myers' Great American Circus and the Great United States Circus sounded modest compared to the Mammoth National Circus, or Stone & Murray's Great Circus, or Sells-Floto Super Combined Circuses. When American impresario Seth Howes took his circus to London in 1856, his posters amazed passers-by: 'People would stand half the day and look at them,' the *New York Times* reported. 'The streets were actually blocked by people viewing them, and the authorities were obliged to order them down.'[8]

In a single season, a circus might use hundreds of thousands of poster sheets: in 1911, for example, the Ringlings posted more than 900,000. After a town was inundated, advertisements appeared in local newspapers. Editors, aware of how important advertising was, inflated their rates for circus agents. With several dailies in each town, advertising was a costly but crucial investment. While excitement built among potential ticket buyers, a contracting agent for the advance team finalized renting the show grounds, ordering food and animal feed and getting a licence to perform. 'Lodgings for the principals must be secured,' reported the nineteenth-century equestrian manager Charles Montague; 'and what is of no less importance, good stabling for the stud of valuable horses . . . The agent in advance is to a travelling circus what scouts are to an invading army.'[9] To make sure there were no dissenting voices, a press agent met with ministers, educators and any town officials who might have opinions about the wholesomeness of circus entertainment. As with farmers, free tickets often assuaged concerns.

Circus poster, Alabama, 1935, photograph by Walker Evans.

Boys like Saroyan, distracted by the mere thought of the circus's arrival, were hopeless once wagons or railroad cars arrived with

Downie Bros posters covering a building, Virginia, 1936.

Circus poster, Omaha, Nebraska, 1938, photograph by John Vachon.

Circus posters, Ohio, 1938, photograph by Ben Shahn.

Wagon maker and his wagon, Sheridan County, Montana, 1937, photograph by Lee Russell.

performers, animals and the scores of workers who would set up a tent at dawn. 'After the circus *reached* town we were just no good at all,' Saroyan admitted. 'We spent all our time down at the trains, watching the gang unload the animals . . . and hanging around the grounds, trying the win the favor of the animal men, the acrobats, and the clowns.'[10] Some towns simply gave up and closed schools on circus days. Thomas Wolfe, growing up in Asheville, North Carolina, remembered waking with tremulous excitement the day that Ringling Bros, or Robinson's, or Barnum & Bailey came to town in the early 1910s. Hurrying through his paper route, he went with his brother to the fields where the circus was being set up. What had been pastoral became, suddenly, wild:

> The receding gulf of lilac and departing night would be filled with the savage roar of lions, the murderously sudden snarling of great jungle cats, the trumpetings of the elephants, the stamp of the horses, and the musty, pungent, unfamiliar odor of the jungle animals: the tawny camel smells, and the smells of panthers, zebras, tigers, elephants, and bears.

Ringlings Bros Circus parade on Market Street, San Francisco, 1900.

Poster showing a
parade travelling
through Dewey Arch
at Madison Square,
New York, *c.* 1900.

The powerful animals were of a piece with the powerful performers, men and women, Wolfe thought, who were so 'strong and
handsome, yet speaking and moving with an almost stern dignity
and decorum, that their lives seemed to us to be as splendid and
wonderful as any lives on earth could be.' After watching them eat
their tremendous breakfast, the two boys felt 'a ravenous hunger' –
for food, which they satisfied at a local lunch room, but even more,
for the splendour of those circus lives.[11] 'The circus was everything,'
Saroyan decided, 'everything else we knew wasn't.'

Before the show began, there would be, as Emily Dickinson
reported, a parade, a preview of what the circus had in store. In the
early nineteenth century, those parades were modest: a few wagons
pulled by four horses, a small troupe of performers, 'no band, no
menagerie, no gauze and spangles, no ringmaster, no tent', but only
'an informal stockade of poles and canvas'.[12] By the middle of the
century, though, the circus pageant had evolved into a spectacle in
itself. Carved and gaudily painted wagons carried clowns, acrobats,
jugglers; riders in glittering costume pranced by on bedecked horses;
the brass band played on; and finally there was the unmistakable
tooting of the steam organ or calliope. A menagerie followed in cages,

CALLIOPE! THE WONDERFUL OPERONICON OR STEAM CAR OF THE MUSES.
AS IT APPEARS IN THE GORGEOUS STREET PAGENT OF THE GREAT
EUROPEAN ZOOLOGICAL ASSOCIATION!
BRITISH MUSEUM. ROYAL COLISEUM. GALLERY OF ART. WORLD'S CONGRESS AND GIGANTIC CIRCUS! 12 Tents! 900 Men and Horses! One Ticket Admits to All!

Calliope!, 1874.

or elephants took the lead, if the circus could afford to buy, feed and care for them. Spectators felt engulfed by the bustle and fervour of the pageant. Young boys lining the street, bursting with excitement, threw themselves into somersaults or handstands; but, as Tarkington realized, 'the ecstasy of all this glittering, shining, gorgeous pageantry needed even more than walking on your hands to express'.[13] The circus parade reprised the experience of being at a fair, where a panoply of entertainment was free and accessible to all. For some, the parade was their only circus experience, available to anyone – including blacks in places where they were barred from entering the tent, children whose parents forbade them to see a performance, or families adhering to their minister's prohibitions.

Exotic visits

Like the Continental circuses, the tent shows that travelled throughout the countryside were small circuses, and it was these that captured
the imaginations of American artists, just as they had inspired their
European predecessors. In the spring of 1929 – at the same time that
the Greatest Show on Earth played Madison Square Garden – 'The
Circus in Paint' opened in New York at the Whitney Studio Club and
Galleries, forerunner of the Whitney Museum of Art. With sawdust
strewn on the floor, balloons wafting through the rooms and con-
tainers of peanuts set out for viewers, the exhibition was a critical – and
popular – success. Except for Reginald Marsh, whose circus paintings
show the press of throngs, artists such as Charles Demuth, Walt Kuhn,
Charles Rocher, William Glackens and John Sloan focused on the
faces and bodies of individual performers, much as Toulouse-Lautrec
and Degas had done before them. 'The Circus in Paint' conveyed the
ambience and enchantment of the heirs to *cirques intimes*.

This was the kind of circus that Emmett Kelly recalled as life
changing. For him, it was the boastfully named Mighty Haag circus,
with its small menagerie. He remembered a tiger and, he said, 'under
gasoline lamps I beheld my first clown, a little white-faced guy who
belonged to the long-gone "talking clown" tradition. One of the acts
was the buckboard kicking mule, and there were trained ponies and
a girl contortionist, but no aerial acts . . . But insignificant as it was,
I couldn't get it out of my mind.'

Later, in a larger town, he saw the M. L. Clark & Sons Combined
Shows. First, of course, came the parade.

This, too, was a small circus, but compared with the one I had
seen it might have been as big as Barnum & Bailey . . . Some
distance from the show grounds, I could see the tents and
I felt my heart begin to pound. The parade was soon in the
streets and the music of the band thrilled me even more. The
musicians wore red uniforms and they were followed by some
mounted people and a couple of cages of animals. There was
a zebra, the first I'd ever seen, and a steam calliope.

Clark & Sons was a two-ring circus with trapeze acts and a few clowns. Nevertheless, the performance only intensified for Kelly the excitement of the parade. 'As I walked away,' he remembered wistfully, 'I looked back and wondered where it had come from and where it was going. The farm seemed far away.'[14]

Growing up in Jackson, Mississippi, in the 1900s, Eudora Welty often saw travelling circus troupes, stopping for one performance in the town's Century Theatre on their way to New Orleans. 'Then, as now,' she wrote, 'my imagination was magnetized toward transient artists – toward the transience as much as the artists.'[15] For Welty, like Kelly, the familiar surroundings of her own town emphasized the performers' exoticism. They seemed like visitors from another world, inhabiting a small community of their own. She was in love, she told a friend, with Picasso's saltimbanques, 'and was wishing they were set down in my little Smith Park.'[16]

Her memory of those performers inspired her short story 'Acrobats in a Park', whose characters are a circus family: Beppo, the father; Nedda, the mother; their sons, Bird and Ricky; their young daughter, Betty; and Bird's wife, Tina. Even a glance at the group picnicking in the shade of an oak tree reveals that they are out of the ordinary: 'Their bodies are smaller and more long-waisted, darker, more hairy . . . Their anatomical structure is both obvious and strange.' If at first the scene seems idyllic, Welty soon reveals tensions: the acrobats, we learn, are worried about being rehired. They need constantly to adapt their act, making it more and more daring, in order to keep working. The night before, though, their signature feat ended badly: 'the Zarro Wall', a structure built up from their interlocking bodies, collapsed. Tina, pregnant, slightly heavier than Ricky expected, stepped into his hand and 'drove catastrophe into his very center', and his arm broke. Now the family cannot perform until he is healed. We learn, too, that Ricky both resents and is attracted to Tina; and when Nedda suddenly exhorts Tina to go across the street to the church to confess, we guess that Tina's child is not Bird's, but Ricky's.

These acrobats are strangers, with no connection to the people or the mores of the community. Their presence fascinates and disturbs the few visitors to the park, and although Tina does go to confession, she seems unrepentant as she walks 'with her easy manner' to join the family as they leave the park and walk towards the 'worn, red van' waiting for them on the circus grounds. As acrobats, they can revive their 'Wall', but their unity has been tested and it failed; what the public will see is an illusion. Yet what entices the public is the mystery, the secrets, that the family harbours; perhaps that is why, when the Zarro Wall collapsed, loud applause 'broke from the audience, the louder because an attempt had failed'.[17]

George Garrett's 'An Evening Performance' takes up a similar theme: the arrival of circus performers to a small town, giving the townspeople a glimpse of another reality, another way of being. First, posters are seen advertising Stella the High Diver. One of the Fabulous Wonders of Modern Times, the posters proclaim: She Dives One Hundred Feet Into a Flaming Cauldron. Then a truck appears in the middle of a field, and a stranger is seen shopping at the supermarket and the hardware store, washing laundry at the Washeteria. He limps, people notice, and talks to himself. There is a little girl, too, with long reddish hair, dressed always in white, and a woman, short, with dyed red hair and a big, ready smile. Soon it is apparent that she is mute, and the family communicates with her through sign language. She is Stella.

One morning, the man begins to erect a tower in the field: a high tower with a rope ladder dangling on one side and, at the top, a plank serving as a diving board. At the foot the man builds a wooden and canvas tank and fills it with buckets of water to a depth of about six feet. He strings coloured lights and aims searchlights on the tower, and then begins to sell tickets. By evening, a crowd is gathered, waiting even as it begins to rain.

Although Stella is worried about the weather, she finally agrees to perform, and the man introduces her:

> The way that Stella does this dive is skill, skill pure and simple. When Stella climbs that tower and dives into the flames she's doing something anyone could do who has the heart and the skill and the nerve for it. That's what's different and special about our show. When Stella sails through the air and falls

into the fire and comes up safe and smiling, she is the living and breathing proof of the boundless possibility of all mankind. It should make you happy. It should make you glad to be alive.[18]

Stella climbs. At the top of the tower, she unhitches the ladder. Suddenly, just as the man lights the gasoline that ignites flames around the tank, Stella jumps. The dive, lit by the searchlights, lasts only a moment. She splashes into the flaming cauldron, and then she climbs out of the tank, still smiling, and makes her way back to the family's small tent.

The next morning, the man and Stella and Angel are gone, but their visit has left its mark. Clergymen call Stella's act the work of the Devil; some in the town, given to telling rambling stories, drunk or sober, recount the dive so often it becomes a legend. One man – the narrator calls him wise – deems it a terrible event. 'It made us all sophisticated,' he says. 'We can't be pleased by any ordinary marvels anymore – tightrope walkers, fire-eaters, pretty girls being fired out of cannons. It's going to take a regular apocalypse to make us raise our eyebrows again.'

'He was almost right,' the narrator tells us, 'as nearly correct as a man could hope to be. How could he even imagine that more than one aging, loveless woman slept better ever after, smiled as she dreamed herself gloriously descending for all the world to see from a topless tower into a lake of flame?'[19]

The evening performance was a display of physical control and athletic prowess. It was a display of sexuality: the posters emphasized Stella's 'buxom magnificence'. It was a display of the exotic, notable in Stella's 'savage makeup, wild, accented, slanted eyes, a mouth of flame, and always two perfectly round spots of red like dying roses on her high cheekbones'. It was a display of the visceral: Stella is mute, and her hands flutter 'as swift as wings', 'like the wings of a wild bird in a cage', when she communicates with the man.[20]

The audience pays to see her risk her life, to be sure, but they pay also for the promise of identifying with her, and part of themselves goes away with her – leaving the small town, the farms, a quiet and circumscribed life – to join a family: magnetized, as Welty admitted she was, by the fluidity of their transience as much as by Stella's spectacular feat.

When the circus arrived in town, mounted a parade and marched through the streets, viewers saw performers outside of the tent, in the parks, shops and streets that townspeople inhabited each day. The performers' appearance marked them as outsiders, and if some viewers found them discomfiting or threatening, others were inspired to dream of possibilities that perhaps were boundless.

Pyrotechnics

Once circuses moved by railroad rather than wagons, parades became an increasingly urban, and increasingly crowded, event. Photographs of cavalcades in the late nineteenth century show miles of horses, chariots, floats and animal cages competing for the road with trams and streetcars. Rather than participating in the cavalcade by doing handstands and somersaults at the side of the road, children had to be hoisted onto their fathers' shoulders to get a view of the passing show above the heads of the throng lining the sidewalks.

Here, for example, is a report from the *New York Times* on Barnum's advent into the city in 1883:

> There was a sound of a hundred musical instruments – the psalter, the fife, the drum, the bassoon, the calliope, the hand-organ, the jews-harp, the viol, the French horn, the flute, the tin whistle, the harmonicom, the accordion, and every other instrument of torture known to science or religion, accompanied by the glare of electric light, blue, green, yellow, pink, red and purple fire, Roman candles, rockets, pinwheels, gunpowder, dynamite, nitroglycerine . . . Nearer they came; louder sounded the music; more gloriously flared the pyrotechnics; more fiercely growled the lions; bass-profundo chorused the tigers; more merrily jogged the elephants; blithely bobbed the camels; grandly rolled the chariots, and the multitude burst into a roar of applause, which almost shook the City to

its foundations, and caused the cobblestones to grind against each other in the streets.[21]

A few years later, the parade seemed even more glorious: 'The great and glittering pageant, heralded by flaring torches, blaring trumpets, and trumpeting elephants, and roaring lions and tigers, will delight the hearts of the small boys next Wednesday, April 1', reported the *New York Times*. 'A thousand torchbearers will march in dazzling ranks on each side of the chariots, while red and blue fire and various novelties in pyrotechnics will make the night brilliant and pale the moon herself.' The march included fox hunters and cavaliers, hippodrome riders and equestriennes, three teams of Roman standing racers and seven caged dens containing lions, tigers, leopards, panthers, hyenas, bears and wolves, along with their trainers.[22]

One of Barnum's parades stretched for nearly 3 miles, with twelve golden chariots and a 30-foot-high Temple of Juno, a revolving Temple of the Muses, three bands and 100 cages and vans. 'The Great Procession', Barnum boasted, 'will be interspersed with grotesque figures, such as automaton gymnasts, mechanical trapezists, globe and ball jugglers, comic clowns, and athletic sports, performing on the tops of the cages and chariots.'[23] Knights in shining armour, a gleaming Goddess of Liberty, mythological and historical figures: the parade was designed to awe.

When the Adam Forepaugh & Sells Brothers' Circus opened in Manhattan in early April 1900, performers paraded at night under blazing calcium lights mounted atop gilded cages, while a twelve-piece band played familiar melodies. Throngs of people filled sidewalks, watched from balconies and stoops and hung out of hotel windows from Madison Square Garden to Union Square, then up Fifth Avenue to 57th Street, across to the West Side, and down Eighth Avenue to the Garden.[24]

Where the parade once had lured people into the tent, the city parade grew to be so large and long that some viewers did not bother coming to performances. After watching a parade for a few hours, what more could they expect to see? Expensive to transport and mount, the parade, reported the *Washington Post* in 1910, is the trial of the circus profession, because it comes in the morning during the greatest rush of the day, and if there is the slightest delay it runs over into the business of the afternoon and gives no time for rest for either the people or the horses . . . More accidents happen during the jam which results from the parade than at any other time during the visit of the circus . . . The proprietors of the Barnum & Bailey show abandoned the parade altogether while in Europe, and found that its withdrawal greatly simplified the handling of the show without affecting the attendance.[25]

When the Ringlings and Barnum & Bailey combined their shows, the new circus was so large and cumbersome that parades were impossible to produce. The last one occurred in 1919, when, Henry North wrote, 'the three-mile-long line of tableau wagons, cages, band wagons, elephants, horses, clowns, and steam calliopes snarled up traffic for hours.' In one parade that season, a brake failure of the band wagon sent 40 horses careening down Boston's Beacon Hill 'like a cavalry charge toward the crowd massed at the end'. Only the quick reflexes of the driver managed to avert disaster.[26]

Instead of the parade, circuses put their efforts into the spectacle, or spec, a production that appeared at the start of each show, featuring as many circus performers, staff and animals as could be rounded up. Some specs were modest entertainments of barely half an hour, but, unsurprisingly, those staged by Barnum often lasted 90 minutes – or half the time of the entire show. The spec often was theatrical, presenting historical, literary or patriotic themes, such as Jerusalem and the Crusades, Cleopatra, Joan of Arc and the coronation of King Charles VII, or a variety of famous battles. The specs, then, reprised the hippodramas that had been so popular in the eighteenth and early nineteenth centuries.

Each spec had its own theme. In 1933, with the United States still in Depression, and a relatively small matinee crowd of 8,000 at Madison Square Garden, the theme was the 'Delhi Dunbar', a celebration of Queen Victoria's ascent to the throne. On opening day in 1943, in the midst of the Second World War, more than 14,000 viewers bought War Bonds in exchange for tickets. The theme that year was nostalgia: accompanied by music from the 1890s – 'Bicycle Built for Two', 'Sweethearts' and 'East Side, West Side' – performers, dressed in turn-of-the-century outfits, strolled around the rings and pedalled on tandem bicycles. The sweetly sedate opening, though, soon gave way to the noisy, glittering procession of horses, spangled aerialists, clowns and chariots. Wild animals had returned as a circus staple: leopards, tigers and lions roared in their gaudy cages. In 1947 the theme of the spec was the 'Wedding of Cinderella', featuring Cinderella in a gilded coach and her fairy-tale attendants, such as Blue Beard, the Old Woman Who Lived in a Shoe, Santa Claus, Little Red Riding Hood and Mother Goose. For adults in the audience, 'The Royal Ascot' displayed legendary historical figures: the emperor of China, the king of Siam, the khedive of Egypt, the Mikado, the shah of Persia, the sultan of Turkey, the infant queen of Holland, King Leopold of Belgium, King Oscar of Sweden, the Infanta of Spain, the king of Italy, the czar of Russia, the president of France, the emperor

Poster for Ringling Bros' Light of Liberty theme show, 1899.

A wagon in the
Great Circus Parade,
Milwaukee,
Wisconsin, 2009.

of Germany – and even Queen Victoria, Washington, Lincoln, Grant, Uncle Sam and the Goddess of Liberty. Each figure rounded the rings with its own fanciful chariot and entourage. The Big Show, reported the *New York Times*, once again delivered 'the rhapsodic verbiage of its heralds'.[27] Once again, it captured the spectators' imaginations and desire: as the poet John Masefield put it: 'what sage is there so wise that he would not give a finger to be able to just do a "jump-up" or a somersault upon the back of a ring-horse, or hold a thousand people spellbound, like the clown in the red and white?'[28]

FIVE

WITHOUT
A NET

It is so delicious to see a man risk his life,
without being in danger oneself.

Charles Dickens

In 1829, when Jean François Gravelet was five years old, he saw a tightrope walker perform in a travelling circus and could hardly wait to go home and try the same feat. His father, a gymnast, caught up in his son's enthusiasm, sent him to the École de Gymnase in Lyons to learn acrobatics. In just six months, he was accomplished enough to perform as 'The Little Wonder'. When his father died four years later, Jean-François found a place for himself with a circus, and went on to perform with troupes throughout Europe until, at the age of 27, he joined the famed Ravel Family Circus in their North American tour. Since the Ravels had a few members of the Javelli family in their group, Gravelet, to avoid confusion, took the stage name Charles Blondin – evoking his blond hair.

Like other aerialists, Blondin devised increasingly daring feats to compete for the public's acclaim. In 1859, when he was 35, he embarked on his most audacious performance: crossing Niagara Falls on a hemp cable more than 1,000 feet long, strung 160 feet above the roiling Falls on one side and 270 feet on the other. Advance publicity stirred up excitement, and on 30 June throngs of viewers arrived by train and boat to witness the spectacle from specially constructed amphitheatres. Some shared the opinion expressed by the London *Times* that Blondin's feat was 'one that fits the performer for the highest place in the lunatic asylum'.[1] But whether or not

Five male trapeze
artists performing
at a circus, *c*. 1890.

viewers believed he was crazy, all agreed that he was uncommonly and astoundingly brave.

If his audience was anxious and agitated, Blondin, slim and agile, comported himself with admirable serenity. The sun reflecting off his spangled costume made him appear, a reporter noted, 'as if clothed in light'. At 5 pm, when Blondin stepped onto the rope from the American side, onlookers held their collective breath: 'The slightest misstep, the merest dizziness, the least uncertainty, would cast him at once into the perdition beneath.'[2] He carried a 38-foot balance pole, but his performance was not merely a walk across the waters. He stopped to wave, stretched himself along the rope, hung from it and did headstands and a somersault. When he stepped off on the Canadian side, he was drenched in sweat, but the audience did not see evidence of his exertion. From their vantage, he appeared to be a tiny man playfully, gracefully, doing something extraordinary.

In subsequent performances, his feats were even more audacious: sometimes he performed blindfolded or on stilts, or toting his young manager, Harry Colcord, on his back; in his second Niagara performance, he carried a tripod and camera, and took a photograph of some onlookers. Once, when he balanced a chair and then stood upon it, a few women in the audience fainted. His performance, which took about an hour, left some viewers exhausted by anxiety. The Prince of Wales was in the audience when Blondin crossed the cable on stilts. 'Thank God it is all over!' the prince remarked with relief when Blondin alighted from the rope at last.

By the time Blondin took his act to London's Crystal Palace in June 1861 he had become a hero, a superman and the subject of songs and poems, such as one with the following chorus:

> The world has seven wonders up,
>   An eighth I will install,
> The Hero of Niagara,
>   And greatest of them all.

Among the thousands who saw Blondin perform there – many were turned away – was Charles Dickens, who wryly noted the

Charles Blondin
crossing Niagara
Falls, photograph by
George Barker.

audience's frenzy: 'Why, the railway station is full', Dickens wrote in
All the Year Round,

> the voluminous gowns are jamming up the ticket collectors'
> turnstiles, statuesquely dressed Guardsmen are losing all sense
> of dignity, and rushing madly up the tedious and endless
> steps, honest tradesmen are dragging their children through
> all obstacles, as if they were taking thieves to prison, everybody
> seems afraid that Blondin may fall before they are able to
> take their seats . . . It is so delicious to see a man risk his life,
> without being in danger oneself, and so cheap too – for only
> half-a-crown.[3]

Blondin gave twelve performances at the Crystal Palace, earning
about four times what other aerialists were paid. Each performance
featured different costumes and props, many reprised from his Niagara
Falls spectacle; in one act, he dressed as a chef, wearing a toque and

apron, and setting upon the rope a table, chair, pan, plates and ingredients for an omelette, which he cooked on a stove; he danced, sat on a chair, turned complicated somersaults and played a drum. Only once, when he pushed his five-year-old daughter across the rope in a wheelbarrow, did the audience rise up in protest. It was one thing to risk his own life, but quite another to subject his child to danger. His wife watched the performance calmly, but no matter: the law stepped in quickly, and Blondin was forbidden to repeat the act.[4]

Blondin's exceptional daring came at a moment when the perfectability of humans was a much-debated topic. Charles Darwin's *On the Origin of Species* had been published in December 1859, generating consternation among readers discomfited by the notion of the survival of the fittest. What, for a human, constituted fitness? To what extent could self-improvement mitigate nature's selectivity? How did Darwin's theories account for the fondly held idea of human exceptionalism? One biographer concludes that Blondin represented for his contemporaries the image of humans 'as standing at the head of the mundane creation'. Physical feats, he says, 'could not take place without a corresponding salutary effect on the nervous system, and, of course, the functions and organs of the brain'.[5] As the historian Peta Tait notes, 'The human body's physical improvement became an unavoidable feature of these new ideas.' Gymnasts, and especially aerialists, came to represent 'the promise of human physicality, its future'.[6] It is no surprise that on 26 October 1929, in the midst of the first 'black' days of the stock market decline, leading to the Great Depression, the *Saturday Evening Post* ran a piece about Blondin that celebrated the Niagara feat. Blondin exemplified dramatically the challenges a man could overcome, the glory he could achieve.

The 'Hero of Niagara' created such a sensation at the Crystal Palace that circus impresarios were quick to copy or even surpass the act. Van Hare, for example, 'transmogrified' his performer Pauline Violante into the Female Blondin, staging a dramatic ascent from the stage to the top of the Alhambra Palace on a telegraph wire. She also crossed the Thames on a rope, with 100,000 astounded people watching. But unlike Blondin, Violante fell, and a hip injury ended her career.

At the same time that Blondin was crossing Niagara Falls, trapeze artist Jules Léotard –whose tight, sleeveless costume was adopted by all future aerialists – performed an apparently superhuman feat: swinging through the air at the Cirque Napoléon in Paris. The *New York Times* reported the performance in breathless detail:

Three trapezes, or pieces of wood about five feet long, suspended from ropes attached to the extremities, hang from the roof of the circus, one in the centre and the others at about forty feet distance at each side. A young man, named LEOTARD, ascends to a small platform arranged for him above the place where the musicians sit, over the passage for the horses into the ring. The trapeze nearest to him being put in motion, he catches it as it flies up, and then, after balancing himself carefully, he seizes it with both hands, and darts into open space. After flying to the utmost extent of the ropes, he comes back with the recoil, and alights in safety on the spot from which he started. When he has done this two or three times to show that the exercise is mere sport to him he again launches himself into mid-air, but not this time to return, as before; for when the trapeze has reached its furthest point, he suddenly lets go his hold, and borne onwards by the impetus imparted seizes the second trapeze, which in turn carries him forward to the length of its rope, where he again quits it, springs to the third trapeze, and, borne forward by it, alights on another platform at the opposite side of the circus, and in face of that from which he had started. The performer again seizes the third trapeze, and flinging himself forward, as before, flies to its furthest limit, and then quitting it, springs to the second, which, however, he does not leave, but permits it to fly back towards the third, then, as it descends, since his back is still towards the trapeze which he quitted the moment before, he all at once lets go with both hands, and turning in the air, seizes it again in time to meet the third, catching which he again reaches the platform. Once more ascending to the platform above the orchestra, he springs forward, hanging by the hands to the trapeze, and quitting it as it approaches the end of its range, he gives a somersault in the air, and seizes the second trapeze as he descends! When it is considered how truly brain, eye, and muscle must respond to each other in these perform- ances, the whole exhibition must be pronounced one of the most extraordinary that has ever been seen of its peculiar description.[7]

Léotard was self-taught. While swimming at his father's gymna- sium and pool in Toulouse, he noticed cords hanging from two roof ventilators. If a wooden bar were attached between the cords, he thought, he could swing on them, and if he lost hold, he would only fall into the pool. He tried it, inventing the first trapeze act. Performing in a circus, though, meant that there would be no pool; the Cirque Napoléon insisted that he provide mattresses to cushion a fall.

In time, he, and the performers who copied him, complicated the act by adding a catcher, and later a third performer who sent the trapeze back to the flyer. When audiences grew jaded about seeing aerialists swinging through the air, performers competed for attention by adding a somersault (or two or three), a pirouette or a twist.

Among the most notorious trapeze artists were the six Hanlon-Lees brothers, who began performing as acrobats in London in 1860. Soon, inspired by Léotard, they devised daring trapeze acts. 'Risking life and limb,' brother George explained, 'William will leap from his pedestal onto the first trapeze, from there to the second, and then the third. From the third trapeze, he will attempt to land on this pedestal. Good luck and God go with you, dear brother William.' The leap took about five seconds, after which William swung on a trapeze to build momentum, let go and did an end-over-end somersault to the second trapeze, and another somersault to the third.

Thomas created another bold feat, L'Echelle Périleuse, a variation on trapeze work in which one brother held a ladder while the others performed acrobatics at the top. A reviewer who saw this act at the Cirque Napoléon felt abject terror:

You cannot look at him [Thomas] without trembling, without bursting, without feeling your heart beat with extreme violence. Hanlon laughs at danger on his ladder . . . We have seen many aerial exercises, but we have never yet seen anything to be compared with his.

In 1861 the Hanlons brought their exotically titled Zampillaerostation to the Academy of Music in New York. Audiences thronged to see them, eager to feel a frisson of terror as they watched the brothers. The Hanlons' biographer Mark Cosdon likens viewers' attraction to dangerous aerial acts to their morbid interest in scenes of Civil War carnage, reproduced as stereopticon slides. 'A blood-lust, not unlike that of the Ancient Romans, had been whetted,' notes Cosdon. 'The Hanlons' death-defying aerial stunts appealed to this very human, very perverse instinct.'[8]

On 14 August 1865 the audience's desire for carnage was fulfilled when Thomas fell 40 feet, piercing his skull on a footlight burner. Although he survived, from then on he could perform only ground acrobatics, and from time to time suffered bouts of insanity. Three years later, while hospitalized for his mental problems, he committed suicide by banging his head against the wall of his room until his skull shattered.

A direct result of Thomas's fall was the widespread use of nets for aerial acts. Inspired by the netting used by construction workers, the nets offered some assurance of safety for performers, provided they learned how to fall without breaking their necks. For audiences, fear gave way to awe and admiration – and a strong interest in emulating aerialists and acrobats. Cosdon discovered that after the Hanlons had performed in New York for six months, the number of gymnasiums in that city increased from two to 32. Colleges such as Harvard, Bowdoin and Amherst added gymnasiums to their campuses. Admirers of aerialists, though, coveted more than sinewy muscles: they sought transcendence.

The advent of Blondin, Léotard, the Hanlons and many other aerial troupes coincided with a craze for ballooning. In the second half of the nineteenth century, thousands of newspaper reports give accounts of intrepid 'aeronauts' and their passengers who sailed aloft. Couples married in balloons high above their hometowns; balloons transported newlyweds on their honeymoon; and entrepreneurs could hardly keep up with tourists' demand for balloon rides over cities. Ballooning was dangerous, to be sure, but how else could one waft above the earth; how else feel such intense exhilaration? Clearly audiences were enraptured with the idea of flying, with defying gravity. One newspaper article described an aerialist as 'a convert to Einstein . . . The Newtonian laws of gravity that affect every one else have no standing with her.'[9] Many artists and writers embraced Nietzsche, who saw in aerial performances a metaphor for humanity's existential plight: 'Man is a rope', he wrote, 'fastened between animal and Superman, a rope over an abyss.' The tightrope walker especially, writes the art historian Janice McCullagh, 'fulfills Nietzsche's urgent declaration: "live dangerously!" Acting out this supreme challenge was the extreme

The Hanlons' 'Voyage en Suisse' production, c. 1900.

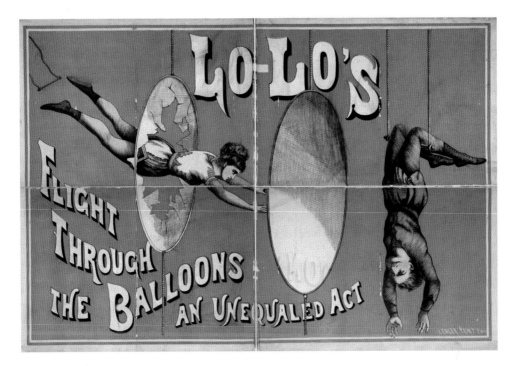

example of the total affirmation of life, the greatest joy and the ultimate freedom.'[10] For Nietzsche, the rope walker's courage was heroic. 'In *The Gay Science*,' McCullagh writes,

> Nietzsche suggested a meaning for the dance on the wire: 'Whenever "the hero" appeared on the stage, something new was attained . . . Life and I and you and all of us became interesting to ourselves once again for a little while . . . In the long run . . . the short tragedy always gave way again and returned to the eternal comedy of existence.'[11]

Part of the thrill of watching a rope walker came from vicariously experiencing risk. Viewers felt exhausted after watching Blondin cross the Falls, for example, not only because they knew intellectually the danger of falling, but, as neurobiologists later discovered, because the brain's mirror neurons create a visceral sense of an aerialist's feat. Empathy for the performer generates the accelerated

Poster for an aerialist
act, *c.* 1890s.

The Miraculous
Melrosas mid-air
cyclists, 1900.

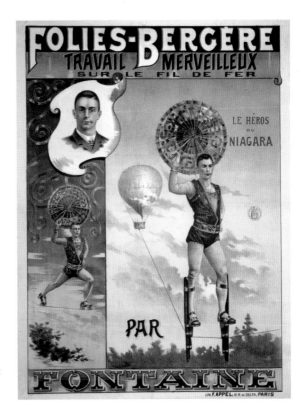

The tightrope
walker Fontaine at
the Folies Bergère,
Paris, c. 1890s.

pulse, the palpitating heart, the breathlessness. Performers emphasized the audience's thrill by incorporating into their acts deliberate 'mistakes': in one famous act, the 'drunk going home', for example, the rope walker, in a clown's costume, wobbles, teeters and misses steps, all to evoke viewers' gasps. Sometimes, says the circus historian Hermine Demoriane, walkers took foreign names so that they would seem exotic, but also because some of the nationalities were enemies of the viewers. 'Perhaps', she suggests, 'the excitement of watching such acts is enhanced for the native onlooker by a pleasurable sense of guilt – his secret sin of hoping the hated foreigner will fall.'[12]

Girlish heroism

If revenge was part of the viewers' delight, it seems not to have been directed at women aerialists, who became increasingly popular beginning in the second half of the nineteenth century. Men's muscularity was impressive, to be sure. 'Woman, you know, loves alone the man who succeeds; the man who fails she only pities,' the *New York Times* concluded at the turn of the century.

> So . . . the young women who nightly crowd the Garden see in the acrobat the man who succeeds . . . The circus presents to the young woman of ideas the man of ideals. She sees here men who perform without failure most delicate feats of precision, calling for all the qualities of a healthy physique, and naturally she exacts more from her male associates of every day who don't have to stand on their heads on trapezes.[13]

The men who crowded the circus arena saw women flyers and rope dancers who also displayed a healthy physique, but they exuded as well a paradoxical combination of power, sensuality and vulnerability. A woman on a wire or trapeze seemed to some viewers to be transformed into a mythological being – floating, weightless and ethereal. Despite her skills, the historian Nicola Haxell suggests,

'Aerialists Supreme',
1892.

Mlle Beeson, the
'High Wire Venus',
1921.

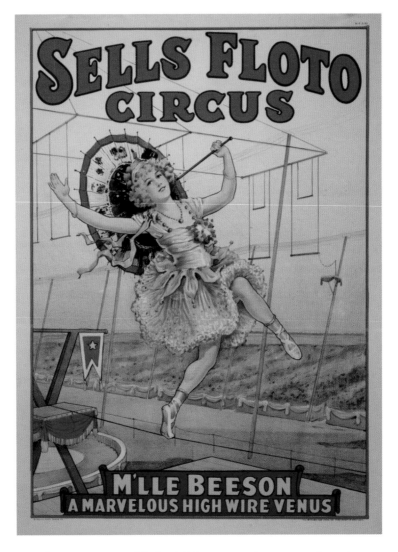

The Vortex sisters'
trapeze act, *c.* 1898.

she was just a publicly visible woman in an age when the
domestic female was prioritized, and one whose autonomy,
costume and the physicality of her *métier* led (men) to view
her as the archetypal Accessible Woman, a blank cipher onto
which could be projected . . . a range of desires and fantasies,
centered primarily around female abasement or fear of/desire
for female domination.[14]

If some men saw women aerialists as angelic, others saw a woman willing to flout convention, in all the titillating ways that transgression could be imagined.

Women's costumes evolved from loose bloomers covering just the top of the thigh to a tight-fitting, sequined brassiere, tight trunks and a sheer, short skirt. Flesh-coloured woollen tights gave way to silk, showing a scandalous amount of leg. Some women aerialists exaggerated their femininity with frills and ribbons, pastel colours and stage names that advertised their vulnerability. Famous among them was Marie Meeker, a buxom aerialist who dressed in flesh-coloured one-piece tights, called herself Dainty Marie and walked the rope carrying a parasol.

No female performer, though, represented power and seduction as blatantly as the legendary Lillian Leitzel, an sensational star of the golden age of the circus. She was born in Breslau, Germany, in 1892; although her mother, grandmother and aunts were aerialists, following in their path was not inevitable. At the same time that she took gymnastics classes, she studied languages and music in Breslau and Berlin, and was talented enough to consider a career as a concert pianist.

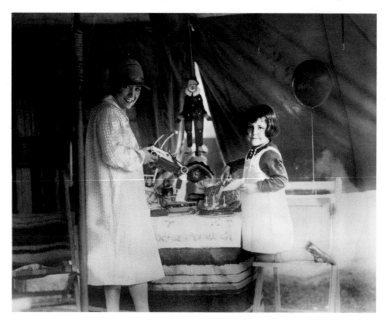

Lillian Leitzel and Dolly Jahn, 1926.

Watching her mother and aunts perform, however, lured her at the age of nine to join them in an aerial ballet. Tiny as she was – even as an adult, she was four feet nine – her agility and stage presence were outstanding; many in the audience came away thinking that the adults 'were more or less window dressing for the tot . . . in the center'.[15] The outburst of applause, the attention and the acclaim made Leitzel determined to spend her life as an aerialist.

The act she devised was strenuous, risky and breathtaking. Henry Ringling North, who watched her for years, described it: 'Wearing silk tights and a diaphanous short-short skirt, Leitzel would go up the web – as the dangling ropes for the aerialists are called – in a series of apparently effortless roll-overs until she reached a pair of roman rings high above the center ring. There was no net beneath them – Leitzel never used a net.' After some acrobatics on the roman rings, she descended, grabbed onto a rope and was pulled to the top of the tent. At that moment, everything else in the arena stopped; nothing competed with Leitzel's main attraction.

'As a single spot focused on her tiny flittering figure,' North wrote, 'she slipped her right wrist through a padded loop attached by a swivel to a hanging rope. Then she got up by momentum and hurled her entire body in a full circle over itself. This is called the full-arm plange, or "dislocate," for each time she did it her right shoulder was dislocated and was snapped back by its powerful muscles.'[16] Drum rolls heightened the tension; the audience chanted the count: 50, 100, 200. 'The crowd would count them in unison, and their chanting in the darkened tent had the feeling of a magic incantation. The chanting crowd, we can see now,' observed the historian John Culhane, 'was a vital part of her act. In a sense, the crowd cast a spell on itself.'[17] And Leitzel cast a spell on the crowd: 'As she spun around,' North recalled, 'her long hair gradually, artfully loosed from its pins and swung free, following the parabolas her body made like a golden comet's tail.'[18] By the time she was finished, her hair had loosed itself entirely: 'She looked like a pastel doll spinning in the halo of flame.'[19]

North called her 'the greatest star of them all, personifying in her tiny lambent person the quintessential glamour of the circus'. With her cascading blonde hair, tiny waist and child's-size feet, she looked fragile except for her muscular arms and shoulders. With her scanty costume, bare midriff and gold mules, she was undeniably sexy. Leitzel deliberately honed her feminine image. Often she was carried into the arena in the arms of a muscular man so tall he appeared to be a giant; always she was attended to by a woman dressed as a French maid, in white cap and apron, who dutifully picked up the ankle-length red cape that Leitzel threw off. Alexander Calder was in the audience once at Madison Square Garden when Leitzel entered 'with the light all on her . . . What I loved', he said, 'was the spotlight on her and the rest in obscurity.'[20] She understood that vulnerability made her even more appealing: 'Quite early, having learned that the crowd's response to a faint was about like the ancient Roman's enjoyment of lions on a Christian diet, she placed herself on a permanently wobbly footing.' She would take a few steps, stagger, hold her hand to her heart and wait for her maid to rush to her side; then, wistfully, bravely, she would continue, a paragon of 'girlish heroism'.[21]

Leitzel revelled in the applause that greeted her entrance. 'She savored and tasted her power,' wrote Robert Taylor in a *New Yorker* profile. 'She stood at ease and looked around, establishing the wonderfully electric connection between herself and her audience. She would giggle slightly, and people would break into roars of sympathetic laughter.' She knew she was a star. And she was a diva, too: emotional, temperamental, demanding. She would not share a dressing room, she fired and rehired her faithful maid several times a day, she insisted on special treatment, and she got it. She seemed to love what she was doing. Her expression, as she whirled in her planges, was radiant, gleeful. 'She looked like a child riding a carrousel and yelling, "Whee!"' Yet once, talking about her career, she admitted that like many aerialists she was terrified by 'an urge to let go. "I have to fight it"', she said. '"You're spinning around way up there, holding by one hand, and all of a sudden you hear a little nagging voice – Why not let go? I've never managed to get over it."'[22]

Besides the abiding dread of a nagging inner voice, Leitzel experienced constant, relentless pain. Underneath her leather wristband, the skin was raw, bloody, scarred, often with festering abscesses. As iron-jaw performer Tiny Kline recalled,

Lillian Leitzel and
clown, 1925.

Her right wrist was everlastingly bruised and chronically
abscessed from the pressure of the loop holding her while
she did those marvelous throwovers. Remembering all this
. . . a feeling of deep reverence possessed me. She became
divine in my estimation of her. Adjusting that band over a
bruised, black-and-blue wrist and sacrificing so much, enduring the torture of live tissue being torn from her, she must have
been a saint.[23]

One physician was so alarmed he told her that he might have
to amputate her arm. Leitzel left his office, wrapped her wrist and

proceeded to the arena. She was vain enough to cover her wrist with a chiffon scarf or hide it in the folds of her skirt for photographs, but she never admitted, or succumbed to, pain. When an interviewer suggested that she alternate arms for her planges, giving the right wrist a chance to heal, she refused to consider it. Then she would have scars on both wrists, she retorted, harder to hide. Even after falling once in the middle of her act, she rose from her knees and continued the performance; the next night, with both legs sprained and bruised, she walked into the ring on crutches, handed them away when she reached the web and carried out her act impeccably.

Audiences adored her, not least male admirers, of which there were many. She married twice early in her career, but her most publicized marriage was her third, to 34-year-old aerialist Alfredo Codona, 'the Adonis of the altitudes'. It was, said one reporter, the marriage of 'two comets'. They were a golden couple: she, the goddess of the air, and he, the most astounding man on the flying trapeze. Known as 'the handsomest man ever to appear with circuses', he was also the most daring, with the same combination of 'grace, compulsion, and careless ease, or glamour' that characterized Leitzel.[24]

Codona perfected the triple somersault, at the time the most dangerous trapeze feat. 'The history of the triple somersault is a history of death,' he once told an interviewer.[25] As the circus historian and artist George Beal explained, 'The difficulty in the triple somersault is a simple one. After the second turn, you see nothing, feel nothing, and have no further control over your muscles. The world goes black and chaos reigns.' The catcher, hanging face down from his own bar, must grasp the flyer coming towards him through the air at great velocity.

He must hold onto the flyer and, with his dead-weight body suspended at arm's length, swinging back and forth through the air, cast him in the direction of his trapeze as it swings back through its giant arc through space. And that casting must be done timed with such accuracy that the flyer, turning, will arrive at his own trapeze as it swings on its outward arc.[26]

The act required split-second precision.

'We must work in the dark to a certain degree; we do not know why we let go at a certain instant, or what clocklike arrangement of our brain gauges that tiny part of a second which forms the starting time,' Codona said. 'We only know that a flashing energy shoots through us and on we go, to the double somersault, the triple . . . to the applause of a well-done act, or to the sympathy of an audience as we fall, spin about, fight for a safe landing and then, rope-burned or bruised, go back to our tricks again.' Unlike Leitzel, he performed with a net, but the net, he made clear,

> is not the beneficent thing which it appears to be. It is danger-
> ous, a friend indeed if you fall into it properly, but otherwise
> a lurking enemy, waiting to snap the bones of an arm or a leg
> – or a neck. Persons have been killed by falls into the net,
> and even on many tumbles which the audience classes as
> uneventful, it seems to possess satanic joy in gouging the
> flesh out of one.[27]

Rope burns were a common hazard of a net, a broken neck always possible.

Codona was as emotionally volatile as his wife, and their marriage, which the media called 'the true love match of the circus world', was tempestuous and passionate.[28] While they performed often in the same circuses, they also accepted engagements individually, which is what occurred on Friday 13 February 1931: Codona was at the Winter Garden in Berlin, Leitzel at the Valencia Music Hall in Copenhagen. She had just finished the first half of her act on the roman rings when suddenly one of the iron swivel rings broke. As always, she had no net, only a rubber mat, and she plummeted more than 40 feet, landing on her head and shoulders. She was conscious, insisting that she was not hurt, but still she was taken to the nearest hospital. Codona, notified by telegram, rushed to Copenhagen. On Saturday, she greeted him cheerfully. She was fine, she insisted again, and told him to return to the Winter Garden. He was back in Berlin on Sunday morning when he learned that she had died.

'Circus Fall Fatal to Lillian Leitzel' read a headline in the *New York Times* the next day. 'Circus Star Loses Life' announced a front-page story in the *Los Angeles Times*.[29] Her fans were incredulous, the circus community desolate. On 17 February, the house lights dimmed at the start of a hockey match in Madison Square Garden for a tribute to Leitzel in the arena where she reigned as queen. Now a mournful crowd sang 'Auld Lang Syne' to her memory. A memorial notice in *The Nation* gave voice to what her fans were feeling:

> Lillian Leitzel, whirling at the top of the big tent, without even a net beneath to cast a doubt upon her perfection, spun out to its finest one of the shining threads by which men throw themselves toward the unattainable. For that she deserved the acclaim and the long roll of the drums that were always hers. And the manner of her death was not inappropriate. She was thrown to the earth because an iron ring, and not a human nerve, gave way.[30]

No one grieved more than her husband, who ended his engagement to attend to her cremation in Copenhagen, then accompanied her ashes back to America. They would have retired in two years, he told reporters, and had planned to settle in Long Beach, California. Now he would bury her ashes there. He said he would never perform again.

In a short time, though, he was back in the air, and on 18 September 1932 he remarried. His new wife was Vera Bruce, who performed with him, and publicity photographs show them radiant, far from the reality of their life. His fellow aerialists found Codona grim and increasingly reckless. They could not account for his risk-taking, and were not surprised when, in 1933, he fell and was seriously injured. His shoulder was dislocated and he was grounded, permanently. In the next few years, he became more and more depressed; finally, in 1937, Bruce sued for divorce. For Codona, losing Bruce was the final degradation of a life that was spiralling downward. At a meeting in her lawyer's office to finalize the divorce, he asked for a few minutes alone with Bruce, pulled out a pistol and shot her, then killed himself.

If Leitzel had any competition as Queen of the Air, it was Jennadean Engleman, known as Bird Millman, a wire dancer who, like Leitzel, took the spotlight alone when she performed with Barnum & Bailey and the Ringlings. Singing, chirping and dancing on an extended wire of 36 feet (twice the length of other acts), she performed without a balance bar or umbrella. What she lacked in daring – her wire was only 7 feet off the ground – she made up for with a winning flirtatiousness. 'How Would You Like to Spoon With Me?' was one of her signature songs. Millman retired in 1924 when she married, and with the deaths of Leitzel and Codona in the next few years, it seemed that the circus had lost some of its most mesmerizing stars. But the show, of course, went on.

Cornelius Sullivan, born into a circus family in New South Wales in 1899, began his career at the age of three, being tossed on his father's feet in what was known as a Risley act. When he outgrew that, he graduated to bareback riding, tumbling and acrobatics. But, determined to be a wire walker, he practiced seven hours a day for several years on a tight wire without any pole for balance. Once he perfected walking, he moved on to tricks. It took five years to perfect the forward somersault, which is more difficult than the backward flip because the performer cannot see the wire before landing; in the next five years he added other moves: flip-flaps and springs to a standing position. As impressive as these feats were, though, they did not comprise an act. So he decided to dance, specifically the Spanish and Argentine tango, and trained with a matador to learn how to swing a cape. Dressed in a Spanish costume, he transformed himself into one of the most adept wire dancers since Bird Millman, with a stage name that evoked an exotic Spanish heritage: Con Colleano. 'He was a proud, tigerish figure as he paced up, down and round his little room with feverish litheness, dressed ready for the show in his yellow and black satin,' recalled the painter Laura Knight, who saw Colleano perform with the Bertram Mills Circus. Travelling with Bertram Mills and drawing and painting performers, Knight found Colleano extraordinary: 'his build was perfect', she wrote. 'His shoulders made a lovely fan shape from his slender waist as he poised on the wire, the sheen on his silk stockings outlining his muscular, finely cut legs.' He was a consummate stylist, the Wizard of the Wire.[31]

Colleano often shared a bill with the Concellos, Arturo and his wife Antoinette, billed as 'the world's greatest aerialists, male and female'. Unlike other performing pairs, the Concellos were not born into the circus, but after seeing aerialists perform, they were determined to make the circus their life. When Arthur Marshall Vasconcello was a thirteen-year-old in Bloomington, Indiana, a circus came to town and Art saw his first trapeze act – and his future. At a local YMCA, he set up a net and two trapezes, enlisted a friend to be his catcher and practised every day for two hours. At the age of sixteen, he was good enough to be hired by the Flying Wards and began touring with them; the following year, he was performing in Springfield, Illinois, when he noticed a beautiful teenager, Antoinette, in the audience. It was, they agreed, love at first sight. Antoinette was a student in a convent school at the time, but Art convinced her to defect, to run away with him and join the circus, in which her sister already was an aerialist. Their marriage in 1930 generated none of the excitement that Leitzel's and Codona's did, but in the 1930s and '40s, the Concellos were stars.

More terrifying than Colleano's dancing and the Concellos' flying was the high-wire performance of the Wallendas, who made their debut at Madison Square Garden in 1928. They had been a circus family since the eighteenth century, starting out as a travelling troupe of acrobats and jugglers. Karl, born in Germany in 1905, first performed on the trapeze with his father, Engelbert, and later joined a wire walker, doing a handstand on his partner's shoulders. In a few years, he and his brother Herman created the wire act that made the family renowned: a human pyramid, first with four men, and later, astoundingly, with seven. 'I was born into show business,' he once told a reporter. 'Our fathers and forefathers didn't know any other trade and we never felt happy in any other business . . . Then comes my wish, when I was a kid, to do something big, very great, to be world-famous in show business.' Their debut performance was met with a fifteen-minute ovation.[32]

On the night of 30 January 1962 the Wallendas were performing at the Coliseum at the Michigan state fairgrounds in Detroit when suddenly Dieter Schepp, a nephew, cried out, 'I can't hold on any longer.' When he lost hold, the pyramid collapsed; Schepp and Karl

Tightrope dancer Con Colleano on a slack wire, *c.* 1920.

Wallenda's son-in-law were killed. An adopted son was paralysed
from the waist down. This was not the Wallendas' first mishap. In 1944
Herman slipped while doing a backflip, dangling from the wire as his
pole crashed to the ground. But he suffered only lacerations and, with
his arm bandaged, resumed his act, crossing the wire on a bicycle.

In Detroit, though, there was a catastrophe: viewers watched,
horrified, as three bodies fell 40 feet, as if in slow motion, landing with
a deathly thud. 'The collapse of the pyramid', Rick Wallenda told
the family's chronicler,

> wasn't just the biggest accident in the history of the circus, it
> changed the way people *looked* at our kind of entertainment
> – the way the public looked at it, the way we ourselves looked
> at it. Suddenly, everything circus people had known for years
> about the risks, but that audiences had never really had to
> confront, was right out there in the open – people heaving
> their last breaths right there in the ring. I mean, even for us
> the vulnerability had been pretty much abstract most of the
> time – now it was this very ugly reality.[33]

Still, the event did not keep Karl, at the age of 65, from walking
across the Tallulah Gorge in Georgia, on a cable of nearly 1,000 feet,
700 feet above the rocks. He stopped twice during the walk to do a
headstand. The audience of 20,000 people included his wife – the
first time in eight years that she had watched him perform. After
1962, she said, she prayed in a back room when her family was on
the wire.

In 1978 Karl embarked on another feat, walking on a 750-foot
cable between two hotels in San Juan, Puerto Rico. The stunt was
meant to draw audiences for the Pan American Circus, where the
Wallendas were performing each night. 'I feel better up there than
I do down here,' Wallenda once said. 'It is my whole life.'[34] He preferred working without a net, claiming that a net would only provide
false security and even invite a fall. Of course, there was no net in San
Juan that day, but there was a strong wind, and the cable he was
walking on began to sway. His troupe, watching the stunt, cried out

to him to sit, but as he started to squat, a sudden gust blew him off the wire. He fell 100 feet to his death.

The Wallendas – members of the biological family, those who married into the family and those who joined the troupe and took the family's name – kept walking on the wire. In 1985 seventeen-year-old Elizabeth Pintye married Steven Wallenda and started training to become a wire walker. Two years later she was diagnosed with cancer, and her right leg was amputated and parts of both lungs removed. Still, with a prosthesis, she got back on the wire. 'When I'm way up in the sky, walking on a thin line with a fake leg, people look up at me and really pay attention,' she said. 'They see that I'm using everything I've got to live my life the best I can. When people think about that, it makes them think about themselves, and some of them see how much better they can live their own lives.'[35] Living better, for the Wallendas, meant living courageously, defying death and overcoming obstacles. It also meant putting oneself on display as a spectacle of physical and mental control.

Liliana Luna, a contemporary aerialist, has perfected an act using a web, or woven cotton hose, packed with cord and suspended from the rafters. From the rings, Luna begins a backward somersault, completing her spin when she feels the web at her back. 'I go into it blind,' she said. 'My only orientation is in being able to feel the web on my back.' But that feeling is abrasion, each time searing away a two-inch oval of skin. After a month's tour, her back, an observer noted, became 'a raku glazing of welts, scabs, and calluses – these on top of the welts, scabs, and calluses already there from years of practice and performance.' Luna performs without a net, aiming to be the first woman to do a double somersault to the web.

Another aerialist performs a 'cloud swing', also without a net, that involved flips and hangs from a web, ending with a dramatic swing that her audience perceives as a free fall, not noticing that she has slipped her ankles through straps that will catch her. She loves to hear the crowd scream as she falls: 'I love hearing that gasp. Some people can't watch. Or they duck. I get a real thrill out of their reaction.' Like Luna, this performer, too, has calloused wrists and ankles, bruised arms and legs.[36]

This exalting of exhibitionism attracted artists who portrayed aerialists as solitary figures suspended in space. Jean-Louis Forain's *Tight-Rope Walker* (c. 1885), for example, is pictured on a low rope, hardly above the heads of a milling crowd. Her legs, arms and balance pole are illuminated against what appears to be the night sky. She is a still figure, transcending the bustle of the spectators. Everett Shinn's *The Tightrope Walker* (1924) also stands alone, a ghostly white figure against the darkness, stepping tentatively along a high wire.

What artists conveyed in their portrayal of aerialists seems to me a visual rendering of a reflection on the circus that appeared in *The Nation* in 1931, at a precarious moment in history:

> On their trapezes and their tight ropes high above a solid earth they act out a dream of perfectability. Defying space and gravity and human weakness they weave a fantasy of human infallibility. And the spectators? There are no spectators. Every last one of us, svelte and lithe and sheathed in silk, is swinging in space, walking on air, leaping to the backs of plunging white horses. There is not a flabby muscle, not an awkward limb, not a sagging knee in the whole tent.

In the summer of 1943, artist and writer Marsden Hartley went to see the Ringling Bros circus at Madison Square Garden. Long a circus fan, he was just finishing a book, *Elephants and Rhinestones: A Book of Circus Values*, in which he celebrated the muscular bodies of the aerialist and acrobat that he so envied. At the age of 66, there was no question that he would run off to join a circus, as much as he wished he could. 'If there is to be a Heaven hereafter,' he said,

> then let me go straight by pelican air service to that division of it set apart for the circus and go pell-mell for the rings and the bars, till I can join the splendid horde all turning and springing and flying through the properly-roped spaces and merge myself in the fine pattern which these superior artists make in what will no longer be 'The Greatest Show on Earth'.[37]

Age, though, did not stop 62-year-old Sam Keen from enrolling in a trapeze class at the San Francisco School of Circus Arts in the 1990s. 'Thus far,' he said, 'I have been a man of gravity – serious, strong, rigid, taut, heavy, and earthbound. It is time for levity, lightness, litheness, and soaring.' Like Hartley, he saw in aerial work a chance for physical, mental, and spiritual discipline: 'the hope', as he put it, 'to transcend the "normal" limits of the human condition'. He knew well that he was embarking on a project far out of the ordinary. 'From the point of view of common sense', he admitted, 'flying, like radical compassion, is an unnatural act. Normal people keep their feet on the ground, their ego boundaries clear, and limit their care to those within their own family, tribe, or nation.' In learning circus arts, Keen was distinguishing himself from 'normal people' and their circumscribed lives. Like professional aerialists, Keen learned that besides rigorous practice to build his muscles and skills, he needed to develop a sense of communion and trust with other performers, especially his catcher. 'The gap that exists between two pairs of outstretched arms is only a few feet that could be traversed in a millisecond,' he said. 'But between the "Hep" and the catch there is a journey across an abyss. No footbridge leads from reason to faith, from doubt to trust. Prior to the leap, fear seems more justified than trust, isolation more fundamental than communion, and the flight of the spirit an impossibility.'[38]

'I heard an acrobat say once,' the painter Laura Knight recalled in her 1936 memoir, '"No matter what we come to, we have lived. I was King of the Earth when I was young, the laws that governed other people did not govern me, I could do anything. I clawed my way through the air back to the net once when I missed my grip on the flying trapeze." It is the feeling of defiance for the laws of nature that makes the circus people a race apart.'[39]

SIX

BEASTS

Out slink the striped cats, snarling and roaring, leaping
at each other or at me. It's a matchless thrill, and life without
it is not worth while to me.

Mabel Stark

I n 1911, when Mabel Stark was in her early twenties, she applied
for a job with the Al G. Barnes Circus, intent on training tigers.
Nothing in her background or her life pointed to this career choice.
In fact, she had recently graduated from nursing school, but suffered
a nervous breakdown soon afterwards. Nursing, she decided, was
not to be her future; it was too stressful, she said. Although there are
several contradictory versions of how Mabel became interested in
tigers, one story she perpetuated had her vacationing with a friend in
Los Angeles and visiting the Selig Zoo, a facility housing hundreds
of animals used in film productions by the Selig Polyscope Company.
She claimed that she performed in a few jungle scenes for the studio
and became 'so engrossed' in the work that she decided to make
tiger training her career. 'My family are not show people,' she added,
'and for a long while frowned upon my circus work', but after several
years of her growing fame, they were 'weaned over to a lukewarm
approval'.[1]

Working with tigers, then, was an act of defiance against her
family, and also against wider social expectations. Nursing was woman's
work, Mabel believed, and she aspired to a profession that was dominated by men; more important, she wanted her work to reflect the
person she believed herself to be: forceful, wilful and wild. She loved

Poster showing
clowns performing
with barnyard
animals, c. 1900.

'the roaming life', she said, and the thrill of danger when the big cats, snarling and roaring, leaped into the cage.

The tiger, she wrote, 'is the most magnificent expression of animal life . . . They are killers because they know their own strength. They can be subdued but never conquered, except by love.'[2] She would love them, but what she expected in return was not love, but obedience to her commands. At the Barnes circus, she begged trainer Louis Roth to allow her to go into the tiger cage. Roth was reluctant. This young, small-boned, soft-voiced blonde did not fit his image of an animal tamer. But she insisted, the circus had her sign a release and, for the first time, she stepped into a cage.

The tigers, she decided immediately, were more fearful than she was. Their fear, though, was what made them aggressive, and she knew intuitively that she had to earn their trust. Somehow she survived that first encounter, and Roth agreed to take her on as a pupil. For more than 50 years, until her death in 1968, Mabel Stark was one of the most famous animal trainers in the world, orchestrating acts with up to twenty tigers. Her body was raked with scars from bites, gouges and rips – wounds that she was proud to display. Unlike aerialists, who hid their bruises and scars to convey the illusion of a perfect body, animal trainers flaunted their wounds. Theatre historian John Stokes notes that a 'strange pride' in showing off scars was shared among animal trainers:

> Like the gashes proudly displayed by chivalric knights – like stigmata even – wounds are visible testimonies of an honourable sacrifice ostensibly made for the sake of an audience, but equally endured by the trainers on behalf of their own vocation . . . The stress on wounds is quite exceptional. It points to a peculiar sense of initiation, a fellowship among trainers, and, even more importantly, of intimacy with the animal who has caused the damage.[3]

This longing for intimacy with big cats is evident in Stark's sensual description of her tigers. She admires their 'rippling muscles', the 'matchless beauty of their tawny bodies', the 'rhythmic grace in their stealthy stride and the long curving arc of their supple bodies'.[4] Her evocation of tigers' wildness and primal strength borders on the erotic. Posters advertising her performances underscored the connection between Stark and her big cats. In one poster, a docile tiger, standing on its hind paws, rests its right front paw on her shoulder, its left through the crook of her arm. They appear to be dancing, or preparing to embrace. In another poster, Stark wears eyeliner, lipstick and a low-cut gown; a tiger, looking at her longingly, leans on one shoulder. As the historians Katherine Adams and Michael Keene observe, 'The tiger appears about as anthropomorphically smitten with her as would be possible before the age of Disney.' Stark claimed to love her tigers, more, apparently, than several of her four husbands. 'I still love the tigers best,' she said. 'They may snarl back at me but they never cause me to be sneered at or talked about, tigers only tear flesh – which heals – but men hurt characters, break hearts, spirits, and souls – and my spirit is easily broken or perhaps I should say pride in myself and work.'[5] Emotionally vulnerable, she was determined to prove her fearlessness in the cage.

By the time Stark entered the field, animal acts had undergone big changes. Early circuses usually did not feature any animals except horses, and occasionally dogs and monkeys; instead, in the eighteenth century, the animals long associated with circus acts, such as lions, tigers and elephants, were shipped to cities and exhibited singly for a fee. The 'Lyon of Barbery', for example, arrived in the American colonies in 1716, a camel in 1721, a polar bear in 1733 and a leopard in 1786. The first elephant arrived in New York in 1796, with tickets priced at a hefty 25 cents.

Animal baiting, an attraction since ancient times, continued as well. In 1830 a circus advertisement announced, 'A Full Grown Bear will be chained out once, at liberty for any person to set their dogs on him; he will be so secured, that any person may view the fight with perfect safety.' By the early nineteenth century, audiences' fascination with exotic animals made travelling menageries profitable. George Wombwell's famous menagerie was a feature at English fairs, where he dabbled in lion baiting, but was more successful in gathering such amazing beasts as an elephant and a buffalo. Eventually menageries trailed as an appendage to tent shows and, later, animal acts were incorporated into circus programmes: dancing elephants, for example, or performances by animal tamers, demonstrations of human courage and bestial rage. Some menageries seemed like travelling zoos: in 1893 one featured

> trained camels, zebras, a hairless horse, a remarkable steer with three horns and three eyes, a horse 7 feet high, a clown elephant that performs comical antics, a dwarf cow only 32 inches high, a miniature zebra 30 inches high, and a great variety of trained goats, monkeys, pigeons, ponies, lions, tigers, hyenas, leopards, and panthers.[6]

Only wealthy circuses boasted one or two elephants. When an elephant was featured, reported the *New York Times*, 'People would sit all night by the roadside, anticipating the coming of the circus, to see the big pachyderm go by, and all they were allowed to behold without paying an admission fee was a seeming haystack covered

Giraffes, elephants, tigers and hippos at Sells Brothers' circus, c. 1895.

Caged animals at John Robinson's Menagerie, 1898.

SELLS BROTHERS' ENORMOUS UNITED SHOWS.

MAGNIFICENT THREE RING CIRCUS,
FIVE CONTINENT MENAGERIE, HUGE ELEVATED STAGES,
AUSTRALIAN AVIARY, AFRICAN AQUARIUM,
ROMAN HIPPODROME,
SPECTACULAR PAGEANTS, ARABIAN CARAVAN AND
TRANS-PACIFIC WILD BEAST EXHIBIT.

RARE ZOOLOGICAL MARVELS SEEN ONLY IN EXTENT AND PERFECTION IN OUR GRAND 5 CONTINENT MENAGERIE THE LARGEST, THE BEST SELECTED AND THE MOST RARE COLLECTION OF LIVING WILD BEASTS, BEAUTIFUL BIRDS AND STRANGE REPTILES EVER ASSEMBLED IN A SINGLE EXHIBITION. THERE IS NOR CAN BE NO DUPLICATION OF THIS INTERESTING DISPLAY IN THE WORLD.

Bostock and
Wombwell's circus:
Captain Bonavita
reading a newspaper
at the centre of a
pyramid of lions,
c. 1903.

with a huge tarpaulin. They could only see its feet move and its trunk squirm. That much thrilled them with awe, and the show was known to take in as much as $75 in a single day.'[7] Circus animals often performed comic tricks – dogs dressed in frilly tutus might be taught to dance – and more often performed in acts that reflected their helpfulness or sympathy to humans. Horses, especially, were considered intelligent enough to form real connections with people, and their performances involved demonstrations of loyalty, such as rescuing or serving humans.

The growing commercial importance of animal acts is reflected in their prominence in the Ringling and Barnum & Bailey Circus. The Ringlings started out with domestic animals, such as trained dogs; in 1886 they bought two lions, a kangaroo, an anteater, an elk, a monkey and a cage of birds. In 1888 they acquired two elephants, along with two camels, another lion, a hyena, deer, emu and 80 horses and ponies. In 1900 they invested in several elephants, at a cost of many thousands of dollars each. Besides the initial cost of the animals were the costs of housing, feeding, transporting and training them, providing veterinary attention and disposing of their bodies if they died of injury or disease.

As more exotic animals from Asia or Africa were incorporated into the circus, the acts conveyed a message justifying colonialism and imperialism. The roaring beasts of the jungle became synonymous with the natives dominated by colonial rule; animals – described in publicity posters as huge, ferocious and bloodthirsty – were tamed by a white man posing as heroic. Audiences, one circus historian claimed, were sadistic, and trainers often created an atmosphere of peril where none existed:

> At the end of the act, red fire would be used to fill the ring with smoke; and out of the smoke would be heard the agonized voice of the 'tamer' shouting for help. And as he stepped from the cage, a waiting attendant would throw a cupful of bullock's blood over him, so that, when the smoke cleared away, he might present an edifyingly gory spectacle.[8]

The bloodier the spectacle, the larger the crowds.

Kings of beasts

Just as Blondin and Léotard are credited with inaugurating an iconic type of aerial performance, the American Isaac Van Amburgh created the modern animal act. Born in upstate New York in 1811, Van Amburgh left home at the age of fifteen, bouncing from one odd job to another until he landed work in a zoo caravan. One day, he volunteered to

substitute for the absent lion keeper and found his vocation. In the next few years, he built up his own menagerie of wild animals, travelling through New York, New Jersey and New England, creating acts that featured his power and daring. Most famously, he prised open a lion's jaws and put his head in its mouth, leaving his audiences aghast. A large man – newspapers describe him as Herculean – Van Amburgh flaunted his strength and his apparently uncanny ability to mesmerize his animals with the intensity of his gaze. He claimed to intuit the animals' essential characters: the tiger, he said, was 'like a reckless, good-for-nothing, drunken rascal'; leopards, 'like cats, playful but easily provoked'.[9]

In 1838 Van Amburgh appeared at Drury Lane and Astley's in London with performances that astonished his audiences: he trained his animals to perform rage, using whips and pistols to cue his tigers, leopards and lions to growl, claw and hurl themselves upon his back.

Edwin Landseer, *Mr Van Amburgh, As He Appeared with His Animals at the London Theatres*, 1846–7, oil on canvas.

One act, called 'The Brute Tamer of Pompeii, or the Living Lions of the Jungle', ended with the animals arranged in a tableau in which Van Amburgh, wearing a gladiator's toga, sat among his animals like a biblical figure exerting his dominion over the beasts of the earth. It impressed the nineteen-year-old Victoria just one year into her long reign: 'One can never see it too often,' she wrote. 'Van Amburgh . . . has great power over the animals, & they seem to love him, though I think they are in great fear of him. He took them by their paws, throwing them down & making them roar, & he lay upon them after enraging them.' The Queen saw six performances in six weeks, sometimes accompanied by the Duke of Wellington. Both commissioned paintings of Van Amburgh from Edwin Landseer, who had painted Victoria's dogs, much to her delight. In the queen's painting, *Van Amburgh and His Animals*, the trainer appears reclining with a tiger and lamb – he famously brought a lamb into the cats' cage – resting in his lap amid his carefully contrived peaceable kingdom. In the Duke's painting, *Mr Van Amburgh as He Appeared with His Animals at the London Theatres*, Van Amburgh strikes a stilted pose, his arm outstretched, while tigers and lions roar menacingly even as they cower. For his contemporaries, the painting recalled the story of Daniel in the lion's den and, for the Duke especially, the lines in Genesis that proclaim man's sovereignty over nature.[10]

Enraged animals subdued by human mastery became a circus staple. In America, George Conklin's animal act ended with the cats worked into a fury by Conklin's firing two or three blanks; as the cats growled and clawed, he pretended to be in fear for his life and ran out of the cage. He admitted to starving his animals to inspire a sensational act – this was an accusation levelled against Van Amburgh, too – and to train them, he used a collar, chain, muzzle, broom and boxing gloves. Van Amburgh used a crowbar. In the second half of the nineteenth century, however, the meaning of animal acts and the training of animals underwent an evolution.

Darwin's *On the Origin of Species* electrified Western culture with the idea that humans and beasts existed on a continuum; that humans were not specially created in God's image. Those who believed that whites comprised a species in themselves, those who resisted evidence of the comparative anatomy between humans and simians, found themselves disturbed and discomfited. The idea that humans were essentially animals affected both trainers and their audiences. Foremost among the reformist trainers was the German animal hunter Carl Hagenbeck who, after a career supplying animals – and people – for circuses, established his own performing menagerie based on a new philosophy of training. 'Brutes', announced Hagenbeck, 'after all are beings akin to ourselves. They will repay cruelty with hatred and kindness with trust.'[11] Hagenbeck's 'gentling method' meant that an animal was not forced to do anything that did not come naturally. The trainer spent time observing an animal's behaviour, alert to anything that might become part of an act. Such trainers were convinced that animals enjoyed perfecting tricks and, furthermore, enjoyed appearing before an audience.

'Hagenbeck's Trained Animals', 1893.

This enactment of joy occurred, for example, at the Crystal Palace in 1891, where Hagenbeck's lions, tigers, bears and leopards performed 'in perfect harmony'. Moreover, they did not growl and attack, but instead playfully rode tricycles, balanced on a see-saw and walked on revolving globes; the bear, reported the London *Times*, seemed 'to fulfil much the same purpose as the clown in a circus'. The innovative performance reflected a new way of training in which, the report noted, 'recourse has never been had to the old fashioned methods of club or red hot iron'.[12] In New York a few years later, Hagenbeck treated viewers to the sight of lions, tigers, bears, leopards, cheetahs and many other wild animals prancing freely into the arena to perform their tricks. Under Hagenbeck's direction, animals were adorable, and their trainers looked on like doting parents.

Other trainers of Hagenbeck's persuasion, though, still believed that audiences wanted to see evidence of human superiority. Frank

Bostock, 'The Animal King', director of one of the largest animal shows, agreed that animals should never be punished. Yet he conveyed his mastery in part by wearing a hunter's costume and in part by showing off his muscular physique. If humans were not superior to animals physically, still Bostock believed that the beasts he trained feared him, as they feared all men: 'The explanation', he said, 'probably is that they are unable to comprehend his habits, to fathom his mental attitude, to learn what he is likely to do next, and are awed by the mystery of his conduct, as we might be by that of some supernatural being of unknown power who came among us and threatened our liberty and our happiness'.[13] Like Bostock, many other trainers reiterate the notion that their animals see them as gods.

Despite many trainers' testimonies that they used only rewards in training, some observers insisted that punishment was unavoidable. 'The most approved method of training wild animals of the feline species,' wrote circus clown Robert Sherwood in the 1920s,

> is to cross-hitch them securely in a small cage wagon, the trainer sitting just beyond the reach of their paws when they plunge forward at him. Each attempt on their part to injure brings a sharp cut across the nose with a rawhide whip; this is kept up until the pupil begins to understand that he will be punished every time he does it.[14]

The process took from 60 to 90 days.

Sherwood confirmed observations by the journalist Maurice Kirby. Mutual affection between trainer and animal was impossible, Kirby concluded, after witnessing trainers using whips, sticks, and iron rods to 'persuade' their animals:

> When it comes right down to actual cases, the sole bond between the domestic man and the wild beast is a good strong stick; and the fiercer the beast, the bigger and tougher the stick. Of the great army of nature fakers, certainly the professional animal trainer is commander in chief . . . When a wild animal is to be broken, the first thing to break is his spirit. It is done with a club.

He witnessed animals being pushed and hauled, dragged, choked and whipped, describing in gory detail how an elephant is taught to lie down: a sharp hook is put into his hide, penetrating deeper and deeper if the elephant resists. 'Finally, when the pain becomes unbearable, he drops on his knees and clumsily rolls over on his side. Immediately the trainer gives him a lump of sugar as a reward of merit, and to show there is no hard feeling. This lesson is repeated until the beast lies down at a sign.' 'Once taught,' Kirby added, 'an elephant never forgets a trick.'[15]

Even if trainers saw themselves as teachers, even if they felt a special sympathetic bond with their animals, the presence of a whip and gun (shooting blanks, but still startling to the animals) upset some viewers. Many believed that animals could not possibly be trained without cruelty; besides, animals were confined in small cages or windowless rail cars when they were hauled from one place to another. By the late nineteenth century, humane reform movements that had focused on the poor, enslaved and children embraced animals. By 1877, the American Humane Association was founded; in 1900, the Wild Animals in Captivity Protection Act was passed in England; and in 1914, the Performing Animals Defence League was established. The writer Jack London became an outspoken supporter of animal rights, urging people to boycott animal acts and support humane societies. By 1924, worldwide membership of Jack London Clubs exceeded 400,000.

Although P. T. Barnum took on his animal rights critics with equanimity and eventually convinced them that his animals were not mistreated, the Ringlings later caved. In 1925, Charles Ringling explained why he was giving up wild animal acts in the Greatest Show on Earth:

There has been enough criticism by the public of wild-animal acts to warrant us in withdrawing them as a quite common impression is prevalent that tigers, lions, etc. are taught by very rough methods, and that it is cruel to force them through their stunts. Many parents object to bringing young children to a show in which men and women enter the cage with ferocious beasts. The delay in hauling the animals into and out of the circus tent and of transferring the animals from their shifting

A crowd watches a keeper feed meat to lions, *c.* 1891.

dens into the arena and back is very objectionable and not altogether without danger.

'The public', he concluded, 'seems to prefer animal acts in which the animals themselves seem to take an interested and playful part, as do dogs, seals, horses, elephants, etc.'[16] When the circus opened on 28 March 1925, Mabel Stark performed in a cowboy and cowgirl act. She hated it.

Despite the Ringlings' announcement, the circus still featured performances by elephants, apparently not considered wild, and other animals that appeared more docile than big cats: giraffes, zebras and sea lions. But by 1930 the Ringlings had rethought their position: audiences, it seems, were hungry for ferocity. That hunger overrode any ethical qualms they might feel, noted *The Nation*:

Animals come first, in any circus. The impossibility of giraffes, the sleepy, now unavailing cunning of leopards, the hugeness

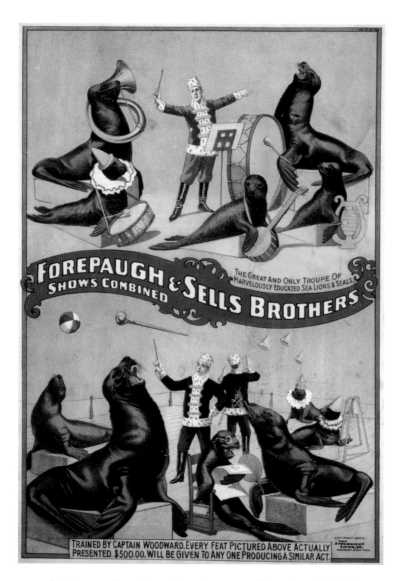

'Marvelously
Educated Sea Lions
and Seals', poster for
Forepaugh & Sells
Brothers, *c.* 1899.

of elephants, the agility of monkeys . . . all caged and labeled
for our pity and our delight. 'Isn't it awful to put anything so
fine and fierce as a lion in a cage?' we exclaim, thinking upon
our own freedom (we are careful not to think too fiercely). 'But
then no doubt they get used to it. They have no consciousness.'
We pass on, preoccupied with popcorn and life in the jungle.

We look deep into the eyes of the supercilious and ridiculous
camel, searching for the fascination of deserts.[17]

When the season opened in 1931, 'roaring beasts of the jungle' were
again part of the show, put through their paces by a charismatic young
trainer, Clyde Beatty.

Born in 1903, Beatty ran away to join the circus, and by the time
he was fifteen was working as a cage boy with Howe's Great London
Circus. For two years he fed animals and swept muck from their cages,
hoping for a chance to perform. When one of Howe's trainers quit, he
got that chance. Like Stark, Beatty believed that he possessed a special
connection to big cats. 'More than once', he said, 'I have confused
people by referring to a lion or a tiger as a friend.' Although he loved
his animals, he admitted that he never trusted them. 'You get accustomed
to the idea that wild animals never lose their primitiveness and that these
are friends that have to be carefully watched.'[18] As a young trainer, he
said, his work was close to being an obsession. He spent all of his time
with his troupe, learning about their personalities and behaviour,
thinking of new acts and new ways to train them.

For his own part in the performance, Beatty, who was about five
feet seven, slight and agile, took on the persona of a hunter, dressed
in white, wearing tall black boots and a gun at his hip, carrying a
whip and a wooden chair to fend off his cats' attack. Though the gun
was loaded with blanks, though the whip had a popper at the end to
augment the sound of the crack, Beatty knew that what audiences
wanted to see was a man mastering ferocious beasts. As the *New York
Times* reported about his first performance, Beatty, 'a young man,
goes into the cage and cracks a whip while his carefree charges growl.
The audience liked it, and that was that . . . New York is said to be
yearning for lions, tigers, pistols and whips.'[19] And for men who
dominated beasts.

Beatty publicized his preference for working with animals that
had been born in the wild, not those that had been raised in captivity and trained by someone else. He wanted his cats, most of which
weighed between 650 and 700 pounds, to retain their fighting spirit
and to get as close to him as possible in the cage. Beatty related how

Ernest Hemingway watched Beatty's act and commented afterwards that 'I put on my best show when I drew an animal as close to me as possible and "fought" him at close range' – 'and of course he was right', Beatty said.[20] That proximity put Beatty in danger, to be sure, but he was exhilarated by the cats' 'basic savagery', their bared fangs, the slap of their treacherous claws.

Early in his career he was seriously injured by Nero, a rampaging lion, and was hospitalized for three months. At the time, circus contracts did not cover injuries – trainers worked at their own risk – but the Ringlings came across with the money to cover Beatty's hefty hospital bills. And Beatty lost no time in returning to the cage as soon as his wounds healed. 'Occasionally an animal attacks and injures me,' he recalled late in his career, 'but when I recover and return to the arena and retain my attacker in the act, I seem to sense – and the animal psychologists will have to decide whether I am right – that I have impressed my cats anew.'[21] Beatty wanted his cats to be impressed by his superiority at the same time that he wanted them to perceive him as another animal, not as physically strong as they, but with advantages – his mental abilities, as well as a chair and whip – that enabled him to dominate them. For his part, he admired cats that seemed to him disciplined, intuitive and self-controlled: the very qualities he prized in himself. His most dependable lion, Pharoah, Beatty said, had 'more natural dignity than any big cat I have ever handled. He comports himself with a kind of majesty that almost seems a reminder to the other animals that he expects them to be respectful in his presence.'[22] Certainly Beatty was respectful of this particular cat, and felt a sense of empathy – and yearning for even more connection. As he once told an interviewer, 'while it might seem like reaching for the moon, I felt that some day we would achieve close communication with wild animals and learn how to exchange thoughts with them on a systematic basis.'[23]

In many ways, Beatty felt closer to animals than he did to non-white, non-Western humans. When African women, with plates in their lips, oversized jewellery and indigenous costumes, were featured as a circus attraction in the 1930s, Beatty noted their 'stubbornly held belief that I was a god'. He claimed to regard them as friends, despite their 'weird' appearance and, he noted, 'childlike charm'. They seemed to be of a species even more foreign to him than his cats.[24]

Vying with him for prominence in the arena was the French trainer Alfred Court, who had performed for the Ringlings as an acrobat in 1914 and returned in 1940 with his huge animal act. Court had been a champion gymnast at school when he ran away, at the age of sixteen, to join the circus, working as a juggler and acrobat and eventually as a ringmaster and circus impresario. A strong, talented, innovative acrobat, Court came to the attention of the Ringlings, later moving on to other circuses in the United States and abroad. He was performing in Mexico when he taught himself to train animals and established his own extensive travelling menagerie, the Zoo Circus. Like Beatty, Court was slender and lithe, and he had a dapper and urbane quality that made him an attractive figure in the cage. In the spring of 1940, the 57-year-old Court arrived in New York with 60 animals and fourteen assistants, hired by the Ringlings once again. Among the animals were eighteen different species; he called his act 'Peace in the Jungle'.

Henry Ringling North recalled Court's method of training, evoking Hagenbeck's 'gentling' method, but with definite modifications:

> He did start off with the animals collared and chained to their pedestals, but he began by making friends with them. He went into the training ring with a leather pouch full of beef cut into small morsels. He would put a piece of beef on the end of a sharp stick and offer it to the animal, whatever it was. Then he would talk to it. Coming closer until he was alongside. The next thing you knew he was stroking it. Of course, it took several days to gain an animal's confidence.

Yet even Court had to resort to punishment at times, using his whip 'in the most sensitive place you can hit either a male or female. He hit, but only because the animal had made a mistake, and had to know, at that very second, that it had done wrong.'[25]

Queens

Mabel Stark was not the first woman to make her reputation with wild animals. Bostock featured Madame Planka in the cage with lions; the English trainer Ellen Bright performed in the 1880s; and Claire Heliot, the daughter of a German professor and herself a former teacher, was profiled in Ellen Velvin's *Behind the Scenes with Wild Animals*, a book dedicated to hunting enthusiast Theodore Roosevelt. Heliot exemplified the woman trainer as ladylike and genteel. In Velvin's book, the frontispiece photograph shows Heliot seated in an armchair, wearing a formal and revealing gown, with her hand extended next to the head of a lion – her favourite lion – seated beside her. Described as 'frail but fearless' and 'as mild and gentle as a woman can be', Heliot claimed that she tamed lions through sentimentality. She admitted to Velvin that the trainer's personality greatly influences animals. 'For a weakling, animals appear to have nothing but contempt,

'The Lion Queen', *c.* 1874.

Bostock's trained animals: 'Lady and leopards', *c.* 1903.

and of a man lacking in personality they take no notice,' she maintained. 'A command from such would have no effect whatever, whereas a man with a strong will and dominating personality has at once influence and authority.' For her part, she translated her strong will into what she insisted was love: she played with her lions, flirted with them, carried them across her shoulders like a boa, lay down across four of them. 'They would not have the heart to kill me,' she said.[26]

Velvin watched her feed her companion, putting a piece of meat inside his mouth: 'This particular lion would take the meat,' Velvin saw, 'but his rage and viciousness were astonishing to behold.' When Velvin

'Vallecita's Leopards', c. 1906.

asked if he had ever bitten her, Heliot replied, 'Lions seldom bite, but he scratches me all the time,' and revealed deep scars.[27] The scratches, Heliot explained, were the results of the lions' playfulness. But in 1907, playfulness or rage resulted in injuries so severe that Heliot's career was ended.

While other women trainers also conveyed a sexual attraction between trainer and animal, like that of Beauty and the Beast, Lucia Zora, a contemporary of Heliot's, was determined to show a woman's strength. Zora was singing in a light opera company and performing on tour in New Orleans when a circus came to town. 'The truth is that I ran away,' she said, 'coldly, deliberately, burning my bridges behind me, with a clear knowledge of what I was doing'. What she was doing at the time was taking a job as a 'generally useful' performer: 'That meant dancing in the ballet, riding in the grand entrée, appearing as the background for other acts . . .'. What she wanted to be doing was working with animals, specifically elephants. While most women that were included in elephant acts only perched upon them in scanty costumes, or were lifted by the elephant's trunk, Zora was determined to train them.

Unlike elephant trainers who subjected their animals to the pain of hooks, Zora was convinced that only reassurance, rewards and repetition were effective in teaching an elephant new tricks, but that strength – physical and mental – were necessary, too: 'animals seem to have a strange ability to discover the failings of the person who seeks to train them,' she said. 'Unless the woman who seeks to train him is dominant, he succeeds in shirking his performance; the woman becomes disheartened and in the end gives up her task.' Zora had no doubt about her power: 'I was one hundred and sixty pounds of strong bone, muscle and sinew, of a type better described as masculine strength,' she boasted. 'The usual softness of feminine flesh was wholly lacking.'

Besides elephants, Zora also trained cats, using Hagenbeck's method of studying animals' behaviour. 'Just as with elephants,' she said, 'I let the animals themselves suggest their own tricks. One tiger loved to climb and seemed to have an excellent sense of balance. Why not make use of it? Why not be the first woman to teach a tiger to walk a "tight rope?"'[28]

Trainers like Heliot and Zora paved the way for Mabel Stark. When the Ringlings reinstated animal acts, Stark returned to the ring with more and more tigers: sixteen, then twenty, then twenty-one. She would raise cubs herself, in her own house, where they would sleep with her, play in the bathroom, ride in her car; she put them in a harness and walked them, and she nurtured them, all the while carefully observing them. 'If Sonny, whenever I pass him, throws himself up on his hind legs, snarling and striking at me, I decide that he can be taught to sit up,' she explained.

> Every time I go past him I throw up my arm as if I were going to tap him on the nose with my whip. Instantly Sonny rears up, spitting like a ludicrous big house cat. Within a few weeks Sonny is a star performer in my act – the first tiger to sit up ... If Nellie happens to land on the ball in the ring when she jumps down from her seat and balances herself there a few seconds before springing to the ground, she has shown me that she can be taught to roll a ball.[29]

But though she claimed to have an almost mystical rapport with her animals, she never fooled herself into thinking that they were tame. They were wild, and they could kill her.

In every performance, Stark risked her life, and many times she was left severely wounded by the cats she had raised from infancy.

> A tiger without his teeth and claws would be as helpless as a person without fingers. Every tiger has eighteen claws – four on each hind foot and five on each forefoot. When he attacks he goes for the head or throat, holding down his prey and ripping with those lancelike points. One ripping blow can tear flesh to the bone – I know![30]

After a particularly bad attack in Bangor, Maine, resulting in nineteen wounds, she insisted that each gash and bite had to be burned out with carbolic acid, a drastically painful treatment. After a few weeks, wrapped in bandages, limping and using a cane, she returned to rehearse the routine.

Rajah II, one of Stark's favourite cats, suddenly attacked in the middle of a much-practised wrestling act: 'Deliberately she put her foot in my face and shoved me away when she threw me,' Stark remembered.

> At the same time she spread her claws. I turned my head, trying to avoid those piercing nails, but I was not quick enough. Her thumb claw caught the skin beneath my right eye, tearing open a two-inch gash. I was wearing a new white suit for the gala show, but it was polka-dotted with red before I got off the stage. The audience cheered uproariously. It was a bigger thrill than they had bargained for.
>
> The week we played in Newark, New Jersey, Rajah grabbed the side of my head. One tusk went into the corner of my eye and tore the tissues loose, almost blinding me. But still I loved her. She did not mean to hurt me.[31]

Stark claimed she was not conscious of pain while being attacked, and afterwards she refused to blame her tigers or to succumb to fear.

Henry Ringling North described the 110-pound Stark as 'an Amazonian lady, with masses of yellow-dyed ringlets on her head and a body covered with scars . . . Without whip or gun or fear in her heart, she worked sixteen of the great cats in the most commanding manner a lady ever had.'[32]

When Stark was in her late seventies, after her circus career had ended, she worked at Jungle Land in Thousand Oaks, California; each morning, it was discovered, she went into the ring with her cats, provoking them into attack, hoping that one of them might injure her fatally. When the park administration found out, they barred her from entering. A few months later, she was dead; friends said she had suffered a heart attack. But the truth was that Stark had found life was not worth living. Hopeless and despondent, she had killed herself.

Nostalgia and compassion

Mabel Stark would find it difficult to perform today. Most circuses have dispensed with animal acts as a result of pressure by animals rights groups, notably People for the Ethical Treatment of Animals (PETA), which publicizes a litany of abuses: animals are hurt, injured, confined, isolated from their natural habitat and social groups, kept in filthy cages and transported for months at a time. Animals, unlike their trainers, have no capacity to consent to perform; therefore they are exploited and, in effect, enslaved. These protestors are not swayed by the claims of some trainers that their relationship with animals is 'a feeling akin to religion, a losing of the small personal ego in a triumphant vision of the unity of all things'.[33] They are suspicious that a trainer can feel – as one admitted he did – an incomparable sense of achievement 'when at last I have transmitted an idea from my mind into the mind of an animal without touching him; when, at last, all barriers are down and we completely understand and respect each other'.[34] Unconvinced by such sentiments, protestors continue to give voice to what they believe animals need and deserve.

The anthropologist Yoram S. Carmeli, a circus scholar, explains these protests in part as caused by the spectator's identification with the animal's body. Focusing on elephant acts, Carmeli finds that they 'do not necessarily involve actual physical torture and circus animals are not necessarily objects of actual human cruelty'. But the viewer sees that the animal is subjugated and that the trainer produces 'forced tamed behavior' that often mimics human behaviour. Although trainers insist that performances reflect the animals' natural movements, the trainer in fact chooses among those movements the ones viewers expect to see: a bear riding a bicycle, an elephant dancing, a lion balanced on a rolling ball, sea lions playing catch, a tiger walking on a tightrope. This uncomfortable anthropomorphism translates for some viewers into discomfort and accusations of cruelty.

Changing beliefs about the place of humans in nature has shaped this discomfort. Carmeli believes that the popularity of the circus as mass entertainment resulted from increasing industrialization and urbanization, during which nature lost its potential as 'a metaphor for objectivity and realness', and, he believes, 'nature and animals turned into an object of nostalgia and compassion.'[35] Viewers feel nostalgia

Ringling Brothers' Marvelous Acting Pachyderms, 1899.

'Louder than a
thousand human
bandmen': poster
for the Ringling
Brothers, *c.* 1899.

not for the circuses of the past, where lions were goaded into lungeing
ferociously and tamers lashed with whips, but for an ideal of nature
as a place for moral sustenance and transcendence. Animal acts, for some
viewers, undermine that desire, representing not nature, but nature
manipulated and deformed. And scholar John Stokes adds another
significant trait of these performances: the difference between animal
acts and all other risky circus performances, he asserts, is 'the almost
complete absence of trust between participants'.[36] The cage, then,
has become a site of anxiety.

Compassion for animals has increased also by the popular con-
flation of trainers with recreational hunters, bullfighters or promoters
of illegal dog fights. Ernest Hemingway, for example, famously loved

animal acts, claiming that he had a special rapport with bears especially, because he was part Native American. But when he was not attempting to communicate with animals in their cages, he hunted them. Fictional creations of animal trainers have fed popular images as well. Joanne Joys has found that in nineteenth- and early twentieth-century dime novels featuring trainers, these men – 'Lion Charly', 'The Boy Beast Tamer', 'Samson, Jr. The Wild Beast Tamer' – were 'vividly stereotyped as brutal, vindictive, conceited and often cowardly'. Although authors were not condemning animals acts, still they portrayed trainers 'as strange, somewhat less than human creatures'.[37] Moreover, she adds, 'in the last thirty years, the characterization of the cagehand has shifted from the innocent small town boy seeking adventure to an emotional cripple running from reality.'[38]

Since the mid-1970s, many circuses have dropped animal acts; but as late as the 1990s, Gunther Gebel-Williams was still performing for the Ringlings, where he had been hired, at great expense, in 1969. Like generations of trainers before him, Gebel-Williams had joined a circus as a child. He was twelve, and the Circus Williams had just opened in Cologne, reviving after the war. Gunther's mother took a job as a seamstress and Gunther began working with horses. When his mother left after a short time, Gunther stayed, eventually appending the Williams surname to his own. He trained elephants and then tigers, at which he excelled.

Like many trainers before him, Gunther was a small man, slim and muscular, and his act reprised much performance history, with bits recalled from Heliot, Stark, Court and Beatty: his tigers leapt onto his back, he stretched out across two leopards, his pumas jumped through a flaming hoop and a leopard stood on its hind legs, with its front paws on Gunther's shoulders. They leaned together in a tight embrace. He worked with nearly as many big cats as Stark did, and he claimed to train them with the gentle method of rewards and infinite patience.

If his animal acts were familiar, his own persona in the arena was original, and more suitable to the late twentieth century than a hunting costume and pith helmet. As one observer noted, he looked like a rock star in spangled tights, with a short bolero revealing his bare chest. 'From the moment Gebel-Williams enters the arena, standing

on the back of a galloping horse and holding an Olympian torch,'
wrote an admiring reviewer, 'we know we are in the presence of an
extraordinarily sophisticated performer, who has a thorough awareness
of his own indelible image, and who understands, the way Marilyn
Monroe did, the value of a platinum-blond head under strong lights.'
He did not use a whip, chair or pistol: in fact, there seemed to be an
'almost mythical rapport between man and beast – a rapport that goes
back to some unknown time . . . with a loop along the way around
a character named Tarzan'.[39] The character named Tarzan was closer
to nature than the character named Clyde Beatty; and Gunther, unlike
Beatty, was not accused of animal cruelty during his performance
career. When he died in 2001, the circus lost its last animal master.

E. E. Cummings once declared that 'a periodic and highly concen-
trated dose of wild animals – elephants, tigers, lions, leopards, jaguars,
bears, wolves, giraffes, kangaroos, zebras, horned horses, camels, hyenas,
rhinoceri and at least one hippopotamus – is indispensable to the
happiness of all mature civilized human beings.'[40] If transcendence
might be gained from a 'dose' of wildness, the circus is no longer a place
where it can be found.

SEVEN

CLOWNS

You asked me what a clown is . . . It's the reduction of ourselves
into our purest desires, to our desperate hunger for approval.
André Riot-Sarcey

Rarely has a clown begun his career clowning. Emmett Kelly was
a cartoonist and later an aerialist; Dan Rice was a jockey and
riverboat gambler before he devised his exuberant clown persona; the
Swiss-born Grock, who amazed Picasso at the Cirque Médrano, was
a contortionist and tightrope walker; George Footit, a favourite of
Toulouse-Lautrec, and Edwin 'Poodles' Hannaford were trick riders;
the Hanlon brothers created their clown act after many years as aerialists. Becoming a clown, for all of them, was a deliberate choice, rewarded
not only by their audience's acclaim, but by prestige and high pay.
In the late nineteenth century the circus chronicler Hughes Le Roux
estimated that there were no more than 30 professional clowns in
the world – by which, no doubt, he meant Paris and London. 'Like star-
tenors,' Le Roux noted, 'they contract engagements for many years in
advance, and receive the emoluments of an ambassador, and their
requirements increase with their success.'[1] No longer synonymous
with court jesters, mountebanks and fools, clowns devised their own
extended acts, called entreés, which took centre stage in the ring. The
clown, wrote Antony Coxe, 'is the soul of the circus'.[2]

Intellectually and emotionally complex, the clown, Coxe said,
'plays with situations, characters and words as the juggler plays with
his clubs, knives, and rings'. He might appear to be a buffoon, but
beneath the comic antics are an inner dignity, grace and 'spiritual

Poster showing 'Five
celebrated clowns',
1856.

179

daring' – as well as impressive physical talents.[3] Joseph Grimaldi, the most famous clown of the early 1800s, never performed in a circus. Still, when he started entertaining, a circus owner gave him this advice:

> My boy, if you want to be a successful clown, first you must be an acrobat, then a trapeze artist and a tumbler; in fact you must be able to do everything, and then you can think about being a clown.[4]

Only a performer who is versatile, agile and deft can manage pratfalls; only an insightful actor can create and inhabit the persona of a clown.

The clown is a performer in disguise, but is no more hidden behind his exaggerated make-up than an animal trainer in his safari costume, or an aerialist in spangles. Like these other artists, he has inherited a lineage from which to choose and adapt. What most viewers call a clown actually comprises three different types: the elegant whiteface clown, wearing a ruffled neck piece and pointed cap; the hapless auguste, dressed in baggy trousers, oversized shoes and a punched-down hat; and the grotesque, whose wide variety of personas may range from a mischievous baby to menacing monster.

Clowns have some prototypes in *commèdia dell'arte* characters: the innocent, the devious cheat, the buffoon, the country yokel, the comic servant. *Commèdia* skits were satirical, especially of pretence, but they also reflected anxieties shared among their viewers: the farm boy coming to the city, intimidated by sophisticates, rules and manners; the would-be lover fearful of rejection; anyone worried about being thought clumsy, awkward, ignorant or gullible. Clowns count on their audience to identify with them, to sympathize with them – and in laughing at them, to laugh

Pulcinella, a character in the *commèdia dell'arte*, French engraving, *c.* 1650.

Polichinelle.

Si Polichinelle a grand mine   Son cœur sçait braver le péril
Armé de Pincette, et de Gril;   Que l'on rencontre à la Cuisine.

Antoine Watteau,
Pierrot (formerly
titled *Gilles*),
c. 1718–19,
oil on canvas.

at themselves. 'We see him bumbling for our attention, desperate for a little love,' contemporary clown André Riot-Sarcey says, 'and because we recognize ourselves in his fumbling, we want to give it to him. Because he is completely open about his intentions, completely vulnerable, we're on his team.'[5]

Although the ancestry of clowns is rooted in ancient times with any entertainer playing the fool, the story of the modern clown begins with two whiteface clowns: the Englishman Joseph Grimaldi, whose career spanned from 1781, when he took to the stage with his father and played a monkey, until his death in 1837; and his French

Paul Legrand at the Royal Adelphi Theatre, London, mid-19th century.

contemporary Jean-Gaspard Deburau, who conceived the clown as a Romantic, even tragic, figure. Both men derived their clown types from earlier players: the cunning Harlequin, the prancing Merry Andrew and especially the Pierrot, traditionally costumed in a wide-collared smock, loose white pantaloons and a soft hat worn over a skull cap or shaved head. The Pierrot was a *commèdia dell'arte* variation of a zanni, or comic servant; some were simple and unworldly, others sly and

Joseph Grimaldi
and Joseph Samuel
Grimaldi, *c.* 1810.

3   **Mr. Grimaldi and Son, as Clowns.**
Printed by Arliss, 35, Gutter Lane, Cheapside, London; for O. Hodgson, Macclesfield Street, City Road.

devious. If the sly player seemed confident of his power, he learned that
the simpleton was not so simple after all, but often found subversive
ways to get what he wanted.

The plight of the little man in a confusing world has been an
enduring theme for clowns, and one that Grimaldi found suited to
Georgian England. As his biographer Richard Findlater notes, at the
time that Grimaldi rose to fame in the early 1800s, changing social
roles provided much material for satire: 'Farmers left rural areas for the
industrial slums, and the clown evolved from the rustic booby to the

metropolitan Clown,' who satirized greed and gluttony and mocked draconian laws, such as the death penalty meted out for petty thievery and pickpockets. Grimaldi, Findlater said, 'was a Cockney incarnation of the saturnalian spirit; a beloved criminal free from guilt, shame, compunction or reverence for age, class or property'.[6]

His costume and make-up became an iconic variation of the Pierrot: whiteface with bold red triangles on his cheeks, the better to symbolize the florid complexion of drunks; a blue wig – a parody, Findlater surmises, of the yokel's traditional red hair; and a costume that pokes fun at servants' livery. The exaggerated facial make-up was both a legacy of the *commèdia dell'arte* and a necessity for projecting emotion in a large theatre such as Covent Garden or Sadler's Wells, where Grimaldi made his solo debut in 1800.

Like Grimaldi, born in 1776, Deburau was the child of entertainers, with whom he performed at the Théâtre des Funambules in Paris, a venue that attracted a mostly working-class audience. His indelible contribution to circus history is his revision of the Pierrot character, dispensing with a neck ruff, simplifying the make-up and projecting melancholy, a trait most certainly drawn from his own personality. Rumoured to indulge in alcohol and the opiate laudanum, Deburau

Joseph Grimaldi on the frontispiece to his memoirs, 1838.

could display a mercurial temper. Once, when walking in Paris, he lashed out at a young boy who was teasing him, hitting him with his cane. The blow killed the child, and Deburau was arrested for murder. His trial was much publicized, not least because viewers who jammed into the courtroom wanted a chance to hear his voice. Although he was acquitted, the event haunted him for the last decade of his life. At the height of his fame, Deburau was praised effusively by influential journalists who saw in his white face an evocation of innocence and purity, and in his introspective air a reflection of the artistic spirit of French Romantics: their

The French mime
Jean-Gaspard Deburau
(1796–1846) as Pierrot.

reverence for sincerity, their sense of vulnerability in the marketplace, their surrender to emotions. For Deburau and his followers, the clown became mystical, complex and profound.

Icons

Toulouse-Lautrec once had his photograph taken wearing the cap of Footit; Picasso, lathered in shaving soap, pretended to be in whiteface, and rendered his self-portrait in his paintings of saltimbanques and harlequins. For many nineteenth- and early twentieth-century painters, clowns represented not foolishness, but rather a fragile and transcendent joy; not glee, but pathos.

In mid-nineteenth-century France, strict reforms proscribed travelling performers in favour of state-sanctioned theatre. Many artists, nostalgic for their intimate connection with acrobats and

Paul Cézanne, *Pierrot and Harlequin*, 1888, oil on canvas.

clowns, mourned the loss. The saltimbanques depicted by Honoré Daumier and Gustave Doré, for example, huddle together at the margins of towns, tired, struggling to make a living. Daumier portrayed the clown as a sad figure, a victim of censorship and restrictions, just as he felt himself to be a victim of laws against political caricature. For Doré, who practised gymnastics as a child and often socialized with acrobats, the strictures against saltimbanques felt like a personal affront. One painting of performers at rest shows a mother and child in a pose that evokes a pietà: the mother's crown like a halo, the child's head wrapped in a bloody cloth. A feeling of identification with wandering entertainers struck Charles Baudelaire as well; he described the saltimbanque as

> pitiful . . . stooped, worn out, a human ruin, leaning back against one of the posts of his shack . . . But what an intense and unforgettable gaze he cast over the crowd and the lights . . . I said to myself: I have just seen the very image of the old writer who has outlived his generation, which he brilliantly amused, or of the old, friendless poet . . . whose booth the forgetful world no longer wants to enter![7]

Although Picasso laughed at the clowns who performed at the Cirque Médrano, his paintings give a different perspective. Apollinaire noted the 'tawdry finery of his slender clowns', whose 'cheeks and brows . . . are withered by morbid sensibilities'.[8] For Picasso's contemporary Georges Rouault, the circus was a site of epiphany when he realized 'the contrast between the brilliant, glittering things made to amuse and a life that is so infinitely sad if we see it from a little way off . . . Then I extrapolated it all. I saw clearly that the "Clown" was me, was us, almost all of us . . .'.[9] Even more than perceiving the clown as a striving artist, Rouault, an ardent Catholic, portrayed clowns as Christ figures, betrayed by the world and sacrificed.

Ironically, early twentieth-century American artists who aimed to render urban, working-class reality also took circus clowns as their subjects. These artists, some of them members of the Ashcan School, and others followers of the New York painter Robert Henri and members of the group known as The Eight, include John Sloan, William Glackens, George Luks and Everett Shinn. Working also as illustrators and cartoonists, they documented in their paintings the daily

Henri de Toulouse-Lautrec, *At the Circus: Performing Horse and Monkey*, 1899.

struggles and simple joys of ordinary people: children playing, beggars in doorways, sellers in a marketplace – and clowns. Sloan, after dressing as a clown for a costume ball, was inspired to paint *Old Clown Making Up*, a portrait of a whiteface clown sitting before a mirror, illuminated by candlelight. The softly lit folds of the clown's costume, the ragged planes of his aged face, make this work a sentimental homage to a sad figure. Luks, too, painted a whiteface clown, his nose and ears a garish red, his eyes mere slits; he holds a single flower. E. E. Cummings might have written a caption for this portrait:

> At positively every performance Death Himself lurks, glides, struts, breathes, is. Lest any agony be missing, a mob of clowns tumbles loudly in and out of that inconceivably sheer fabric of doom, whose beauty seems endangered by the spectator's least heart-beat or whisper.[10]

The whiteface clown recurs in other portraits: Walt Kuhn's *White Clown*, for example, and Edward Hopper's *Soir Bleu*, in which a clown, wearing the traditional ruff and white costume, sits on a café terrace with two male companions, one a soldier, smoking a cigarette. Behind him stands a prostitute wearing make-up that echoes the clown's red lips and eye accents. Conflating the clown with the prostitute recalls Daumier's and Picasso's saltimbanques, scorned as vagrants. But Hopper's clown is urbane as well, one among many Parisian types out for the evening; and he is a self-portrait of the 32-year-old aspiring artist. Except for the clown, Hopper's *Soir Bleu* is of a piece with Hopper's other work depicting the loneliness and isolation of urban life. He returned to the clown image late in his career: in one of his last paintings, he depicts himself and his wife as *commèdia dell'arte* performers, again imagining himself as a whiteface clown.

The French artist Fernand Léger, a regular at the Cirque Médrano in the early 1900s, turned to circus themes throughout his career. Besides individual paintings, Léger also designed clown costumes for the famous Fratellini brothers, and in the 1940s, he decided to publish 63 circus lithographs as a book. Wanting a text to accompany his illustrations, he asked Henry Miller, whom he knew to be circus fan, to write for him – a task with which Miller struggled. Finally, unwilling to wait for Miller to come up with something, Léger wrote his own text. Eventually Miller's ruminations led him to publish *The Smile at the Foot of the Ladder*, a homage to clowns. 'I thought of my passion for the circus,' he wrote,

> especially the *cirque intime*, and how all these experiences as spectator and silent participator must lie buried deep in my consciousness. I remember how, when I was graduating from High School, they had asked me what I intended to be and I had said – 'a clown!' . . . And later I discovered to my surprise that my most intimate friends looked upon *me* as a clown.

For Miller, a clown was 'a poet in action. He is the story which he enacts. It is the same story over and over – adoration, devotion, crucifixion.'[11] Like Léger, who envisioned the action of the circus as 'an enormous bowl in which circular forms unroll', Miller saw the circus as an organic, continuous form.[12] The joy it generated, he said,

> is like a river: it flows ceaselessly. It seems to me that this is the message which the clown is trying to convey to us, that we should participate through ceaseless flow and movement, that we should not stop to reflect, compare, analyze, possess, but flow on and through, endlessly, like music. This is the gift of surrender, and the clown makes it symbolically. It is for us to make it real.[13]

Power and pretence

While both Grimaldi and Deburau achieved their fame in theatres, in early nineteenth-century circuses, the most common clown acts were accessories to equestrians and acrobats. The clown to the rope act made fun of rope walkers; the clown to the horse – Billy Saunders and Fortunelly were the most celebrated – spoofed riders. In 1816, 'Monsieur Claune' appeared in Paris, playing the role of a farmhand or peasant, enemy of the acrobats. Small circuses featured speaking clowns whose banter involved puns and misunderstandings, and whose themes were often bawdy.

The auguste clown, which most historians believe was created in 1864, underscored themes of power and pretence. According to circus lore, one evening, a drunken jockey rider ambled into the ring at the eminent Renz Circus in Berlin, stumbling, bumbling and grinning stupidly. '*Auguste* – idiot!' the audience cried out, which the rider took as a sign of approval. The next night, when the circus allowed him to return, he appeared with his nose reddened, dressed in an oversized suit, and repeated his act. This time, the audience was charmed, and the 'auguste' became a new kind of clown, transformed later into the tramp clown, whose famous interpreters include Otto Griebling, Buster Keaton, Emmett Kelly and Charlie Chaplin.

The whiteface and auguste formed an odd couple, negotiating the world in far different ways: the whiteface, aspiring for success, planned for the future; the inept, messy auguste seemed defeated from the start. The anthropologist Kenneth Little described a typical routine based on that stark opposition

> between the authoritarian, exacting, and sophisticated character of the whiteface and his rather clumsy and disheveled partners, the augustes . . . The whiteface clown attempts to accomplish some fantastic task for his audience, but his plans are forever interrupted by the intruding grotesques, the augustes . . . Disorder rules as the whiteface's dream is shattered.[14]

While Grimaldi and Deburau were honing their reputations in Europe, Daniel McLaren, who had run away from home in New York City at the age of eight to work at race tracks, began his long career in the circus. Joining Nicholls Circus in Pittsburgh, he changed his name to Dan Rice, trained in gymnastics, weight lifting and clowning, and soon fashioned himself as a particular clown personality, an irreverent gadfly: wearing red and white breeches, a blue jockey blouse and cap, and striped stockings, he became 'Yankee Dan', and his aim was satire. Rice was a talking, singing, dancing clown whose songs were often political satires, and whose patter was often burlesque versions of Shakespearean plots. 'A successful clown must possess more intellect, ability, and originality than a comedian,' Rice once said. 'He must be a crack mimic, an elocutionist, a satirist, and so ready witted that he, to the ringmaster, is a stupid fool, a buffoon; to the audience a wise man whose every remark is impregnated with philosophy as well as humor.'[15] A contemporary of Barnum, Rice was no less a self-promoter: he ran for political office, including president, several times; and he made and lost a fortune. Once paid $1,000 a week for performing, he declared bankruptcy in 1875, claiming that he had given his money away to charities. Once an alcoholic, he took to the road as a temperance lecturer and evangelist. The lecture circuit, though, was not as satisfying as the circus ring; in the mid-1880s, Rice revived his clown act. But audiences had changed, and Rice's controversial political views – he had opposed abolition and aligned himself with conservatives – offended potential ticket buyers. When he died in 1900, few remembered him.

As the American circus expanded from one ring to three, the talking clown could not be heard by audiences numbering in the tens of thousands, and clowns' performances featured physical pranks, pantomime and slapstick. 'As early as 1885,' reports historian John Culhane, 'all the clowning with Barnum & Bailey was silent, and there was at one time a rule that any clown who spoke would automatically be fired.'[16] Circus clowns became buffoons, and the finely drawn characters of the whiteface and auguste began to appear instead in vaudeville and movies, interpreted by such performers as the Marx Brothers and Laurel and Hardy.

Charles Adrien Wettach, the Swiss-born performer who took the stage name Grock, made the transition from circus to music hall before the First World War and never returned to the ring that had enchanted him as a child. When a travelling circus came to the Swiss town of Col des Roches, the young Adrien noticed with amazement 'a big, jovial man at their head, with a white-chalked face and scarlet nose and mouth. For the first time in my life,' he recalled, 'I beheld a CLOWN, and for the first time also felt something stir within me that was not just mere childhood excitement. That something said to me: I WILL. I *will* become what that man is there upon the platform.' The path to reaching that goal was circuitous: first, he practiced contortion, working for hours each day to perfect his twists and bends; then he mounted the tightrope that he erected behind his house. If neighbours stopped by to watch, he ignored them: 'All I beheld was the utmost summit of success, attended by world fame.' For him, this meant performing at the Cirque Fernando. His debut as a rope walker was as momentous as he had imagined:

> I could feel the sympathy of my audience all around me, and I was possessed with a feeling of *lightness*; I felt light as a feather, and scarcely even sensed the touch of the rope on my feet. Like a sleep-walker I continued on my perilous way, with a sense of poise so acute it could be hardly called of the body alone, for it included a sense of harmony with the entire world, and I was filled with a feeling of ecstasy I had never known before.[17]

Finally, he made the transition to clowning, as rapturous an experience for him as aerial acts. 'There's something about my profession that's irresistible, or so I think,' he said, ' – this mastering by will-power, this transforming the little, everyday annoyances, not only overcoming, but actually *transforming* them into some[thing] strange and terrific.'[18] When he was 23, he devised a clown act with another performer, known as Brick. Adrien decided that he too needed a stage name: he called himself Grock. The partnership with Brick was short, followed by a more productive connection with the clown Antonet, who became his mentor and partner. Antonet put Grock through rigorous training in music, miming and acrobatics, and at the end of three intense months, he emerged able to play the fiddle, clarinet, piano, drum, hurdy-gurdy and concertina, as well as being proficient in pratfalls. The two rose to popularity on the Continent before appearing, to great enthusiasm, in London in 1911. Eventually, Grock went out on his own, quickly earning the epithet of 'the funniest clown in the world'. When he made his New York debut in 1919, the acerbic critic Alexander Woollcott advised his readers to travel miles, if they had to, to see Grock's 'infinitely mobile face' and inventive musical antics. This clown, Woollcott

Bust of Grock
(Charles Adrien
Wettach).

raved, with his deft miming and Cockney outbursts, was 'colossally funny'.[19]

Grock eventually appeared in movies, giving his contemporaries Buster Keaton and Charlie Chaplin a new rival. Their clown personas, derived from the auguste, developed into the tramp clown, the sad bumbler trying to make his way in a cruel world. In 1933, Emmett Kelly brought the little tramp to the circus as 'Weary Willie', inspired in part by homeless wanderers during the economic depression of the 1930s, in part by a character Kelly had created years before as a cartoonist. 'I am a sad and ragged little guy who is very serious about everything he attempts – no matter how futile or how foolish it appears to be,' he explained. 'I am the hobo who found out the hard way that the deck is stacked, the dice "frozen," the race fixed and the wheel crooked, but there is always present that one tiny, forlorn spark of hope still glimmering in his soul which makes him keep on trying.' Children loved 'Weary Willie', whose futile efforts seemed endearingly childlike, and adults identified with the message of powerlessness and deep-seated faith that his character conveyed. 'All I can say . . . is that there must be a lot of people in this world who feel that way and that, fortunately, they come to the circus,' Kelly wrote.

> In my tramp clown character, folks who are down on their luck, have had disappointments and have maybe been pushed around by circumstances beyond their control, see a caricature of themselves, and realizing that they have done this gives them a sort of spiritual second wind for going back into the battle.[20]

Emmett Kelly in
a publicity shot
of *c.* 1945.

New wave comics

By the mid-twentieth century, influenced by mime, puppetry, dance and
innovative theatre, new types of clowns emerged within and outside of
the circus ring. These performers were no longer interested in slapstick
routines where a whiteface clown dominated a woebegone auguste.[21]
Instead of drawing from past archetypes to create their clown identity,

new clowns saw their stage persona as a second self. As the social geographer Lindsay Stephens discovered from interviews with contemporary performers, 'Clowns often speak of their clown as another person, referring to "her" as distinct from "me" and even sometimes describing potential conflicts between their desires and those of their clown.'[22] New clowns aim not so much to amuse their audiences, but to make them think. 'For the new clown,' Kenneth Little wrote, 'laughter is not always the standard by which they judge the success of their and others' work. It is the individual poetic object that counts, and that does not necessarily need to be funny.'[23] Their object, instead, is to get the audience to see the world in a new way.

New York Times theatre critic Mel Gussow used the term New Vaudeville to describe these innovative clowns, but performers were quick to distinguish themselves from Old Vaudeville, which presented a roster of singing, dancing, acrobatics and comedy acts in music halls and later on television variety shows. New Vaudeville was more determinedly political and more likely to emerge from street corners than theatre houses. These performers strived to make a deep connection to their viewers. 'Good clowns make you laugh,' said new wave clown Avner 'the Eccentric' Eisenberg, 'but great clowns can make you cry, too.'[24]

Some new wave clowns aim to provoke discomfort and even fear – as in the sinister figure of Krusty, Bart Simpson's idol in Matt Groening's animated series *The Simpsons*. Krusty, notes Karal Ann Marling, 'is no benign Bozo, no bumbling Clarabell, no vacuous Ronald McDonald. Groening draws upon the tradition of jesters and clowns as transgressive figures who upset the rules of everyday life, much as red-nosed Shriners on tiny, noisy motorcycles disrupt the Memorial Day Parade.' Unlike Grock or Kelly, clowns like Krusty are sly tricksters:

> Krusty stands for the grafter who shortchanges the rube buying a ticket to see wonders that are merely grotesque. Krusty exposes the make-believe tears of Weary Willie and his ilk. What lurks behind the comic make-up could scare you half to death.[25]

Or, like Stephen King's murderous clown in his novel *It*, the grotesque persona could incite coulrophobia, a neurotic fear of clowns.

Not all contemporary clowns can be considered part of a new wave. Some simply want to be part of the circus, in a role that does not require swinging from a trapeze or taming lions. These aspiring clowns flocked to a clown college begun by the Ringling Bros in order to fill out their diminishing roster of clowns. For 30 years, beginning in 1968, it gave classes in make-up, improvisation, gag development, costumes and various clown antics such as stilt walking and juggling. The school was so popular that it added venues in various cities throughout the United States. Bill Irwin trained at the school, as did the magician Penn Jillette; so did hundreds of other would-be clowns whose careers were far less illustrious. The circus historian David Lewis Hammarstrom is among many who criticize most of the Ringlings' graduates: 'What they all bore in common in the early years', he wrote, 'were pretty coloring book faces and a buoyantly acrobatic approach to their work. What they fell woefully short on was character. A good clown is much more than a cute face. The clown who engages our attention is a figure of discernible quirks and flaws.'[26] Ernest Albrecht added that the clown college never helped students discover their unique clown personality, but only to learn shopworn gags. 'There is little patience', he noted, 'for the subtle, the delicate, the thought provoking, or the time-consuming.'[27] The Ringlings saw clowns as quick acts that kept their huge show moving; at best, they were purveyors of fun.

Fun and an outlet for self-expression has led to a proliferation of circus arts schools and camps, some requiring an application process and some open to anyone with the desire to be a clown. Their classes are usually far from rigorous, unlike the courses Moscow Circus star Oleg Popov undertook in his native land. Popov told an interviewer that he had studied for five years, six days a week, at Russia's State School of Circus and Variety Show Arts, graduating in 1949 after taking classes in dancing, acrobatics, balancing and the history of the circus, among many others. Still, he claimed that being a clown 'is an art . . . You cannot learn it. You have to *have* it.'[28] By 'having it', he meant that a clown personality was inextricably drawn from the performer's identity, not just created by a costume or mask. What Popov expressed was a wistfulness,

Oleg Popov in
his characteristic
make-up, 1979.

a gentleness, that elevated his clowning above slapstick; he brought to
clowning 'an almost philosophical approach to his craft'.[29]

New wave or New Vaudeville clowns find philosophical support
in such postmodern thinkers as Michel Foucault and Gilles Deleuze,
who proposed in their writings the possibility of unstable, shifting
identities; a clown personality might emerge from hidden layers of
consciousness, or expand a performer's potential for self-definition.
Charlie Chaplin admitted that his Little Tramp character came into
being when he put on baggy trousers, a tight jacket and a tiny bowler
hat, a costume he hoped would be funny. The moustache was an
afterthought: an effort to make him look older. Suddenly he was
someone else. 'Both clowns and aerialists', Lindsay Stephens discovered, 'expressed a fluidity or redistribution of subjectivity' that affected

even physical sensations. One aerialist told her that when he rehearses while portraying his created character, he feels aches and pains that he never feels in his non-performing identity. 'I don't feel it at all,' he said, 'it doesn't hurt in the slightest.'[30] The noted mime Marcel Marceau talked about his character Bip as if he were an independent being who, over the years, has 'become more profound; he has matured. At the beginning of my career,' Marceau told an interviewer, 'Bip was fighting in the metro or he was ice-skating or cruising on the sea. Today, Bip protests against the war . . . or is confronted with the machine age and with the future.'[31] Former clown John Towsen noted that new wave clowns typically come from theatre backgrounds, schooled in drama and with experience acting in repertory companies. For these performers, Towsen said, a clown is 'an actor who performs not a role but something of his own personality, of his alter ego . . . They feel the clown is a character or a theatrical being.'[32]

Although slapstick clowns with red noses and floppy shoes were still appearing in circuses, many twentieth-century viewers found new wave clowns refreshingly innovative. In 1988, when Cirque de Soleil opened in New York, Mel Gussow criticized the troupe's clowns as the weakest links in the show: 'One wishes for one of the Olympian gymnasts of New Vaudeville comedy to enter the ring,' he wrote.[33] Bill Irwin's foiled attempts to operate a remote-control device, Jacques Tati's bewilderment at the complexities of travel, Samuel Beckett's characters, dismayed at trying to communicate with one another – these clowns are the heirs of Grimaldi and Deburau, of saltimbanques and jesters, of Pierrots and wise fools.

Like many of their predecessors, some new clowns take their performances out of the arena – often far out, in hospitals, prisons and refugee camps. As Kenneth Little wrote about Pitu, a contemporary clown he studied,

> Some of the new clowns say that their work is created to "make people think," so that through the clown, the audience members can become more clear-sighted observers of the world around them.[34]

That goal of changing perspectives and attitudes is embodied in such clowns as Wavy Gravy, who inhabits, rather than performs, a clown persona in his role as a social and political gadfly and activist. Among his many projects is Camp WinnaRainbow, centred on the circus arts, mostly for children, some of whom may never have seen a circus, but also as a week-long camp to offer a kind of spiritual liberation for adults: a chance that the circus has always offered – to try on a new identity.

Like Wavy Gravy, physician Hunter Adams aims to change the world through his Gesundheit Institute and his clown persona Patch Adams. The Gesundheit Institute's mission is to provide community-based free health care. Patch Adams has a broader goal of changing the ambience of daily life. Lecturing and performing throughout the world, Adams encourages irreverence: behaving like a silly clown in public can be a precursor to speaking up for equality and justice. Because he was the subject of a Hollywood movie, Adams is best known for combining his clown persona with his work as a practising physician, bringing laughter, as well as medical skill, to his patients. The Big Apple Circus's Clown Care Unit is a similar project, sending clowns to paediatric wards in New York City hospitals.

If clowning does not cure disease or feed the starving, still many activist clowns believe it brings hope. In 1993, after performing in a refugee camp in Croatia, a Spanish clown established Clowns Without Borders, modelled on the volunteer physicians' organization Doctors Without Borders. Two years later, American clown Moshe Cohen set up its American branch. It is now one of eight international groups that travel to sites of floods and hurricanes, famine and war and perform for children and families.

'Joy', Wallace Fowlie once wrote, responding to Picasso's rendering of clowns, 'is vastly different from comedy. It is far away from comedy, detached, living apart in a sphere closed to weakness, irony, bitterness.'[35] New performers redefine clowning as an art form, cognisant of the power of joy to effect change, not only for an individual, but for the culture of communities.

EIGHT

FEATS

Every show it's something else. Every day it's like wrestling with fate.
Sean Thomas, 'human cannonball'

When Hugo Zacchini was a soldier in the Italian army during the First World War, his battalion faced the problem of how to infiltrate enemy lines. Zacchini had an idea: soldiers could be shot from cannons, unfurling parachutes – newly adopted by the military – after they crossed into enemy territory. That idea did not go far; Zacchini's superiors could see that the soldiers, wafting down through the air, would be vulnerable to sniper fire. But Zacchini did not let go of the possibility, and after the war he and his brothers created a circus act. 'The gun was built, and found to work, and circus contracts in Europe were easy to get . . . Bruno shoots Hugo from the gun, the sister marches in the circus tournament, and the wife stands admiringly beside the cannon.'[1] In venues throughout the world, the act involved the whole Zacchini family: six brothers, two daughters, three sons and a daughter-in-law. All, at one time or another, were blasted out of cannons during the Zacchinis' 35 years in the circus.

Although for years Hugo kept secret the process of propelling a human out of a cannon, towards the end of his career he was willing to share how it was done: the performer stands in a cylinder that fits into the barrel of the cannon; the cannon is elevated, sliding the cylinder towards the base. When the cannon is fired, Hugo told an interviewer, 'a blast of compressed air (a hundred and seventy-five pounds per square inch for a man, a hundred and fifty for a girl) slams the cylinder forward. The cylinder stops at the mouth of the cannon,

'La Femme Mélinite', human cannonball, Cirque d'Été poster, 1887.

but the human cannon ball does not. To heighten the effect, a charge is exploded and smoke released at the moment of impact.'² Some cannonball acts set off firecrackers to enhance the atmosphere of danger. Hugo's daughter admitted that the first time she blasted out, she was terrified; but the applause was as deafening as the explosion, and quickly she came to love performing.

The human cannonball act, an unlikely feat to be sure, was invented in 1875 by William Leonard Hunt, self-styled the Great Farini, a performer determined to achieve notoriety. Born in New York near the Canadian border, raised in Ontario, Hunt saw his first circus as a child and, despite his parents' vehement disapproval, trained himself as an acrobat. He gave amateur performances for friends and neighbours, and in 1859 performed professionally as a tightrope walker. He was among the viewers when Blondin crossed Niagara Falls, and apparently took the Frenchman's feat as a dare: he could do the same, he decided. In 1860, with as much fanfare as he could muster, he did.

The human cannonball was his idea: a person would be shot from a cannon, fly through the air and land safely in a net. Although in Hunt's cannon the performer was launched from a spring, gunpowder would provide the necessary effects for the audience to believe that the cannon really was fired. Hunt found an appealing performer, a demure fourteen-year-old aerialist – some newspaper reports referred to her as his pupil – Rosa Matilda Richter. Taking the stage name Zazel, she debuted at London's Royal Aquarium on 2 April 1877: perched on a sinister-looking black cannon suspended by ropes above the arena, she climbed over the lip into its mouth, heard a sharp explosion of gunpowder and shot out into the air, flying in an arc about 30 feet before landing in a net. The flight lasted only a few seconds, but for the audience it was an indelible experience of thrills and fear – more perilous, surely, than Zazel's tightrope walking, accomplished as she was on the wire.

The human cannonball, from the viewer's perspective, appeared to have no control over her body or the course of the flight, succeeding only through faith and luck. But in fact, as an experienced aerialist, Zazel learned how to hold her body rigid, and to turn at just the right moment to land safely. Many less skilled cannonballs who copied her

'The Human Cannon Ball', American poster, *c.* 1879.

act were killed when they landed outside of the net. Zazel repeated her performance in London and Paris, causing, newspaper reports agreed, a furore wherever she appeared. Naturally, Barnum heard about her, and in 1880, she made her New York debut in his circus, performing for the 4,001st time.

Even among audiences inured to dangerous performances, some viewers found Zazel's too frightening. Young girls should not be subjected to such risk, viewers protested; the act should be banned. Barnum was quick to reassure everyone: the net was especially constructed for her act, he said; it was inspected before each performance and changed every two weeks. Zazel was not being exploited; far from it: he paid her – most likely, he paid Farini – an extraordinary salary of $250 a day. Publicity posters touted her beauty as well as her daring. By the age of twenty, she had become an international star, not a likely outcome if she had continued as one among many tightrope walkers. 'It is only by doing something which has never been done before,' Thomas Frost wrote, 'or by performing some feat in a very superior style to that of previous exhibitors, that a circus artiste can emerge from the ruck, whether he is a rider, a tumbler, a juggler, or a gymnast.'[3] Zazel, and the many Zazels who copied her, chose to make as grand a spectacle of themselves as they could.

In the 1880s, Adelaide Wieland, like Zazel, performed an act invented by a man, in her case circus director W. H. Wieland, her father. A talented trapezist, she took the stage name Zaeo when she performed a feat known as the great fall. Standing on a platform about 50 feet above the ring, she would dive into the net, turning a backward somersault in mid-flight. Wieland admitted feeling 'joyous exultation' from walking on a wire, and even more when she heard the thunderous applause of 12,000 viewers awaiting her flight. She felt, she said, 'no fear, no sense of being in a dangerous position', only 'dazed wonder'.[4] Wieland also performed as a projectile, catapulted across the ring from a ballista, a siege weapon dating from the Middle Ages, similar to a giant crossbow.

'Why did these projectile feats become so popular?' asks Peta Tait.

> They certainly provoked more cultural anxiety than other aerial acts, not least because of their theatricality with the use of cannon symbolism that heightened an impression of danger and death. At a time when plots in melodrama routinely featured a helpless damsel in distress needing to be rescued, projectile action presented females who willingly endangered themselves.[5]

When men willingly endangered themselves, though, the effect on viewers was not anxiety but envy. During his travels with a circus,

Edward Hoagland recalled seeing a male cannonball who seemed not helpless, but rather impudent and rebellious: 'We, the Elmers, the hicks, the towners, the hayshakers, had just put down good money to watch somebody shoot himself out of a cannon on the assurance that it was going to be genuine and he might really die before our eyes,' Hoagland admitted.

But he landed succinctly on his back in the L-shaped net, swung to the ground, acknowledged our claps – and didn't then thank his lucky stars and settle down to a productive existence like ours. *Eat your heart out rube,* was part of his message. *We'll be gone tomorrow. We'll see Chicago. We'll be in Florida. You stay here and milk your cows!*[6]

Devils and floating girl, poster, 1870.

Like the human cannonball, the human arrow, who was most often female, gave audiences an exhibition of a woman in apparent danger. The human arrow was fired from a cross-bow at a paper bull's eye that moved when she hit it, allowing her to fall into a net, or, in the case of the famous arrow Pansy Zedora, to be caught by her sister on a trapeze. Zedora, billed as Alar, began her career as an arrow when she was sixteen and performed in Barnum's circus for five years. In 1897, after an accident made it impossible to continue that act, she put her efforts into learning another feat that was even more difficult and more painful to learn.

The iron jaw

When Zedora performed the iron jaw act, far from appearing to be a woman in peril, she revealed herself to be a woman of astounding strength. The iron jaw itself was a thick strap with a leather mouth-piece at one end, around which she fitted her teeth. At the other end, a swivel hooked over the bar of a trapeze or was attached to a pulley that lifted her towards the top of the tent or arena. Thus suspended, she entertained with acrobatics and weight lifting.

Degas' Miss Lala was an iron jaw performer, and although the painter depicted her dangling alone high above the ring, in fact her act was more complicated. Hanging from a trapeze bar by her knees, she suspended a rope and pulley from the iron jaw in her mouth. A boy first, then a woman and finally a man took turns raising themselves on the pulley until they reached the height of her mouth. She then spun them, an observer said, 'with an amount of rapidity . . . conducive to a shocking attack of giddiness'. After this feat, still hanging upside down, Lala lifted three men, two hanging from her arms, another hanging from her teeth and performed a stunning finale: 'Six men strain their muscles to lift to her a cannon of no mean dimensions. This also she supports by her teeth alone, never leaving her hold even when, the match being applied, the gun is fired and gives a tremendous report.'[7] Newspapers called her 'the human gun carriage' and 'the cannon woman'.

The iron jaw act was as risky as projectile acts. In 1885, Lottie Watson, performing with Van Amburgh's circus in Albany, New

York, copied Miss Lala, holding a cannon from her mouth, which was discharged while she hung in mid-air. Watson fell in her 1 July performance, as did 25-year-old Anne Barreta, whose act featured a long slide from the roof to the stage while suspended by the iron jaw. Performing in Baltimore in 1887, to the horror of her viewers, she slipped, falling 20 feet to the ground. To avoid the risk of the jaw contraption's failing, some women contrived a variation on the act, hanging instead by their long, braided hair, and juggling or engaging in acrobatics or contortions while they were suspended.

For men, having an iron jaw was more often attributed to prize-winning boxers than to circus performers. Still, iron jaw acts were not limited to women: one Monsieur D'Atelie, for example, was known as the 'Man with the Iron Jaw' when he performed with Barnum's circus in 1872; on the same programme, Mlle Angela was billed as 'The Female Samson'. The ironic stage name only heightened the incongruity of the strong woman act. Many strong women were billed as graceful and beautiful, and posters showed them in scanty costumes, with soft, curly hair and cheerful expressions. An interviewer of one nineteenth-century strong woman insisted that she had no overdeveloped muscles, no manly traits, but appeared gentle and even maternal. While strong men were advertised as Hercules, women usually were named after one goddess or another: Venus and Minerva were popular epithets.

Katie Sandwina, one of the most famous strong women, was the stage name of Catherine Brumbach, born in 1884 into an Austrian circus family; both parents performed feats of strength. As a child, Katie trained in acrobatics and weight lifting, and when she reached her full height of about 6 feet, she broke weight-lifting records. By 1905, Katie and her husband Max Heymann were performing as the Sandwinas – the name a feminized version of Eugen Sandow, a renowned strong man. Among other feats, Katie lifted her husband, who was 6 inches shorter and 50 pounds lighter than she was, over her head with one hand. Billed as 'The Wonder of Female Strength', she appears on one publicity poster bare-legged in a costume that revealed powerful thighs, lifting three men on a bicycle; another poster proclaimed her the 'Strongest Woman That Ever Lived'. After

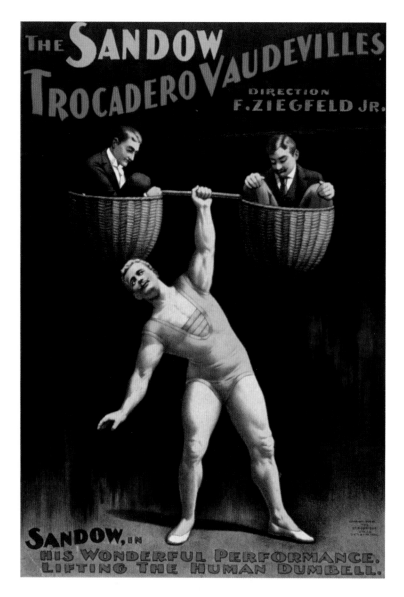

The strongman Eugene Sandow lifting the 'Human Dumbell' [sic], 1894.

performing in vaudeville in America and in several European circuses, by 1911, she and her husband were centre-ring performers for Barnum & Bailey.

Sandwina's acts were not limited to weight lifting. Antony Coxe recalled seeing her in Dublin, where she made her entrance into the

Katie Sandwina,
'Lady Hercules',
holding three men.

The Lady Hercules
Katie Sandwina

circus arena in a Roman chariot, and proceeded with a performance that Coxe deemed remarkable: 'Motorcars were driven across her prostrate body; merry-go-rounds holding four men were supported by her diaphragm; blocks of granite, set on her torso, were shattered by road gangs wielding sledgehammers as she lay across a bed of nails; and she caught a cannonball on the back of her neck.'[8] Coxe notes that such feats became suspect, as audiences wondered if the weights of the cars and granite were as heavy as they seemed, and demonstrations of strength instead focused on hand-to-hand balancing or the lifting of people.

Finger balancers were one speciality act, where a performer supported his entire weight on one index finger. Even if the balancer used an iron splint as an aid, the act required enormous strength in the wrist and arm. Richard Risley Carlise famously balanced his sons on his feet, tossing them into the air, where they did somersaults and landed back on his feet. Risley did not perform in a circus, but circus performers copied his act of foot juggling, known throughout circus history as the Risley act.

Eldora, 'premier equilibrist and juggler', 1892.

Physics

'There is something tremendously basic about the circus arts,' Duncan Wall discovered when he studied at the École Nationale des Arts du Cirque, one of France's premier circus schools, supported by a Fulbright grant.

> They are really just physics; each act is about bodies exerting themselves against unseen forces, about wills and forces colliding. The tension is beautiful: an act seems at odds with everyday reality and is yet natural and satisfying. The lesson applies most concretely to juggling. Balls travel in arcs, and every toss is a little science experiment.[9]

Balls, he soon learned, were not the only objects jugglers tossed into the air: plates, hoops, knives, bowling pins, clubs, fruit – one juggler tried for nine years to perfect catching eggs, until he realized that his viewers would have no idea how hard it was to learn, and so he turned to something else. Juggling, after all, was more satisfying if it elicited rapturous applause.

Juggling dates back thousands of years, even as far back as the Stone Age, according to some scholars, and likely began simply as play. In the Roman arena, jugglers provided diversions, along with acrobats and clowns. At fairs in medieval Europe, jugglers were a staple, admired for their dexterity, but suspect, too, like magicians and mountebanks. Anyone able to move objects faster than the eye could see made some viewers wary: the juggler, after all, tossed balls as quickly as con artists

moved shells in the duplicitous form of gambling known as a shell game. In nineteenth-century circuses, Japanese, Indian and Chinese jugglers dominated the profession, giving performances an aura of the exotic and mysterious. American and European jugglers emulated them, and some, notably Enrico Rastelli and Bobby May, became juggling celebrities.

As Duncan Wall noted, juggling is physics. Objects travel in two kinds of arc: showering, in which they follow one another in a circle; and cascading, in which their paths cross in midair, caught in one hand and the other. Variations include 'tennis', where one ball is tossed over the other two, and 'box', where two balls are tossed up while a

J. T. Doyle
juggling burning
clubs, *c.* 1902.

third shuffles from one hand to another. Jugglers used to compete over how many objects they could catch, but when they juggled more than five or six, viewers had a hard time distinguishing how many were in the air. Distinction had to be sought in other ways: juggling on the wire or slack rope, while rolling a globe beneath one's feet, or balancing on a ladder. Some famous jugglers added visual effects, such as tossing a knife that slit open an envelope in mid-air, or catching a plate on a stick held in the mouth. In the 1920s, Enrico Rastelli was the most famous juggler of the day; he could 'juggle seven balls, twirl three rings on one leg and spin balls on a mouthpiece while he balanced on a board mounted on a rolling cylinder – all at the same time'.[10]

Although juggling doesn't elicit the fear and wonder of aerial acts or human projectiles, performers who choose to master the art still hope to dazzle their viewers. Jay Gilligan, who saw a juggling act when he was nine, immediately began practising. Soon he was at it eight or nine hours a day, increasing the number of objects he could keep in motion. But by the time he was seventeen and touring, he admitted that what once had been a challenge had now become rote: 'With numbers juggling, you can kind of turn your brain off,' he said, and he decided to change his act so that juggling was the central skill of a complex performance that involved music and movement.[11]

Bobby May had created that new kind of juggling act in the 1930s, when he rose to fame. Unlike Rastelli, he was not interested in tossing more objects or combining juggling with balancing or acrobatics. Instead, May and the jugglers who emulated him conceived of a performance that focused on movement, rhythm and dance. Like musical stars of the time, May performed in a top hat and dinner suit; he was elegant, suave, graceful – and dextrous.

Like wire walkers, jugglers are masters of concentration and patience. Two years of constant practice, for example, are needed to learn a four-ball cascade. Performers must be proficient not only in various techniques, but in moving seamlessly from one to the next, creating their own unified routine. 'When you see somebody throwing seven objects in the air at a circus and keep them going,' said Larry Pisoni, founder of the Pickle Family Circus, 'that person is balanced. That person is centered. He's controlling the trajectory of inanimate objects. His heart and mind is going a mile a minute. It's an amazing thing to see.'[12] Amazing and, in some performances, seemingly impossible. Juggling combines what appears to be child's play with sly conjuring and well-honed skill. The historian Arthur Chandler – a juggler himself – suggests larger implications: 'Objects fly through the air, stars wheel through the universe. All fall eventually . . . If we achieve peace within the intervals of rising and falling, we find grace.'[13]

Children who see their first circus might run home to practice juggling, tumbling or acrobatics; string a line in their backyard and try to walk a tightrope; or invent a clown costume and skit. But some circus performers frustrate any child's desire to imitate them: human cannonballs, escape artists, sword-swallowers and contortionists.

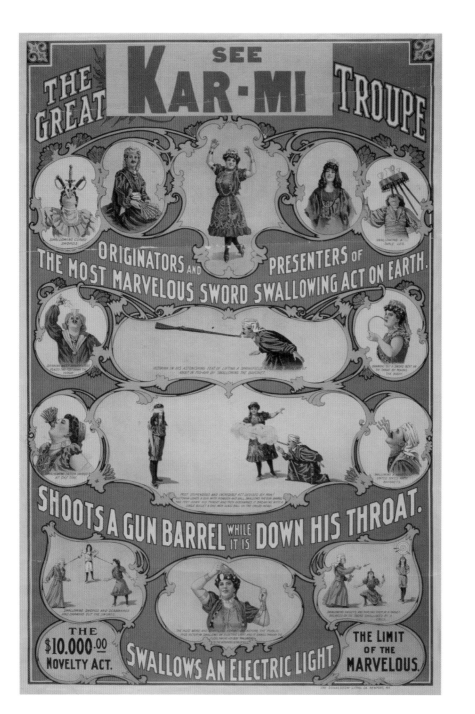

Incomprehensibles

Men and women who bend backward and touch their head to the ground, place their feet around their neck while standing on one leg, roll themselves into a ball, take the shape of a frog: these performers were known as posturers, india-rubber men, elastic incomprehensibles or nondescripts before the term 'contortionist' came into popular use in the nineteenth century.[14] What was incomprehensible was the ability of an individual to manipulate his or her body as if it appeared to have flexible bones. Viewers who witness this physical distortion often admire the performer's athleticism and even grace, but even fans of contortionists admit that they can be disturbing to watch. 'The grotesque never rises into the beautiful,' one observer noted, 'but the beautiful may degenerate into the grotesque.'[15]

In ancient art, contortionists were depicted as shape-changers: magical, sinful or depraved monsters. Figures of gargoyles – leering and menacing – often represent contortionists: the deformation of the body suggests deformation of the spirit. Many performers emphasized this association by wearing costumes that evoked the skin of serpents or reptiles. Yet if these contortionists appeared as forbidden temptations, still it was hard for audiences to look away from demonstrations of apparently supernormal ability. In some early circuses, contortionists were relegated to sideshows, along with performers exhibited as freaks of nature: the fat and exceptionally skinny, the tall and exceptionally short.

Even with their rare talent, though, contortionists looked for ways to distinguish themselves from their competition, and sometimes took foreign stage names to emphasize their exoticism. The circus impresario G. Van Hare came across a sixteen-year-old boy who had practiced bending and was doing odd jobs around the circus. He took him on as an apprentice, and after he had practised for a few weeks, Van Hare deemed him good enough to join the circus. He commissioned special costumes to be made, and, he wrote,

The great Victorina Troupe sword swallowers, c. 1900.

I transmogrified him into a Persian Prince; I wrote a book with this heading, on the front, viz., *Van Hare's Last Wonder. Life*

and Startling Adventures of Sadi Djalma, the Persian Prince,
surnamed The Serpent of the Desert: with a brief History of
Persia; a highly interesting Country, but little known to the
British Public. 'He is a mystery to the Faculty, and the marvel
of Creation.' *– Times.*[16]

The Persian Prince had talents other than bending: he walked up
and down a moving 14-foot ladder, stood at the top and played the
'Carnival of Venice' on the violin.

One Irish posturer in Pablo Fanque's company took an Italian
stage name, but apparently even this change in nationality was not
sufficiently exotic; he decided to transform himself even more dramatically by shaving his head, staining his skin with a yellow tint and
posing as Chinese. He wore a Chinese costume and was billed as
Ki-hi-chin-fan-foo, written on posters in ideographs that may or may
not have been authentic renderings of Chinese. When he performed
in Glasgow, two Chinese residents asked repeatedly to see him, but
he refused and they finally went to the local police, certain that their
countryman was being held against his will. Pablo Fanque reluctantly
admitted the hoax.[17]

Besides the benders, some contortionists were dislocationists
whose performance involved forcing their bodies into impossibly
small spaces. Joe Allen, called the 'Human Corkscrew', wriggled
through a 13½-inch hoop. King Brawn, the 'World Famous Dietician
and Escape Artist', thrust himself through tennis rackets and keyholes
and wriggled out of strait jackets. Walter Wentworth called his act
Packanatomicalization, and in it he packed himself into a box meas-
uring 23 by 19 by 16 inches before having an assistant press dozens
of small soda bottles around him.

In the 1910s and '20s, Harry and Friede DeMarlo were husband
and wife aerial contortionists whose act was called 'Frog Paradise'
and involved back bending on a trapeze while dressed in frog costumes. Harry later performed 'Devil on the Trapeze', dressed in red
as Satan; and Friede, calling herself La Marletta, developed a special
iron-jaw act, 'The Whirl of Death'. Suspended by the iron jaw, she was
whirled by a motor as she performed a repertoire of bends. A fall

Contortionist in
a tuxedo jacket,
c. 1892.

Contortionist in a tuxedo jacket, c. 1892.

ended that act, but she and Harry continued as aerial contortionists for several years after.

Some fans of contortionists were nothing less than obsessed with the spectacle of a human body deforming itself. Bruce Kattenberg, a hotel clerk in the Midwest, assembled a huge collection of photographs, articles and memorabilia – a collection that now resides in Harvard University's Houghton Library – focused particularly on male contortionists. In the 1930s, Kattenberg began a correspondence with another ardent contortion fan, a Chilean businessman who used the pseudonym Eduardo Titus. 'What people like about contortionists is a complicated matter,' Titus wrote to Kattenberg, 'a mixture of curiosity, appeal of the uncanny . . . something similar to what a kid feels when

he breaks a beautiful toy, with the additional pleasure to see it restored as it was before.'[18] For Titus and Kattenberg, though, the pleasure was indeed more complicated, and decidedly erotic.

Titus's fascination with contortion began when he was twelve and attended a performance of a travelling circus in Chile. From then on, he took every opportunity to see such acts, and by the time he was a teenager, he focused his interest on female contortionists, whom he found sexually arousing. He remembered especially two women: Alice Lee, whose movements were particularly graceful, and whose costume of shorts and a bra was particularly alluring; and Irene Vermillion, who appeared to be nearly naked: 'For a contortionist,' he wrote to Kattenberg, 'the real hit of her performance come [sic] from the exhibition of her body and they should make a generous display of bare skin.'[19] Titus praised France for allowing women contortionists to

'Phenomenal Acts of Contortion', poster for Forepaugh & Sells Brothers, 1899.

perform nude, sometimes in private clubs for all-male audiences; in trips to Europe, especially in Paris and Berlin, Titus made sure to attend as many displays of contortionists as possible.

The eroticism of contortion acts made its way into romance fiction in the mid-twentieth century, in which the strong man and muscular trapeze artist were already cast as objects of women's desire. In Letitia Preston Osborne's *Through Purple Glass*, a contortionist tries to get a woman to run away with him, and she is tempted, imagining the delights that might ensue: 'She kept wondering what a contortionist might – well, might do.'[20] Similarly, Jeanet Philips enticingly titled a romantic short story 'Double-Jointed Romeo'. Images of male benders, with their heads protruding beneath their genitals, fed these erotic fantasies.

Although rumours abounded that contortionists were congenitally different from other human beings, in fact, flexibility and strength came from long years of training begun in early childhood, even in children as young as two. One performer described the arduous and

East Asian acrobats in a poster of *c.* 1891.

The 'Four Novelty Grahams' acrobat family, photographed by Lewis Hine, 1910.

painful process: padded splints were strapped around each knee, the ankles strapped to cords suspended from the ceiling, two other cords were attached to a belt. Thus tethered, the child swung with one leg extended one way and the other in the opposite direction. When the cords attached to the belt were let down, the child's weight forced the legs apart in the splits. Being in that position for half an hour, the performer remembered, was slow torture. Even when painful contraptions were not used, the exercises were strenuous and needed to be practised for hours every day. Becoming a contortionist required physical flexibility as well as a compliant nature and willingness, certainly, to

William Glackens,
*The Human Lizard
and the Human Frog,*
1899.

endure pain. Contortionists, one circus performer reflected, 'tend to be pretty hard on themselves, which in a way is good, since your success as a contortionist is totally determined by how hard you're willing to push yourself'.[21]

Contortionists, some of whom first trained in ballet, now take centre stage in circuses. Rather than evoking fear and repulsion, they are praised for their elegance and skill. No longer do audiences think they should be viewed in the sideshow, with the sword-swallowers, the giants and the missing links.

"Carolina Twins,"

MILLIE AND CHRISTINA.

NINE

PRODIGIES

Why is it entertainment, if we're not gawking
at a caricature of ourselves?
Edward Hoagland

In the summer of 1851, conjoined daughters were born on a plantation in North Carolina to the slaves Jacob and Menemia, both owned by Jabez McCoy.[1] The girls' bodies were fused at the lower portion of the trunk, their spinal columns united at the base, forming one large bone common to both and one anus. Their parents named their daughters – their eighth and ninth children – Millie and Christine, and the girls learned to walk, and even run, on their outer limbs, stand sideways with their arms around each other, and give each other kisses. When they lay down, one reclined on her back, the other on her side. Their bodies, apparently, were less a constriction on their freedom than their status as slaves.

When they were ten months old, McCoy saw their potential for making money, and he sold them for $1,000 to a man who planned to exhibit them in freak shows; he, in turn, sold them to another, and finally they came into the possession of one Joseph P. Smith and his wife, with whom they lived when they were not on exhibition. Smith, who paid tens of thousands of dollars for his prize, displayed the girls throughout the Gulf States as 'living curiosities', enabling him to earn back his investment from carnivals and circus sideshows. In 1854, when they were three, they appeared at Barnum's American Museum in New York.

At some point in his venture, Smith engaged a booking agent, but instead of working on Smith's behalf, the agent kidnapped the girls

'Carolina Twins', Millie and Christina, 1866.

223

and exhibited them privately to 'scientific bodies'; he then sold them to another man, who took them on tour throughout Canada and to Philadelphia, where, in 1856, the buying and selling of the twins was briefly interrupted. According to the girls' memoirs, someone who saw them on exhibit 'went to the authorities and said we were slaves, brought into a free state, where we were unjustly deprived of our liberty'.[2] The whistle blower sued the court to appoint a guardian, but before that could happen, the girls' current owner spirited them away to Europe, paying a woman to claim that she was their mother. The five-year-old twins were a lucrative property.

Meanwhile Smith managed to discover the girls' twisting trail; wronged and angry, he and Menemia sailed after them. In England, Menemia testified in court that she was the girls' mother, and won. Smith then proposed a co-partnership that gave the girls, their mother and himself rights to receipts. Their drama was not over, however; the girls' owner refused to comply with the court's decision and threatened Menemia and Smith, and only with difficulty was Smith able to extricate himself and the family.

By the time they were twenty, Millie-Christine, as they were billed, were well known among freak show and circus attractions. They had special success in England, where they were summoned by Queen Victoria, who, they recalled, 'talked tenderly' to them. They learned to read and write from Mrs Smith, and their memoir, most likely produced for publicity, reveals sophistication and intelligence. Although they understood that others saw them as a freak, they were proud, not at all demeaned, to be exhibited. 'We wish to be viewed as something entirely void of humbug – a living curiosity – not a sham gotten up to impose upon and deceive the people,' they wrote. 'We are indeed a strange freak of Nature, and upon the success of our exhibition does our happiness and the well-being of others depend.' Indeed, the money they earned provided enough for their father to purchase McCoy's plantation, and throughout their adulthood the girls contributed generously to their thirteen siblings and many charities. At the age of 32, they joined John B. Doris's Great Inter-ocean Museum, Menagerie, & Circus as the troupe's leading act, paid handsomely at $25,000 per year. They insisted that they considered themselves neither inferior nor deprived. 'One thing is certain,' they proclaimed: 'we would not wish to be severed, even if science could effect a separation. We are contented with our lot, and are happy as the day is long. We have but *one heart*, one feeling in common, one desire, one purpose.'[3]

Proud to be a freak of nature, proud to make a living for themselves and their family by exhibiting their body: this sense of agency is echoed by other men and women who performed in American and British circuses and sideshows willingly, and often represented by agents who negotiated benefits and terms of display. When impresarios advertised in *Billboard*, the most prominent circus magazine, for the most aberrant or exotic bodies, their advertisements were answered by a sufficient number of performers to keep freak shows well staffed. In some cases, parents of legless, armless, hirsute, tiny or tall children saw in the circus a viable future for their unusual offspring and hired them out, or sold them, to managers. When physical 'marvels' were not forthcoming, shows made do with tattooed bodies, always in abundant supply; improvised with costumes and make-up to produce such attractions as a bird girl or mermaid; or hired so-called synthetic freaks, those who manipulated their bodies – by overeating, starving or piercing –for the purposes of display.

The testimony of some performers and the ease of staffing freak shows complicates our understanding of the relationship between performer and voyeur, and of the motivation for some people to assume the label of 'freak' and to display themselves. The historian David Gerber, among others, asks if we can take people at their word when they claim to have freely chosen a career as a freak; he assumes that their choice, after all, is between destitution and participation in a vulgar form of entertainment. But other scholars argue that these performers knowingly colluded in creating the sensationalism of the freak show; that they were not exploited but treated with respect and paid fairly.[4]

According to a newspaper report in 1908, their earnings reportedly were on a par with other circus performers, with pay varying depending on the nature of their oddity. An acrobat or aerialist might earn $25 to $50 a week, taking huge physical risks; in the same show, Charles Tripp, the armless wonder, earned $25 a week; Eli Bowen, the legless acrobat, earned $25; and Lionel, the Human Skye Terrier, because of the nature of his 'rarity' earned $120. A bearded lady earned $15, as did John Hayes, the human pincushion. With lodging, meals and transportation provided, freaks could manage well financially, saving enough to support themselves when they were not performing.[5] In addition to their circus salary, they might augment their income by selling autographed souvenir programmes or copies of their memoirs. Some invited viewers to pose with them for photographs for a fee.

Certainly publicity about freaks' autonomy assuaged viewers' anxieties about staring at another person's body. Audiences preferred to think that freaks were not coerced or enslaved but, like other circus performers, chose to be part of the circus community, sharing in the glamour and benefiting from the chance to travel the world. Articles attesting to the performers' free will persisted well into the twentieth century. 'A freak is usually happy in sideshow life,' wrote Alva Johnston in a *New Yorker* article in 1934. 'In his own family or in his own community, he is an isolated, lonely being; in the circus or carnival, he has the society of others who failed to receive their human birthright. They are at ease with one another.' Besides finding an accepting community, they felt increased self-esteem from being gazed at: 'some of them', Johnston noted, 'begin to regard themselves as favored children of nature. There is a touch of hauteur, of aristocratic condescension, about a typical freak in his contacts with persons of normal size and the routine number of legs, heads, and sexes.'[6]

That touch of hauteur was evident in a profile of the bearded Lady Olga, the stage name of Jane Barnell, who at 69 had been performing in circuses since she was four years old. Married several times, and preferring quiet apartment living to exhibiting herself, she admitted nevertheless that 'her self-esteem suffers least of all when she is working in circuses, where sideshow distinctions are rigidly observed' and 'born freaks . . . are the aristocrats of the sideshow world'. Although she was proud of having what she believed was the longest female beard in history – an attribute that made her feel superior to other performers – still she confessed that 'a snicker or brutal remark made by someone in an audience' could spark depression lasting for a week. 'When I get the blues,' she said, 'I feel like an outcast from society.'[7] The protective community of the circus was not without its emotional risks; still, Barnell did not regret the life she had chosen for herself – a life of exhibitionism, of flaunting one's prodigality and difference.

Humanity askew

As for viewers, their motivation also seems complicated. Freak shows seem part of an unenlightened past, a time when dwarves performed as court jesters in ancient Egypt; when, at medieval fairs, parents charged viewers for the sight of their children with birth defects; when anomalous bodies were thought to portend doom. Yet freak shows coincided with the golden age of the circus, in Britain from around 1840 until after the First World War, and in America for even longer. Queen Victoria sought out Millie-Christine and Barnum's famous midget, Tom Thumb. When the prince and princess of Wales attended a performance of the Barnum & Bailey circus in London in 1898, the princess had one request: 'We want to see the freaks.'[8] In the decades before public and scholarly conversations about disabiity generated anxieties about gazing at freaks, their exhibition flourished, seeming to contradict the underlying theme of joy, magic, enchantment and celebration of skill that the rest of the circus conveyed. The same people who applauded trapeze artists and Risley acts were eager to gape at those displayed as human curiosities.

A generous interpretation of the attraction of freak shows holds that their proliferation in the mid-nineteenth century coincided with a growing interest in human diversity among physicians, scientists and the lay public. Public curiosity was sated also at museums such as Barnum's American Museum, filled with all manner of nature's anomalies, including a few frauds, such as the Feejee Mermaid and Woolly Horse; Philadelphia's Mütter Museum, begun in 1858 as part of the city's medical school, which featured such displays as foetal or skeletal conjoined twins, the conjoined liver of the twins Chang and Eng, and skeletons of giants and midgets; or the even older Musée Fragonard, just outside of Paris, a repository of anatomical oddities.

Freak shows often highlighted their didactic purpose: as proof that the bodies on exhibit truly were unique, a showman or 'professor'

Nellie Lane and
Major Mite, 1922.

Commodore Nutt,
Lavinia Warren,
'The Giant' and
General Tom
Thumb, c. 1855–65.

might introduce the performer with a lecture or provide a pamphlet with
anatomical and biographical details. Circus impresarios encouraged
scientists' validation of their exhibitions so that they could advertise
their performers' authenticity. Millie-Christine were repeatedly investigated until, as adolescents, they refused to allow anyone to probe their
bodies. By then, their authenticity had been amply confirmed. In 1885,
seventeen-year-old Fedor Jeftichew, whose face and body were covered
with hair – a result of hypertrichosis – was promoted as Jo-Jo, a freak in
P. T. Barnum's circus. Billed as the 'Human Skye Terrier', the teenager
became a focus of medical interest, and Barnum received many requests

Susan Barton, the
'Mammoth Lady',
1849.

from doctors who wanted to examine him. One afternoon Barnum granted permission, and Jo-Jo was escorted to the stage of Madison Square Garden and stripped to the waist for perusal by a team of fourteen eminent physicians, accompanied by naturalist Frederick Barnard, president of Columbia College. 'The doctors examined Jo-Jo critically and thoroughly,' reported the *New York Times*, 'but the only opinion they ventured was that he was an extraordinary freak of nature.'[9] For the circus, that was the only opinion that mattered.

The public attended freak shows, however, for more than simply a panoply of human diversity; concepts of normality and abnormality

Fedor Jeftichew, 1880s.

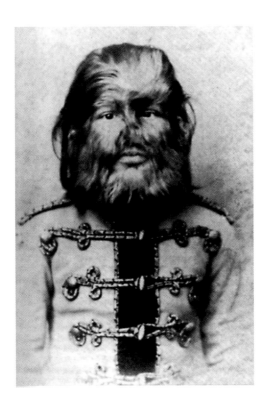

The Rossow midgets,
American poster,
c. 1897.

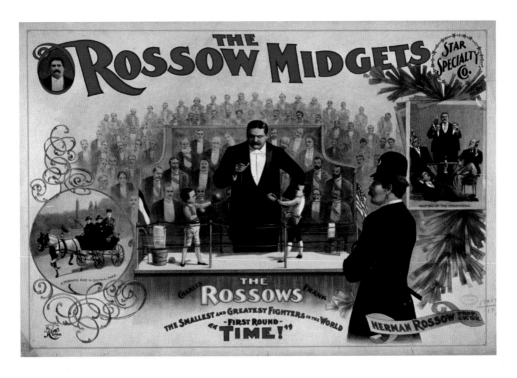

became associated not only with nature's capriciousness, but also with worth. Darwin's writings, from the time his *On the Origin of Species* was published in 1859, imbued discussions of bodily difference with questions about the moral implications of fitness. Were performers displayed in sideshows merely different, or were they monstrous? What was the connection between physical difference and intelligence? Between physical difference and moral goodness? Where was the line between beast and human? Most disturbingly, where was the difference between the freak and the viewer? Often newspaper reviews of freak shows reflect changing responses to those questions depending on how freaks were described, what attributes they were supposed to have and how viewers' reactions were framed.

A newspaper article reporting the investigation of Jo-Jo at the age of seventeen described him as childlike, leaning on his attendant's shoulder and gazing at him affectionately. Physical appearance, it seemed to a reporter in 1885, reflected mental ability. But 22 years later, a reporter meeting Jo-Jo as an adult characterized him as a man 'of superior intelligence . . . He understands and writes Russian, German, French and English,' and conversed intelligently on all manner of sophisticated topics.[10] Jo-Jo was no longer defined by his physical appearance; the reporter noted that during their conversation, he found himself unaware of the long hair covering Jo-Jo's face, transfixed as he was by the gleaming intelligence emanating from his eyes.

Chang Woo Gow, billed as the 'Great Chinese Giant', presented himself in his publicity memoir as a man among men, a giant in gentility, thoughtfulness and culture. Patient with the 'vulgar curiosity' of the populace, he conducted himself with uncommon dignity. 'It is not so much that Chang is one of the largest men of modern times,' commented the London *Daily Telegraph*, 'as that the effect of his extraordinary stature is somehow very strongly brought out, making him really appear as belonging to a distinct race of beings.' He was, reported the British medical journal *The Lancet*, 'a remarkable specimen of humanity; a very finely-made man; a gentleman and a scholar, occupying himself constantly in literary pursuits.'[11] Reports of other sideshow performers also frequently cited intelligence and refinement, qualities that set them above, or at least connected the performers to, their viewers.

Performers pushed for this change in the public's perception of them. Being called a 'freak' seemed demeaning; being stared at for one's uniqueness was not. In 1903, the *New York Times* reported that a group of Barnum & Bailey performers, including the Armless Wonder, the Human Pin Cushion and the Lion-faced Boy, met in Madison Square Garden to protest the use of the derogatory term 'freak'. They insisted on the use of 'prodigies' in advertisements and programmes. Their protest followed a similar revolt four years earlier in London, against the same circus, in which Bailey conceded to their demands; now, they rallied for change in the u.s. By 1907, they had organized themselves officially into the Human Prodigies Society, much like a union, fraternal lodge or benefit organization that provided support for ill or aged performers. 'The new organization would bring the living prodigies together in a social way,' the members announced. 'We would have our own dances, and our own annual dinners, where no one not a "human curiosity" would be admitted.'[12] Whether the organization was motivated by the performers or incited by a creative manager, there followed a spate of newspaper articles attesting to the 'humanity' of so-called 'freaks', and, in some cases, their intellectual superiority and urbanity. Such articles underscored the idea that physical appearance did not correlate with intelligence, contradicting phrenologists, who said they could evaluate personality by feeling bumps on one's head, or self-proclaimed criminologists who maintained that criminals had identifiable facial and bodily characteristics. Still, even in articles

Francesco Lentini, the 'three-legged boy', 1901.

attesting to the mental superiority of their subjects, reporters took the position of evaluators and judges, often showing amazement in response to articulate, multilingual, well-read 'freaks'.

In Britain, freak shows had a shorter history than in America, largely as a result of the First World War. As soldiers who had lost limbs began returning home, legless and armless bodies were not the object of curiosity or amusement, but pity and concern, spurring debate about the government's role in compensating men who had been wounded. As the historian Nadja Durbach notes,

> The category of the 'disabled' took shape . . . at a particular historical moment when the British government was forced to reevaluate the rights and responsibilities of citizenship, and when British society was compelled to rethink the social meanings attached to bodily disfigurement.

Although freaks were not looking for pity, although their bodies were not the result of war injuries, the new category of 'disabled' had an impact on freak shows. Freaks, Durbach writes, 'were heavily invested in their status as "able-bodied"' and 'the armless and legless invariably incorporated into their acts demonstrations of their skills and

Poster for Barnum & Bailey's 'Marvelous Living Human Curiosities', 1899.

234

capacities.'[13] Nevertheless, by the 1920s, freak shows were becoming rare in Britain.

In America, though, they persisted as an integral part of circus entertainment. The Ringling Brothers Barnum & Bailey Route Book for 1943 includes in the sideshow a Snake Trainer, Giant and Giantess, Armless and Legless Girl, Comedy Jugglers, Sword Swallower, Tattooed Strong Man, Magician, Fat Girl, Rubber-armed Man, Long Haired Girl, Smallest Man, Living Skeleton, Pueblo Indian Sculptor, World's Smallest Performers, Midget Musician, South American Troubadours, Black-face Minstrels and a Human Dynamo.[14] In 1908, though, pressure to exhibit more and more spectacular prodigies had led the Ringlings to cut down the freak show, an announcement that caused such strong public protest that by 1913 they reinstated it to its full range of 'humanity gone askew'.[15] That epithet was continuously redefined.

The romance of the 'other'

Circus needs for 'exotic' humans, like the need for wild beasts, generated an international trade in luring or capturing people who could fulfil the role of 'savages' and 'missing links'. In the nineteenth and early twentieth century, freak shows increasingly featured displays of non-Western people as bodily spectacles, underscoring the notion that whites were normative, more highly evolved than non-whites and morally superior; people of different colours were nature's mistakes or early trials. Sometimes exhibitions served as warnings: African-American children suffering from vitiligo, depigmentation of the skin causing white patches, were billed as African 'Leopard Boys', representing the dire consequences of miscegenation.

Many exhibitions emphasized the sexuality – even hypersexuality – of exotic humans: non-Westerners, like the beasts they lived among, were driven by their base instincts. No exhibition more starkly conveyed this message than that of a Black Venus, a title bestowed on many women after the notoriety generated by the South African Sara Baartman, the infamous 'Hottentot Venus'. A member of the Khoikhoi, called Hottentots by Dutch and British settlers, Baartman was born in the late 1770s, according to her recent biographers, and lived as a servant or slave in the rural Camdeboo valley. She was brought to Cape Town in 1800 by Pieter Cesars, in whose household she served. By the time she left Cape Town ten years later, she had been pregnant three times, and lost each child either before, or shortly after, its birth; her biographers speculate that one child was the result of rape.

One of few Khoikhoi women in Cape Town, Baartman was living with Hendrik Cesars, Pieter's brother-in-law, a man in perennial debt who decided he could make some money by 'showing' Sara to sailors being treated in a local military hospital. Because a genetic condition known as steatopygia had resulted in her having enormous buttocks and elongated labia, Baartman, as her biographers put it, 'became a special kind of show, a Hottentot Venus'.[16] Cesars charged sailors to look at her, possibly to touch her, perhaps even to have sex with her. Soon famous for exhibiting herself at the hospital, Baartman came to the attention of a local surgeon, Alexander Dunlop, who, like Cesars, always had an eye out for making quick money. Baartman, he thought, with her 'extraordinary shape', could be the answer to his mounting debts, and he convinced her and Hendrik – she refused to leave without him – to go with him to England and reap the profits of show business.

Baartman arrived in London in the summer of 1810, and in September began a five-year career as Sartjee (the diminutive of Sara), the Hottentot Venus. She wore a short, tight-fitting costume that matched her skin colour and made her appear naked, and was adorned with beads and face paint, the better to evoke her wild African homeland. Publicity posters emphasized her buttocks, and in one poster, although a decorative cloth covers her genitalia, the pattern suggests elongated labia. On stage, at fairs and in private showings – sometimes displayed in a cage – the Hottentot Venus was a hit of the season, summoned by aristocrats for private performances that included 'native' dancing and thorough inspection by male viewers.

One of these showings came to the attention of the noted abolitionist Zachary Macaulay, who became suspicious that Baartman was not in London exhibiting herself of her own free will. Slavery had

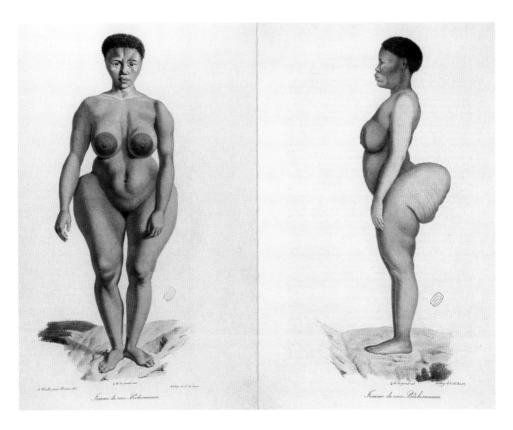

Saartjie Baartman, the 'Hottentot Venus', illustration from Etienne Geoffroy Saint-Hilaire and Georges Cuvier's *Natural History of Mammals*, 1815.

recently been outlawed in the British Empire; it would not do to have an enslaved woman in London, and Macaulay appealed to the King's Bench for an investigation. Although the plaintiff made clear his uneasiness with the display of a half-naked caged woman, the court noted that the 'delicacy' of the exhibition was not their concern; they were charged only 'to ascertain how far the exhibition gives her pain as a sentient being' and whether she was in England by her own free will.[17] Perhaps coached or intimidated by Dunlop, perhaps believing that she really would share in the money that she earned, she told the court that she had no complaints; she had agreed to a contract; she would prefer to stay in England, not return to Cape Town. Dunlop produced a contract, certainly fraudulent, but the court accepted his defense and ruled in his favour. And Baartman remained in England, now even more famous because of publicity over the court case, until 1814, when she was taken to Paris under the management of yet another man, and performed there until her death in 1815. During her brief Paris appearance, the scientist Georges Cuvier became obsessed with investigating her body, interested as he was in anthropology. She consented to pose for drawings, but no more; yet Cuvier succeeded, after all, once she was dead. To further the cause of science, apparently, the French police turned over to Cuvier Baartman's corpse.

First he made a cast of her body, then dissected her, excising and preserving her genitals. When the autopsy was done, he boiled her down to the bones, which he reassembled into a skeleton. The Hottentot Venus, at Cuvier's hands, lived on in multiple macabre displays in Paris museums. Her reputation did not die with her either: instead the epithet of Hottentot Venus, in various forms, came to be applied to other black women whose sexuality became their identity: staged, packaged and sold.

For European and American audiences, racial difference was often synonymous with savagery and violence. In 1856, Howe and Cushing's Great American Show landed in Liverpool with a troupe of so-called Red Indians. When George Sanger went to see the show, he noticed that one member of the 'tribe' was a black man whom he had employed a dozen years before. Not wanting to be outdone by the Americans, Sanger, accompanied by a detective he hired to find 'some savages', trolled 'some dreadful slums, where in half an hour I engaged eight wild men and two savage women . . . A little red ochre for skin tint, some long, snaky black hair, feathers, skins, and beads did the trick properly, and I had as savage a lot of Ojibbeways to look at as ever took a scalp.' He exhibited them in an iron-barred cage, the better to protect viewers, within which they performed war dances and tribal ceremonies. 'My! It was a swindle,' Sanger admitted later, 'and now and again my conscience troubled me fearfully about it, but when I thought of Howe and Cushing I always felt justified.'[18]

Although he was no stranger to the occasional swindle, in 1882, P. T. Barnum hoped to present in his circus real 'specimens of . . . uncivilized peoples' collected from around the world, and 'to exhibit to the American public not only human beings of different races, but also, when practicable, those who possess extraordinary peculiarities, such as giants, dwarfs, singular disfigurements of the person, dexterity in the use of weapons, dancing, singing, juggling, unusual feats of strength or agility, &c'. In a handwritten circular letter, Barnum solicited help from consular officials living abroad, and anyone else who might be able to contribute to his plan for a 'Congress of Nations'. He would provide travelling expenses and board, and, in lieu of salary, 'fancy articles such as are always acceptable and a small allowance monthly'. Like Noah, he hoped to find pairs of these 'specimens', although he granted that he might take 'a group of 3 to 6 or even 10' if they were 'specially novel'.[19]

His global connections proved helpful, and for the 1884 season, Barnum was able to feature an 'Ethnological Congress of Savage Tribes', described in the show's programme and advertisements as including Fudians, Burmese, Todas Indians, Haughty Svrians, Hindoos, Ferocious Zulus, Bestial Australian Cannibals, Afghans, Botocudos from the Amazon, Sinuous Nautch Girl Dancers, East Hindoos, Mysterious Aztecs', as well as the prodigies Chang, the Chinese Giant; Admiral Dot, Midget Actor and Orator; Major Atom, Smallest Man Alive; Fat Women; Living Skeletons; Armless Men; Bearded Women; and other curiosities. The Ethnological Congress paraded around the ring at the start of the show, along with Barnum's recently acquired, and no less sensational, 'Sacred White Elephant'.

A few years later, the animal trainer Carl Hagenbeck contributed to such racial displays with his 'anthropological-zoological exhibitions'. Using the same group of hunters who captured lions and leopards for him from Africa, Hagenbeck rounded up families or small groups from communities in Africa, Lapland and Asia, offered them contracts and brought them to Europe, where he promoted them not as freaks, but as characteristic types.[20] He created 'human zoos' where non-whites were shown in their 'natural' surroundings, engaged in typical activities using tools, with their domesticated animals, dressed in their typical clothing or outfits provided for them by their recruiters. In these habitats, visitors wandered through the exhibition and could interact with those on display.

Those encounters had unforeseen consequences. As historian Eric Ames notes, 'anecdotes of midnight liaisons between spectators and performers can be found throughout the Hagenback material, suggesting that interracial romance was a minor yet continuous part of the show's appeal.' Although the exhibits were meant to convey a message of racial hierarchy, these encounters, Ames says, made evident 'forces of passionate identification . . . that transgressed and destabilized both the social and physical barriers that were intended to construct distinct spaces of identity'. When Hagenbeck exhibited young Nubian men in Germany in 1887–8, so many German women became infatuated with the lean, bronze-skinned, half-naked Egyptians that the press called them 'Nubian-crazed'. The relationships developed to such an extent that in Berlin, the Nubian troupe refused to leave, 'goaded by their new girlfriends', and police intervention was needed to separate the couples. Some young male Germans became just as infatuated with Nubian women. Although human zoos were designed to convey an image of German superiority over colonial blacks, the romantic interactions undermined that message, and the exhibitions became the subject of debate by the Colonial Society, which promoted German imperialism.[21]

Sideshow act displaying people dressed in costume from different countries, *c.* 1900.

Like Hagenbeck, Barnum displayed an assortment of non-whites whose dress and behaviour perpetuated stereotypes. Native Americans dressed in feathers and animal skins whooped and danced; blacks grunted and took savage poses; various performers were billed as 'missing links', as was William Henry Johnson, a black man from New Jersey exhibited during a 60-year career as the 'Man-Monkey', 'Missing Link' and, most famously, as 'Zip, the What Is It?'. Barnum insisted that he remain mute during his exhibition, where he usually wore a grass skirt and held a spear. His small head gave rise to speculation that he was microcephalic, but testimony by circus performers contradicts that portrayal. He was, they said, just an ordinary man.

In 1882, a six-year-old hirsute girl was brought from her native Thailand to England – captured, according to some historians; sold by her parents, according to others – and promoted as Krao, 'The Half-way Point in the Evolution of Man from Ape'. Although British scientists were led to believe that her parents, apparently dead, were more 'monkey-like' than she, her features seemed unremarkably human, and they deemed 'Little Krao', as they called her, to be nothing other than a bright child with hypertrichosis. Despite those scientists' scepticism, the impresario William Leonard Hunt, known as the Great Farini, who managed and later adopted her, nevertheless exhibited her in American dime museums and circuses as the 'Missing Link'. A poster proclaimed that she had been born 'Mongst the Giant Branches of the Mighty Trees of Laos – a Human Being Covered Entirely With Long Hair, Subsisting on Nuts and Grasses. Using Her Hands and Feet With the Facility of an Ape in Climbing To and From Her Hut of Twigs High Up in the Trees of Her Native Country'. This 'Greatest Enigma of the Century', the poster insisted, had endorsements from 'Leading Scientists, Physicians, Ministers and the Press'. Her publicity photograph shows her dressed demurely, standing beside a delicate side table that holds a vase brimming with flowers; a tufted pillow lies behind her. Her dress and the setting of a Victorian parlour are meant to point up the anomaly of the black hair covering her arms and legs, and likely also to unsettle viewers who would identify with everything about the photograph except the hair.

In 1853, a debate ensued over two El Salvadoran siblings promoted as the 'Aztec Children', or 'Aztec Lilliputians', Maximo and Bartola. Microcephalic midgets, they were investigated by physicians and naturalists when exhibited in London and generated much debate; a spate of letters in the London *Times* focused more on their provenance than their physical attributes, arguing about whether their purported homeland was really Iximaya, and about the language of their unintelligible utterances. One visitor tried to speak to them in Mayan and, getting no response, concluded that they might be Toltek, not Aztec as advertised, and therefore speaking a lost language. Others doubted that they were Mexican at all, nor specimens of a unique race. Once again, British scepticism did not cross the Atlantic with them. In New York, a distinguished roster of scientists was convinced of their authenticity as exotic pygmies, whose small heads, protruding lips and general demeanour were characteristics of their race. The siblings joined the Barnum & Bailey circus, dancing and singing, for the next 50 years. Their popularity inspired imitators: one 'Aztec' boy was recruited from the exotic realm of Ohio.

Other whites, too, joined the bandwagon of anthropological curiosities. In 1882, Nora Hildebrandt displayed her tattooed body, the result, she claimed, of abduction by savage Lakota Indians while travelling through the west with her father. None other than Sitting Bull forced her father to tattoo her, but her father refused to complete the job because the needles caused her so much pain. The Lakotas therefore killed him and held Nora captive. After being rescued by a cavalryman, Nora said she came to the attention of the Forepaugh Circus, where she was hired into the sideshow. At 25, Hildebrandt was the first tattooed woman who earned a living by her decorative body, and quickly she inspired copiers with similar abduction stories. In reality, Hildebrandt was born in London in 1857 and tattooed by her common-law husband Martin, who ended his days institutionalized in an insane asylum. Nora, though, had a long circus career.

As late as the 1930s, American circus audiences flocked to see 'savages'. Roland Butler, publicity director for the Ringlings, whipped up interest in Burmese women he dubbed 'Giraffe-necked' because of the many inches of stiff brass necklaces piled on their necks. Uncertain

'Little Krao', the bearded lady of P. T. Barnum's circus, *c.* 1883.

whether viewers would think their necks long enough to count as 'freak', Butler bought a wooden spool, wrapped it with wire and superimposed its photograph on a publicity shot of the women. An accompanying press release stated, 'The Burmese national sport is necking', and claimed that the neck rings served to keep the women's lovers from choking them because of their promiscuity. Butler invented other enticing details, as well: the women were 'kidnappers, savage stealers of men'; they worshipped spirits; they foretold the future by looking at chicken bones; they were dangerous, wild aborigines.

Although some viewers noticed that the women's necks were not so long as publicity posters advertised, and the women themselves seemed notably serene, on the whole they saw what Butler told them to see. After being exhibited for two seasons, the women returned to Burma, having earned enough money to achieve their goal of building a small mission.[22]

Butler had similar success with a group from French Equatorial Africa whose custom it was to insert discs to extend their lower lips. Persuaded to come to America with promises of salt and jewellery, five men and eight women arrived in New York in April 1930 and went directly to Madison Square Garden. Butler named them Ubangis and promoted them as 'The World's Most Weird Living Human! – New to the Civilized World! . . . Monster-Mouthed Ubangi Savages with Mouths and Lips as Large as Those of Full-grown Crocodiles – from Africa's Darkest Depths!' This group stayed for two years, wresting themselves from the control of Eugene Bergonier, the French 'explorer' who had contracted with the Ringlings, and taking charge of their own earnings, with which, Butler learned, they returned to Africa and bought a cattle ranch. Their exhibition in the 1930s brought in the largest audiences in Ringling history.[23]

Besides feeding curiosity about human diversity and propagating racism, anthropological exhibitions confirmed in white Americans their own national identity at a time when the country was growing and becoming increasingly urban. Away from rural towns and villages, communities felt fragmented and individuals isolated. What historian David Gerber called 'a sundering polity' felt bonded, then, by 'the collective act of looking'.[24]

Mirrors

The collective act of looking was also a singular act of making a connection to individuals that seemed, to some viewers, to speak to their own identity in unexpected ways. It is notable that articles about freaks published early in the twentieth century emphasize the normality of their lives off stage. They lived in bourgeois homes, decorated their parlours with plants and pillows, cooked and cared for their spouses and shared the same hopes and fears as those in their audience. The *New Yorker* profile of Lady Olga, for example, revealed her to be 'a violently opinionated Republican' and 'a veteran reader of Hearst newspapers', whose claims, she said, she believed fully. She was a devoted care-taker of her cat, Edelweiss, which she indulged to such an extent that he weighed 16 pounds. She indulged her husband, too, by trying out new recipes that she clipped from newspapers. She was suspicious of corporations, unions and doctors, and she admitted a phobia about New York water; sure it contained some lethal acid, she boiled her drinking water for fifteen minutes. She considered herself an actor – like Ethel Merman, Lynn Fontanne or Vera Zorina, whose plays were advertised in the same issue as her profile – and she was proud of her performance in the circus. 'If the truth was known,' she said, 'we're all freaks together.'

Because freak shows emphasized the health and often surprising abilities of the performers, they conveyed a message of triumph over adversity. Armless or legless individuals performed as acrobats; con-joined twins were aerialists. As a child, 'Otis, the Frog Boy', a dwarf with limited use of his limbs, hopped around the ring; when he grew into adulthood, he was billed as 'The Human Cigarette Factory' and rolled and lit a cigarette using only his mouth. In daily life, these perform-ers were as successful as those who paid to gape at them. Midgets, dwarves, giants, fat men and women, bearded women and hairy men: they married, had children, established stereotypical stable homes. And they were famous besides. At the same time, then, that freak shows pro-moted a shared definition of 'normal', they undermined the idea that physical 'abnormality' meant social, political or economic failure; instead the shows consoled viewers with a broad conception of what 'survival of the fittest' could mean. They celebrated physical difference.

An article in *The Nation* published in 1931 called the freak show 'the boldest, the crudest, the most canny form of showmanship'. After all, the writer asserted,

> We are all cripples of a sort. Each carries about with him
> the knowledge of some defect. One is too plump, another is
> not beautiful enough, one is too tall, another too short. The

ugliest man in the world, the fattest woman, the bearded lady, the giant, the pygmy – these extremes induce a sense of normality beyond words soothing to the human spirit.[25]

The essayist Edward Hoagland, looking back on the golden age of the circus, recalled that

> the sideshow used to be called 'The Ten-in-One' because it had 'Ten Different Freaks Under One Tent for Only One Dollar! Can you beat that, folks?' as the barkers yelled. Only, I suppose, by looking inside oneself. People too fat or too small, too thin or too tall, remind us of a certain unwieldy, weird, but shrinking-violet personage whom we know all too well – as does the Knife-thrower, the Escape Artist or Contortionist, the Tattooed or Albino Lady, hefting a boa constrictor, perhaps, and the knuckle-walking Wild Man, bearded all over, or the Living Skeleton, and the kinky but outwardly clean-cut gentleman who is wed to the swords and fireballs that he swallows a dozen times a day for our entertainment. Why is it entertainment, if we're not gawking at a caricature of ourselves?[26]

Painters and sculptors rarely took freaks as their subjects, but photographers often documented human anomalies. Mathew Brady, photographer of Civil War carnage, had his studio across the street from Barnum's American Museum, well located so that he could serve as photographer for freaks' *cartes de visite*. Edward J. Kelty took an annual portrait of each year's 'Congress of Freaks' in the Ringling Brothers Barnum & Bailey Circus. His photograph of the season of 1929 inspired Donald Platt to consider, in a poem, the difference between freaks and their viewers: himself, for example, or his 'senile / demented father', or his mother, her back deformed from scoliosis, or his brother with Down syndrome – 'his chromosomes / a tongue twister God the stutterer couldn't get right'. His brother, Platt thinks, 'is a member / in good standing / of this congress of freaks. But aren't we all?'[27]

If freak shows, during America's 'swift and chaotic modernization', once aimed to convince viewers that they were, as Rosemarie Garland Thomson argues, 'bound together by their purchased assurance that they are not freaks', surely they inspired, as well, a desire 'in some sense to be extraordinary marvels instead of mundane, even banal, democrats in a confusing cultural moment'.[28] Admired, special, fantastic: for many viewers, the freak represented as liberating an image as the most transcendent aerialist.

TEN

TRANSFORM= ATIONS

A circus is rooted in rootlessness; it's part of the romance, part
of the mystery . . . The merry band of gypsies; the special
brotherhood of necromancers; world travelers; children of the
wind. The circus is mobile, all energy and flash and laughs and
see ya next year . . . People, after all, don't join the circus to
stay home; people join the circus to run away.

Terry Lorant and Jon Carroll

Shana Carroll, a founder of Les 7 Doigts de la Main Circus, sat on
a leafy terrace in her hometown of Berkeley, California, talking
about her transition from trapeze artist with the Pickle Family Circus
and the Cirque du Soleil to directorship of the small Canadian group
about to open on the University of California campus in the spring
of 2013. Like modern dance, she said, the circus has developed in a
multiplicity of directions, incorporating mime, dance, aerial and
acrobatic acts, music, clowning and satire. The circus as sensational
communal spectacle still exists as the gigantic multimedia Cirque
du Soleil, ubiquitous in Las Vegas, Nevada; but hundreds of small
circuses have reinvented the genre, some creating a magical, dream-
like space of imaginative transformations, others redefining the circus
as transgressive and dangerous.

Les 7 Doigts was founded in Montreal in 2002, partly in reaction
to the huge Cirque du Soleil, which also has Canadian roots. Its seven
founders were its original performers: dancers, acrobats, aerialists,
musicians and jugglers, some of whom trained at the National Circus
School in Montreal, others at France's famous circus schools: the École

Les 7 Doigts de la
Main.

Nationale de Cirque de Châtellerault, the École de Cirque Balthazar in Montpellier, or the École Nationale des Arts du Cirque de Rosny-sous-Bois. Gypsy Snider was born into a circus family, in Snider's case the Pickle Family Circus of San Francisco. Isabelle Chassé saw an advertisement for a circus school in a Montreal newspaper when she was eleven and persuaded her mother, a teacher, to allow her to take classes in juggling, tightrope walking and unicycling. Then a Chinese contortionist taught a class, and the young Isabelle was hooked. Starting relatively late for a contortionist did not hold her back, and in two years she was so adept that the Cirque du Soleil signed her up. She performed as an aerial contortionist with that company for more than a decade.

If Chassé knew as a child that she wanted to be a circus performer, Sébastien Soldevila and Patrick Léonard had far different goals in mind. After becoming a Canadian roller-skating champion, Léonard went on to study chemistry, and Soldevila was studying biochemistry with the goal of becoming a doctor when both began performing as acrobats and balancers. The physicality of their acts was exhilarating; the spotlight, alluring. Les 7 Doigts' founders, now involved in choreographing new works, directing and producing, bring new circus talent to their shows, most of whom began with gymnastic or dance training as children.

Les 7 Doigts' recent show, *Psy*, is typical of the company's themes. Set partly in a psychiatrist's office, partly in dream scenarios, partly in public spaces such as a park, a bar and a city street, the show's theme is consciousness, the subconscious and various mental aberrations. Although its themes are sophisticated, Les 7 Doigts aims its shows at both children and adults. Carroll, who trained and worked in France, commented that European circuses do not see children as their only audience, nor does Les 7 Doigts.[1] Aerialist Tino Wallenda agrees: 'The trouble with the circus in America,' he told an interviewer, 'is the idea that it's supposed to be for children, but it's not. The circus has never been strictly for children.'[2] Children who come to *Psy* may not understand allusions to the workings of the mind, but can respond to its quirky inventiveness and the performers' feats; adults appreciate the complexity of such characters as Michel, who hears voices; Danny the manic; Jacques the hypochondriac; and Dexter, with multiple personality disorder.

Les 7 Doigts focuses on the mind and the heart: how people behave when facing disaster, experiencing grief, aspiring for success or feeling thwarted in love. The troupe may consider social and political issues, but its underlying themes are humanistic and its mood poetic. Other circuses, though, take satire as their goal, seeing themselves in the tradition of court jesters who made fun of the nobility, *commèdia dell'arte* clowns who caricatured human foibles, and a predecessor like Dan Rice who directed his clown banter at the pretences of his contemporaries. In the 1970s, some new circuses made civic issues their major themes and, at a time of divisive social unrest, aimed to represent an exemplary kind of community. Foremost among them was the Pickle Family Circus.

Larry Pisoni worked as stage manager at the psychedelic nightclub Electric Circus in New York City before he moved to San Francisco in 1970 with the aim of starting his own circus. For a few years, he performed with the San Francisco Mime Troupe, where he met Peggy Snider and her six-month-old daughter Gypsy. For reasons no one can recall, Pisoni and Snider named their troupe the Pickle Family Circus. Within a year, several new members joined them: musicians Michael Margulis and Randy Craig, clowns Geoff Hoyle and Bill Irwin – the first clown to win a MacArthur Fellowship – Terry Lorant, Zoe Leader, Don McMillan and Michael Nolan. Everyone had multiple jobs, everyone pitched in and, in the zeitgeist of the 1970s, they hoped to run their circus democratically, cooperatively, as a non-profit organization. They succeeded in not making profits: at one point, a member recalled ruefully, each performer – working more than 40 hours a week – earned $1.25 a show. But their goal of democratic, non-hierarchical governance proved harder to attain. Anarchy reigned at meetings, even though Pickle performers believed that they shared ideals and a desire to nurture one another. 'I believe everybody is seeking community,' Michael Margulis remarked. 'The Circus is its own community; if you're looking for that, it's right here.'[3]

'What is most important to remember is that we are a chosen family,' Peggy Snider added.

We chose each other, and we choose to be a family . . . But
what happens, I think, is that the idea of family extends even
beyond our large group of Pickles past and present. It reaches
out and embraces the audience, and the sponsors, and the
towns that we visit . . . We're like the crazy uncle that comes
to visit once a year, and tells jokes and sings songs and does
tricks. And you're always sorry when he's gone.[4]

Snider and Pisani's son Lorenzo tells a different story about the circus
family in which he grew up: trained – mercilessly, he recalled – to
practise pratfalls over and over again, asked by his parents to sign a
contract at the age of six, and touring with his father as a miniature
Pickle clown. Now grown, he has created a one-man autobiographical
show that he has titled 'Humor Abuse'.

Nevertheless, despite some personal tensions, the Pickle circus
tried to be true to its ethical and philosophical beliefs. Juggler and
clown Judy Finelli compared the Pickles to Circus Oz, an Australian
group begun around the same time:

Circus Oz comes right out and says, 'We're the non-sexist,
non-racist, anti-nuke Circus Oz.' I can't see the PFC doing that.
But simply ignoring what's going on isn't it either. Something
should creep in. We just have to do our best to speed along
the next pendulum swing back to a more humane state in
the world, whatever it was that was cooking during the Sixties.
If we keep slugging in there, maybe it'll come a couple of
days sooner.[5]

Circus Oz sprang from a similar impetus in the late 1970s, and,
as Finelli noted, made overt their message of social change. Bringing
together two established small circuses, Soapbox and New Circus,
Circus Oz aimed to incorporate rock'n'roll, theatre and satire into
its new show. Its founders had a clear political bent, insisting that
the circus have no animals and that it promote social justice and human
rights, including the rights of indigenous Australians. The exuberant,
irreverent troupe describes itself as anarchic and subversive.

Performing for the first time in Melbourne, Australia in 1978, Circus Oz remains a small group of about a dozen performers who, like the Pickle Family troupe, perform multiple tasks. Of the current company, for example, Mel Fyfe is a dancer, acrobat and tour manager; others are musicians and aerialists, jugglers and clowns. Besides performing at theatrical venues throughout the world, they have mounted a show at a refugee camp and have performed for indigenous Australian communities. An outgrowth of their community work is Circus Active, which offers public classes in circus arts; Blakrobatics, aimed at attracting Australian Aboriginals as trainees and guest artists; and Melba Spiegeltent, which offers a variation of vaudeville.

Not all new wave circuses offer humour as gentle and playful as the Pickles and Circus Oz. In 1986, Pierrot Bidon, after ten years as a tightrope walker, decided to create a circus that reflected what he perceived as the violence and dehumanization of the industrialized world. The result was Circus Archaos, whose noisy, strident and disturbing productions incorporated such props as acetylene torches and chainsaws, and such acts as stabbing and decapitation. Clowns battered one another with hammers, wearing costumes that included corrugated iron; performers enacted revolting assaults on one another, more in keeping with slasher movies than the circus arena. Some critics would not call Archaos a circus at all, but instead terrifying street theatre. Risk-taking has always been part of the allure of circus acts, but Archaos, as Circus Oz's Mike Finch put it, invented stark new images for danger.[6] If clergy and educators condemned nineteenth-century circuses as sites of wickedness and temptation, Circus Archaos intensified that position of marginalization: it flaunted itself as deviant.

Apple and sun

Quite different from Archaos, and also from social activist circuses like the Pickle Family, were circuses aiming to revive the intimacy of European one-ring troupes. Among the small circuses begun as protests against the commercialization of the Ringlings, the Big Apple Circus, founded by Paul Binder, has been undeniably successful.

Growing up in New York City, Binder was an enthusiastic fan of Broadway musicals; at Dartmouth, where he studied European cultural history, he brought that enthusiasm to the stage, acting in some campus productions. Hoping to make a career in show business, he began a graduate programme in theatrical direction, but dropped out and later earned an MBA from Columbia. For a while, no job felt like a good fit: first, he worked as a stage manager for a Boston public television station, then as a booking agent for producer and television host Merv Griffin. In 1970, he decided to reinvent himself as a performer and headed to San Francisco, with the goal of joining the already famous San Francisco Mime Troupe. His audition – a comedy routine that he had learned by watching Danny Kaye – won him a place, and Binder spent three years with the troupe until he left to join a colleague, Michael Christiansen, with whom he travelled through Europe as street performers. 'It was a gypsy life filled with romance and adventure,' Christiansen told circus historian Ernest Albrecht; sometimes their earnings came only from a passed hat; but one day they appeared on a television show and came to the attention of Annie Fratellini, descendent of the famous Fratellini clown family and herself a founder of the first French circus school.[7] Impressed by their act, she invited them to join the Nouveau Cirque. That experience, along with his observations and investigations of such famous European circuses as France's Cirque Gruss, Switzerland's Circus Knie and Germany's Circus Schumann, inspired his dream of establishing his own troupe: a one-ring American circus focused on artistry and, as he put it, 'poetic vision'.

In 1977 Binder returned to New York intent on making his dream a reality; with Michael Christiansen in charge of clowns, the Big Apple Circus was born. 'Circus, when done right,' said Binder,

> has the capacity, in its magic circle, to create a briefly intensified collective 'life'. Its roots are deep in the community rituals that evolved from spontaneous popular street fairs and marketplace festivals of the earliest known cultures . . . The circus is the single theatrical force that most closely keeps faith with this original exuberant ritual: music, clowning, processions, animals,

sexuality, joy, and most importantly, personal triumph over life's obstacles.[8]

Dosov Troupe at the Big Apple Circus.

Binder's philosophy was shared, at its conception, by the now notorious and gargantuan Cirque du Soleil. In the early 1980s Guy Laliberté was a Canadian street performer when he decided to start a circus. With his friend Guy Caron, who had trained at the Hungarian State Circus School, Laliberté went to Europe to observe, as Binder had done, the famous Cirque Gruss and Circus Knie. They learned how to create a sense of ensemble, how to stage a programme and how to handle finances, and after a year, the pair returned to Quebec ready to recruit talent: acrobats and jugglers, aerialists and clowns – but no animal acts. Animals, they decided, were too expensive. Like the Big Apple and Pickle Family circuses, they hoped to revive the intimacy of the one-ring circus, and in its early days performers took on multiple roles. By 1984 the team had put together enough backing – from private investors and Canadian grants – to mount their first show in Canada, and in 1987 the Cirque du Soleil – so named because Laliberté loved sunshine – opened in Los Angeles. They were an instant hit, and in 1988 they debuted in New York.

From its beginnings, the Cirque du Soleil emphasized its theatricality: each show was built not around the skills of different performers, but around a story line, much like a story ballet, and enhanced by original musical scores played on synthesizers. Their fresh approach and talent earned them acclaim. The Cirque, critics wrote, was an antidote to overblown, 'computerized, over-amplified' Broadway musicals. Critic Mel Gussow called the show a 'cohesive theater piece – conceptual art in perpetual motion'. He singled out the aerialists especially for effusive praise, but remarked that the clowns seemed weak.[9] Circus performances designed around a theme were not new – Barnum had done that, after all – but Laliberté envisioned not one theme, but continually changing themes as the circus moved from one destination to the next. Instead of travelling with a stable troupe, each new story line required new acts. Acts that did not fit were

Equestrian trainer Jenny Vidbel and her charges, Big Apple Circus.

John Kennedy Kane,
Ringmaster at the
Big Apple Circus.

simply dropped. Unhappy with Laliberté's artistic decisions, especially because of their impact on performers, Caron left the show in 1988.

As the Cirque evolved into a big, and then bigger, business, its aesthetics changed to focus on spectacle rather than stars. It serves the Cirque's business model to deliberately efface personalities. Instead of promoting individual performers, the Cirque hides all of them under heavy make-up so that in case of injury one troupe can substitute for another. Rather than foster a sense of community, an important lesson learned from Cirque Gruss, the Cirque du Soleil instead attracts an international roster of performers who socialize mostly with members in their own act. Offstage, there is rarely the camaraderie that defines other circuses. Circus Oz's Mike Finch remembers an after-show party at which a troupe of amazing Russian acrobats came in, got no recognition or acclaim from their peers and were left drinking

Billy Smart's Circus,
1950s.

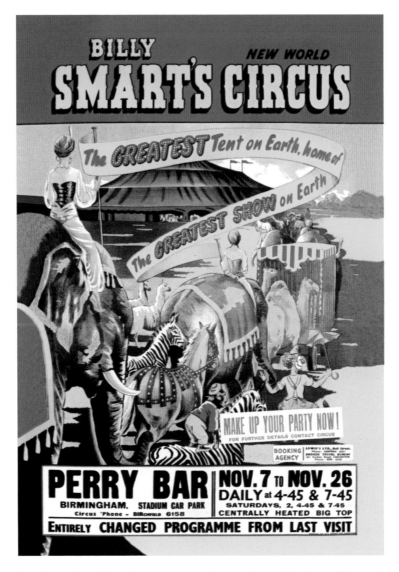

by themselves. The Cirque seems to have taken a hint from Gussow's
criticism, though, and put effort – and a competitive pay scale – into
attracting top clowns.

Unlike the Big Apple Circus, which performs under a tent, the
Cirque – which began as a tent show – evolved into a theatre production, set up on a stage, with the audience – primarily adults – seated

in front, usually in tiers. Even if they could recognize one performer or another, they would need binoculars to identify them. The Cirque soon rejected its 'less is more' attitude and turned the enterprise into extravaganzas that have performed in about 200 cities. They dominate the entertainment scene in Las Vegas with different theme shows in different venues, and dwarf any over-amplified Broadway production. Special effects animate all the productions: in *O*, for example, the stage is flooded with water for startling aquatics; acts follow one another in flawless precision; the lighting is dazzling; the music, amplified. The Cirque du Soleil is very, very loud.

Cities attract big circuses, but in rural areas, small tent shows still open on fairgrounds and mall parking lots, with horses, clowns and maybe a lion or two for entertainment. In the 1970s one such show was Jerry Booker's Royal Horse Fair. Booker got his first taste of circus life when he accompanied his father, a career officer, who had been sent by the army to investigate the logistics used by the Ringlings in transporting their huge cast of people and animals. Booker fell in love with the circus, and after a number of other career moves – including as a male model for the Marlboro Man ads – he decided to form his own troupe. Under a striped red and white tent, Booker snapped his whip as ringmaster in what he called, nostalgically, J. P. Booker's Early American Circus. His friendship with animal trainer Clyde Beatty led to his incorporating a lion, leopard and peacocks into the show, but equestrian acts were the main attraction, and the circus evolved into the Royal Horse Fair. His son Randall, like Lorenzo Pisoni, performed, too, with decidedly more pleasure: the circus, he said, offered a parallel existence for him. Most of the year, he was a regular high-school student; when the circus travelled, he became a rider and acrobat, sharing in his father's childlike joy in being part of the circus world. At home, he was surrounded by the circus: his father's collection of memorabilia, photographs and Booker's drawings and paintings of circus scenes. Like nineteenth-century American circuses, Booker's was a family affair.

Also a family affair was Britain's Billy Smart's New World Circus, which first performed in April 1946 and quickly became one of the most famous troupes in the country. Initially, Smart's eleven children filled out the ranks of performers, from clowns to trapeze artists; twelve-year-old Billy Smart Jr was an assistant ringmaster. Soon the circus, gaining in popularity, grew to expand into ever bigger tents; by 1958, its billowing white big top seated 6,000. Scores of horses pranced around its huge hippodrome, and dozens of elephants took centre stage. Besides touring, Smart took advantage of the new medium of television: for nearly three decades, full circus shows and individual acts were featured throughout the year, with a special Christmas extravaganza. Smart died in 1966, and a few years later the circus stopped touring; however, by 1993 his grandchildren had revived the troupe as a smaller, one-ring production. For generations of British families, Smart's defined the circus experience.

Vagabond angels

At the same time that the Pickle Family, Big Apple and Cirque du Soleil were forming in America, the *cirques intimes* of nineteenth-century France was revived as well, partly in reaction to failed imitations of huge American circuses and partly as a creative outlet for actors, mimes, dancers and artists. Some began as street performances, recalling saltimbanques and other nomadic troupes. In 1973, Christian Taguet formed the Cirque Baroque, featuring mostly clowns and acrobats, moving to a tent only in 1979. Jean-Luc Courcoult gathered 'inventors, stuntmen, poets and scrap-dealers' as Royal-de-luxe. Starting out in Aix-en-Provence, the group first performed in streets and public spaces. They aimed to combine 'urban culture, objects from modern life, and a taste for the unorthodox' with the spirit of the circus, superficially like Circus Archaos, but in fact playful and joyous. Cirque Plume, founded in 1984 by nine performers and directed by Bernard Kudlak, underscored their mission to 'bring together the spirit of celebration, of politics, dreams, vagabond angels, journeys, poetry, music, and the human body, all in a non-vibrant and popular desire for fraternity'. The Plume's first efforts were 'fragile, amateurish, and innocent', but by 1988, they had honed their acts into a slick programme and moved from the streets into a big tent.[10] They had, in a sense, come of age.

Aerial act in the
Cirque Plume
30th anniversary
spectacle, 2013.

Acrobat in the
Cirque Plume,
2013.

Although all of these new troupes recognized, and some even honoured, the circus tradition, they saw themselves as creating a new aesthetic for the late twentieth century, focused on visual images and grounded in political and social awareness. One group, though, rejected an association with circus history – although it seems firmly connected to Astley's original offerings and the popular hippodramas of the past. Clément Marty, growing up in Paris, was fascinated with horses and hoped to become a jockey. At the age of eighteen, though, his dreams took a different turn: christening himself Bartabas, he assembled a travelling circus of horses, dogs, falcons, rats and humans and began performing around France. By 1984 he had decided to focus solely on horses and founded the equestrian circus Zingaro. An expert trainer and rider, he designs shows around whatever his horses – 45 of them, with 50 trainers – can do. Although admired for his equestrian skill, he claims that the circuses of the past made a spectacle of technique; he, on the other hand, is interested in emotion. Zingaro, he insists, is 'a little theater, a little music, a little dance, and not at all circus.'[11] Although Zingaro's acts comprise acrobats leaping from horses, along with the antics of clowns, Bartabas has designed shimmering, ephemeral visual images that distinguish his company from other troupes – but not from Le Cirque Imaginaire.

The Cirque Plume troupe.

Clown,
Cirque Plume.

A Zingaro show, 2012.

Bartabas' equestrian show Zingaro, 2012.

In the early 1970s Jean-Baptiste Thiérrée saw a magazine article about Charlie Chaplin's eighteen-year-old daughter Victoria. At the time, Chaplin was considering a new movie project, *The Freak*, about a young girl who awakens to find that she is sprouting wings. He decided that his graceful daughter Victoria would star. The movie, which would have involved many actors flying through the air, seemed a logistical nightmare, and his wife, Oona, secretly quashed the project, fearing the strain would take a toll on her husband's health. Nevertheless, he continued to work on the screenplay, while Victoria, living at home with her family in Lausanne, studied ballet. But the article revealed that she had her own dreams: she wanted to become a circus

Jean-Baptiste Thierée,
Cirque Invisible,
2013.

Victoria Chaplin,
Cirque Invisible,
2013.

Thierée and Chaplin, 2013.

clown. Thiérrée, an actor and cabaret performer, had an idea for a new kind of circus, and he wrote to her inviting her to join him. Their first meeting led to many others, which they kept secret from Chaplin. When he learned that they had eloped, he was, as Victoria knew he would be, furious.

The pair first created Le Cirque Bonjour, which performed in France in 1971 and at Les Halles a few years later, with a cast of about 30. Over the next twelve years, they pared their company down, first to two – Victoria and Jean-Baptiste – and finally to four, with the add-ition of their son James and daughter Aurelia. 'Serene Simplicity and Fleeting Magic of the Small Circus' was the headline for *New York Times* critic Jennifer Dunning's review of Le Cirque Imaginaire when it opened in New York in 1986. Victoria took on the roles of all the aerialists, tightrope walkers and acrobats; she walked on stilts, blew a tin horn and never uttered a word. Dressed in a costume studded with bells and beads, 'she enfolds herself and unfolds intricate designs', wrote Mel Gussow; 'she becomes animated origami.'[12] Jean-Baptiste represented all the clowns: not only all the clowns in any single circus, but all clowns throughout history. His inspirations, he said, were Grimaldi and Grock. 'Minimal but never minimalist', Dunning wrote, Le Cirque Imaginaire took its place 'on the periphery of the new-vaudevillian movement'. Simplicity and distillation, Chaplin and Thiérré believed, were essential to reinvigorate the new circus. 'The magic of circus performing actually is that it's there and then it's gone,' Le Cirque's artistic advisor David Gothard told Dunning. 'And I think that's where the real delight comes from. Something happens. There is laughter. It's gone . . . And the performer only exists so long as that fleeting moment of magic is being created.'[13]

The circus may respond to changing social pressures, look back nostalgically to real or imagined innocence, incorporate slick technologies and turn the spotlight on performers so agile and daring that they take the breath away – but it has one constant. From the moment a contortionist bent backward to touch the ground with his head, from the moment a daredevil walked on a rope from one church steeple to another, from the moment a wandering family leapt and cavorted on a Paris street corner, the circus has celebrated the fleeting moment of magical spectacle. There is laughter, awe, desire, envy. And then, it's gone.

REFERENCES

INTRODUCTION

1 Hermine Demoriane, *The Tightrope Walker* (London, 1989), pp. 25–6.
2 Nathaniel Hawthorne, 4 September 1838, *Passages from the American Note-books* (Boston, MA, 1891), p. 192.
3 John Evelyn, quoted in Kenneth Richards and Laura Richards, *The Commedia dell'Arte* (Oxford, 1990), p. 23.
4 E. E. Cummings, 'The Adult, the Artist and the Circus', *E. E. Cummings: A Miscellany* (New York, 1958), p. 47.
5 George Speaight, *A History of the Circus* (London, 1980), p. 161.
6 George Van Hare, *Fifty Years of a Showman's Life* (London, 1888), p. 59.
7 Naomi Ritter, *Art as Spectacle: Images of the Entertainer since Romanticism* (Columbia, MO, 1989), pp. 3–4.
8 Ibid., p. 2.
9 Joanne Joys, *The Wild Animal Trainer in America* (Boulder, CO, 1983), p. 265.
10 Josephine DeMott Robinson, *The Circus Lady* (New York, 1980), pp. 2–3.
11 Kenneth Little, 'Talking Circus, not Culture: The Politics of Identity in European Circus Discourse', *Qualitative Inquiry*, I/3 (September 1995), p. 358, n. 3.
12 William Dean Howells, *A Boy's Town* (New York, 1890), p. 95.
13 *The Knickerbocker*, XIII/1 (January 1839), quoted in Matthew Wittmann, *Circus and the City: New York, 1793–2010* (New Haven, CT, 2012), p. 188.
14 Joys, *The Wild Animal Trainer*, p. 227.
15 E. B. White, 'The Ring of Time', *Points of My Compass* (New York, 1954), pp. 51–5.
16 Quoted in Ritter, *Art as Spectacle*, p. 314.

17 Edward Hoagland, 'Circus Music', *Sex and the River Styx* (White River Junction, VT, 2011), p. 84.

18 Ibid., p. 87.

19 American Sunday School Union, *The Circus* (Philadelphia, PA, 1846), pp. 11, 12.

20 American Sunday School Union, *Slim Jack* (Philadelphia, PA, 1847).

21 C. David Heymann, *A Woman Named Jackie* (New York, 1989), p. 30.

22 Robinson, *The Circus Lady*, p. 1.

ONE
TRICK RIDERS

1 Charles Montague, *Recollections of an Equestrian Manager* (London, 1881), p. 99.

2 H. Barton Baker, 'Philip Astley', *Belgravia* (June 1879), p. 473.

3 Handbill, London, 1786. Eighteenth Century Collections Online, Gale Research, document no. CW3305300803, www.gdc.gale.com.

4 Charles Dickens, 'Philip Astley', *All the Year Round* (27 January 1872), p. 206.

5 Ibid., p. 207.

6 'Dead Circuses and Vanished Playhouses', *Saturday Review* (15 July 1893), p. 67.

7 Dickens, 'Philip Astley', p. 210.

8 Quoted in James S. Moy, 'Entertainments at John B. Ricketts's Circus, 1793–1800', *Educational Theatre Journal*, XXX/2 (May 1978), p. 188.

9 Marius Kwint, 'The Legitimization of the Circus in Late Georgian England', *Past and Present*, 174 (2002), pp. 86, 88.

10 Ruth Manning-Sanders, *The English Circus* (London, 1952), p. 49.

11 *New York Daily Times* (16 May 1853), p. 4.

12 Nicola A. Haxell, '"Ces Dames du Cirque": A Taxonomy of Male Desire in Nineteenth-century French Literature and Art', *Modern Language Notes*, XXV/4 (2000), p. 795.

13 Shauna Vey, 'The Master and the Mademoiselle', *Theatre History Studies*, XXVII (2007), pp. 39–59.

14 Thomas Frost, *Circus Life and Circus Celebrities* (London, 1881), p. 126.

15 Marsden Hartley, *Adventures in the Arts* (New York, 1921), pp. 177–9.

16 Nellie Revell, *Spangles* (New York, 1926).

17 Baker, 'Philip Astley', p. 471.

TWO
CIRQUES INTIMES

1 Anne Roquebert, 'Last Work', in *Toulouse Lautrec*, ed. Richard Thomson et al. (New Haven, CT, 1991), p. 486.
2 Julia Frey, *Toulouse-Lautrec: A Life* (New York, 1994), p. 471.
3 Quoted in Corinne Bellow, ed., *Lautrec by Lautrec* (New York, 1964), p. 205.
4 Henry Miller, *The Smile at the Foot of the Ladder* [1948] (New York, 1959), p. 48.
5 Phillip Dennis Cate, 'The Cult of the Circus', in *Pleasures of Paris: Daumier to Picasso*, ed. Barbara Stern Shapiro (Boston, 1991), p. 39.
6 Fernande Olivier, *Loving Picasso: The Private Journal of Fernande Olivier*, trans. Christine Baker and Michael Raeburn (New York, 2001), pp. 200–201.
7 Georges Brassai, *Picasso and Company*, trans. Francis Price (New York, 1966), p. 20.
8 Wallace Fowlie, *Clowns and Angels* (New York, 1973), pp. 129, 155.
9 Antony Hippisley Coxe, *A Seat at the Circus* [1951] (Hamden, CT, 1980), p. 115.
10 'Two Amateur Circuses', *New York Times* (5 May 1889), p. 16.
11 'Viaud Joins the Immortals', *New York Times* (22 May 1891), p. 1.
12 George Ruskin Phoebus, 'Physical Culture and Mental Culture', *Physical Culture*, III/6 (September 1900), p. 273.
13 'A Fashionable Circus', *Washington Post* (18 May 1889), p. 14.
14 Quoted in George Speaight, *A History of the Circus* (London, 1980), pp. 161–2.
15 Quoted in James J. Sweeney, *Alexander Calder* (New York, 1951), p. 26.
16 L. Joy Sperling, 'Calder in Paris: The Circus and Surrealism', *Archives of American Art Journal*, XXVIII/2 (1988), pp. 4, 7.
17 Cleve Gray, 'Calder's Circus', *Art in America*, 52 (October 1964), p. 24.

THREE
THE BIGGEST TENTS

1 Quoted in Robert Sherwood, *Here We Are Again: Recollections of an Old Circus Clown* (Indianapolis, IN, 1926), p. 126.
2 Booth Tarkington, *The Gentleman from Indiana* (New York, 1899), pp. 122, 126.
3 Earl Benson, 'The Circus', *New Yorker* (3 November 1951), p. 125.
4 Letter to William Winter, 12 October 1872, in *Selected Letters of P. T. Barnum*, ed. A. H. Saxon (New York, 1983), p. 173.

5 Letter to Schuyler Colfax, 3 August 1878, ibid., p. 208.

6 Letter, 18 November 1882, ibid., p. 231.

7 Letter to Mark Twain, 19 January 1875, ibid., pp. 189–90.

8 Letters to James Bailey, 12 October 1885; 2 April 1891, ibid., p. 271, p. 334.

9 *The Times*, London (12 November 1889), p. 7.

10 Josephine Robinson, *The Circus Lady* (New York, 1980), pp. 153, 157.

11 Thomas Frost, *Circus Life and Circus Celebrities* (London, 1881), p. 238.

12 *New York Times* (12 March 1882), p. 14.

13 John Culhane, *The American Circus* (New York, 1990), p. 241.

14 Donna Gustafson, ed., *Images from the World Between* (Cambridge, MA, 2007), p. 80, n. 22.

15 Jerry Apps, *Ringlingville USA* (Madison, WI, 2005), p. 79.

16 Mark St Leon, *The Wizard of the Wire: The Story of Con Colleano* (Canberra, 1993), p. 129.

17 Emmett Kelly, *Clown* (Englewood Cliffs, NJ, 1954), p. 175.

18 Henry Ringling North and Alden Hatch, *The Circus Kings* (Garden City, NY, 1960), pp. 256–8.

19 'The Circus has Reached its Limit', *Washington Post* (17 July 1904), p. A8.

20 North and Hatch, *The Circus Kings*, pp. 256–8.

21 '14,212 Patrons Roar Welcome as the Circus Opens in Garden', *New York Times* (10 April 1943), p. 19.

22 Ibid.

23 Meyer Berger, '139 Lives Lost in Circus Fire at Hartford', *New York Times* (7 July 1944), pp. 1, 11.

24 Duncan Wall, *The Ordinary Acrobat* (New York, 2013), p. 229.

25 'The Talk of the Town', *New Yorker* (6 May 1950).

26 St Leon, *The Wizard of the Wire*, p. 140.

FOUR

CAVALCADES

1 Robert Sherwood, *Here We Are Again: Recollections of an Old Circus Clown* (Indianapolis, IN, 1926), p. 139.

2 Emmett Kelly, *Clown* (Englewood Cliffs, NJ, 1954), p. 62.

3 Booth Tarkington, *The Gentleman from Indiana* (New York, 1899), pp. 100–101.

4 William Saroyan, 'The Circus', in *My Name is Aram* (New York, 1940), p. 182.

5 Charles Murray, 'In Advance of the Circus', *McClure's Magazine* (August 1894), p. 252.

6 Ibid., p. 253.

7 Antony Hippisley Coxe, *A Seat at the Circus* (Hamden, CT, 1980), p. 37.

8 'The Circus in America', *New York Times* (12 March 1882), p. 14.

9 Charles W. Montague, *Recollections of an Equestrian Manager* (London, 1881), p. 29.

10 Saroyan, 'The Circus', p. 182.

11 Thomas Wolfe, 'Circus at Dawn', in *The Complete Short Stories of Thomas Wolfe*, ed. Francis E. Skipp (New York, 1987), pp. 202–4.

12 'American Circus', *Washington Post* (24 November 1907), p. A7.

13 Tarkington, *The Gentleman from Indiana*, p. 108.

14 Kelly, *Clown*, pp. 23–4.

15 Eudora Welty, *Stories, Essays and Memoir*, selected by Richard Ford and Michael Kreyling (New York, 1998), pp. 929–30.

16 Letter from Eudora Welty to William Maxwell, 24 April 1978, in *'What There Is To Say We Have Said': The Correspondence of Eudora Welty and William Maxwell*, ed. Suzanne Marrs (Boston, 2011), pp. 341–2.

17 Eudora Welty, 'Acrobats in a Park', *South Carolina Review*, XI/1 (1978), pp. 26–33.

18 George Garrett, 'An Evening Performance', in *The Norton Anthology of Short Fiction*, ed. R. V. Cassill, 5th edn (New York, 1955), p. 676.

19 Ibid., p. 678.

20 Ibid., p. 674.

21 'Barnum's Invading Hosts', *New York Times* (25 March 1883), p. 2.

22 'The Circus is Coming to Town', *New York Times* (29 March 1896), p. 8.

23 Barnum quoted in Thomas Frost, *Circus Life and Circus Celebrities* (London, 1881), p. 232.

24 'Big Circuses' Pageant', *New York Times* (3 April 1900), p. 10.

25 'The Circus is Coming', *Washington Post* (25 March 1910), p. 11.

26 Henry Ringling North and Alden Hatch, *The Circus Kings* (Garden City, NY, 1960), p. 235.

27 Irving Spiegel, 'Cirucs Opens to Cheers of 14,000 with Array of Nerve-tingling Acts', *New York Times* (10 April 1947), p. 27.

28 Quoted in Mildred Sandison Fenner and Wolcott Fenner, eds, *The Circus: Lore and Legend* (Englewood Cliffs, NJ, 1970), p. 208.

FIVE
WITHOUT A NET

1 *The Times*, London (18 July 1859), p. 12.
2 'An Exciting Scene', *New York Times* (4 July 1859), p. 3.
3 Quoted in G. Linnaeus Banks, *Blondin: His Life and Performance* (London, 1862), p. 66.
4 Ibid., pp. 79, 83.
5 Ibid., p. 115.
6 Peta Tait, *Circus Bodies: Cultural Identity in Aerial Performance* (New York, 2005), p. 15.
7 'Marevelous Gymnastic Feats', *New York Times* (5 December 1859), p. 6.
8 Mark Cosdon, *The Hanlon Brothers: From Daredevil Acrobats to Spectacle Pantomime, 1833–1933* (Carbondale, IL, 2009), p. 83.
9 'Circus Opens Doors', *New York Times* (13 April 1927), p. 30.
10 Janice McCullagh, 'The Tightrope Walker: An Expressionist Image', *Art Bulletin*, LXVI/4 (December 1984), p. 635.
11 Ibid., p. 644.
12 Hermine Demoriane, *The Tightrope Walker* (London, 1989), p. 31.
13 'Why They Go to the Circus', *New York Times* (13 April 1900), p. 9.
14 Nicola A. Haxell, '"Ces Dames du Cirque": A Taxonomy of Male Desire in Nineteenth-century French Literature and Art', *Modern Language News*, CXV/4 (2000), p. 800.
15 Robert Lewis Taylor, *Center Ring: The People of the Circus* (New York, 1956), p. 225.
16 Henry Ringling North and Alden Hatch, *The Circus Kings* (Garden City, NY, 1960), p. 183.
17 John Culhane, *The American Circus* (New York, 1990), p. 187.
18 North and Hatch, *The Circus Kings*, p. 183.
19 Taylor, *Center Ring*, p. 221.
20 Calder quoted in Cleve Gray, 'Calder's Circus', *Art in America*, 52 (October 1964), p. 24.
21 Taylor, *Center Ring*, p. 220.
22 Ibid., p. 217.
23 Tiny Kline, *Circus Queen and Tinker Bell: The Memoir of Tiny Kline* (Champaign, IL, 2008), p. 244.
24 Taylor, *Center Ring*, pp. 247, 246.
25 Alfredo Codona, in Courtney Ryley Cooper, 'Split Seconds', *Saturday Evening Post* (6 December 1930), pp. 96–7.
26 George Beal, *Through the Back Door of the Circus* (Springfield, MA, 1938), p. 247.

27 Codona, 'Split Seconds', pp. 96–7.
28 'Circus Fall Fatal to Lilian Leitzel', *New York Times* (16 February 1931), p. 11.
29 'Circus Star Loses Life', *Los Angeles Times* (16 February 1931), p. 1.
30 *The Nation* (11 March 1931), p. 273.
31 Laura Knight, *Oil Paint and Grease Paint* (London, 1936), pp. 319–20.
32 Gregory Jaynes, 'Karl Wallenda, 73, Patriarch of the High-wire Troupe, Dies in 100-foot Fall', *New York Times* (23 March 1978), p. 23.
33 Charles Wilkins, *Circus at the Edge of the Earth: Travels with the Great Wallenda Circus* (Toronto, 1998), p. 97.
34 Gilbert Millstein, 'Why They Walk the High Wire', *New York Times* (18 February 1962), p. SM10.
35 Lawrence Van Gelder, 'Angel Wallenda, 28, A Flier Despite a Life of Obstacles', *New York Times* (4 May 1996), p. 50.
36 Wilkins, *Circus at the Edge of the Earth*, pp. 112, 248.
37 Justus Nieland, 'Marsden Hartley's Light Figures', *Modernism/Modernity*, XI/4 (2004), p. 632.
38 Sam Keen, *Learning to Fly: Trapeze* (New York, 1999), pp. 71, 148, 56.
39 Knight, *Oil Paint and Grease Paint*, p. 299.

SIX

BEASTS

1 'Tells of Taming Tigers', *Los Angeles Times* (16 September 1923), section 2, p. 12.
2 Mabel Stark with Gertrude Orr, *Hold That Tiger* (Caldwell, ID, 1938), p. 248.
3 John Stokes, '"Lion Griefs": The Wild Animal Act as Theatre', *New Theatre Quarterly*, XX/2 (May 2004), p. 144.
4 Stark, *Hold That Tiger*, pp. 14–15.
5 Katherine H. Adams and Michael L. Keene, *Women of the American Circus, 1880–1940* (Jefferson, NC, 2012), pp. 99, 165–6.
6 *New York Times* (13 May 1893), p. 8.
7 'Evolution of the Circus', *New York Times* (7 April 1895), p. 19.
8 Ruth Manning-Sanders, *The English Circus* (London, 1952), p. 215.
9 *The Times*, London (19 September 1838), p. 6.
10 Stephen Duffy, 'Landseer and the Lion-tamer', *British Art Journal*, III/3 (Autumn 2002), pp. 25, 26.
11 Hagenbeck quoted in Joanne Joys, *The Wild Animal Trainer in America* (Boulder, CO, 1983), p. 19.

12 *The Times*, London (16 May 1891), p. 12.
13 Bostock quoted in Stokes, '"Lion Griefs"', p. 148.
14 Robert Sherwood, *Here We Are Again: Recollections of an Old Circus Clown* (Indianapolis, 1926), p. 97.
15 Maurice Brown Kirby, 'The Gentle Art of Training Wild Beasts', *Everybody's Magazine*, 19 (October 1908), pp. 435, 440.
16 'Circus Man Explains Ban on Animal Acts', *Washington Post* (21 June 1925), p. 10.
17 *The Nation* (11 March 1931), p. 272.
18 Clyde Beatty and Edward Anthony, *Facing the Big Cats* (New York, 1964), p. 131.
19 'Thrills Galore', *New York Times* (9 April 1933), p. x3.
20 Beatty and Anthony, *Facing the Big Cats*, p. 16.
21 Ibid., p. 211.
22 Ibid., pp. 124–5.
23 Ibid., p. 298.
24 Ibid., p. 334.
25 Henry Ringling North and Alden Hatch, *The Circus Kings* (Garden City, NY, 1960), pp. 299, 300.
26 'Claire Heliot – Most Daring of Lion Tamers', *New York Times* (29 October 1905), p. SM1.
27 Ellen Velvin, *Behind the Scenes with Wild Animals* (New York, 1906), pp. 107, 74.
28 Lucia Zora, *Sawdust and Solitude* (Boston, 1928), pp. 7, 29, 80.
29 Stark with Orr, *Hold That Tiger*, pp. 148–9.
30 Ibid., p. 198.
31 Ibid., p. 212.
32 North and Hatch, *The Circus Kings*, p. 178.
33 Manning-Sanders, *The English Circus*, p. 226.
34 Alex Kerr, quoted in Stokes, '"Lion Griefs"', p. 150.
35 Yoram S. Carmeli, 'The Sight of Cruelty: The Case of Circus Animal Acts', *Visual Anthropology*, 10 (1997), p. 9.
36 Stokes, '"Lion Griefs"', p. 148.
37 Joanne Joys, *The Wild Animal Trainer in America* (Boulder, CO, 1983), pp. 44–5.
38 Ibid., p. 238.
39 Natacha Stewart, 'Animal Master', *New Yorker* (4 June 1979), pp. 29, 30.
40 E. E. Cummings, 'The Adult, the Artist and the Circus', in *E. E. Cummings: A Miscellany*, ed. George J. Firmage (New York, 1958), p. 46.

SEVEN
CLOWNS

1 Hughes Le Roux, *Acrobats and Mountebanks*, trans. A. P. Morton (London, 1890), p. 278.

2 Antony Hippisley Coxe, *A Seat at the Circus* (Hamden, CT, 1980), p. 213.

3 Ibid.

4 Richard Findlater, *Joe Grimaldi, His Life and Theatre* (Cambridge, 1978), p. 75.

5 Riot-Sarcey quoted in Duncan Wall, *The Ordinary Acrobat* (New York, 2013), p. 216.

6 Findlater, *Joe Grimaldi*, pp. 158, 160.

7 Baudelaire quoted in Jean Clair, ed., *The Great Parade: Portrait of the Artist as Clown* (New Haven, CT, 2004), p. 207.

8 Leroy C. Breunig, ed. *Apollinaire on Art*, trans. Susan Suleiman [1960] (Boston, MA, 2001), pp. 13, 16.

9 Rouault quoted in Clair, ed., *The Great Parade*, p. 105.

10 E. E. Cummings, 'The Adult, the Artist and the Circus', in *E. E. Cummings: A Miscellany*, ed. George J. Firmage (New York, 1958), p. 48.

11 Henry Miller, *The Smile at the Foot of the Ladder* [1948] (New York, 1959), pp. 44, 46.

12 Léger quoted in Clair, ed., *The Great Parade*, p. 119.

13 Miller, *The Smile at the Foot of the Ladder*, p. 47.

14 W. Kenneth Little, 'Pitu's Doubt: Entrée Clown Self-fashioning in the Circus Tradition, *Drama Review*, XXX/4 (Winter 1986), p. 52.

15 Rice quoted in John H. Towsen, *Clowns* (New York, 1976), p. 134.

16 John Culhane, *The American Circus* (New York, 1990), p. 197.

17 Adrien Wettach, *Grock, King of Clowns* (London, 1957), pp. 33, 74, 110.

18 Ibid., p. 52.

19 *New York Times* (30 December 1919), p. 18; (4 January 1920), p. XX2.

20 Emmett Kelly, *Clown* (Englewood Cliffs, NJ, 1954), pp. 125, 126.

21 Little, 'Pitu's Doubt', p. 55.

22 Lindsay Stephens, 'Rethinking the Political: Art, Work and the Body in the Contemporary Circus', PhD diss., University of Toronto, 2012.

23 Little, 'Pitu's Doubt', p. 55.

24 Eisenberg quoted in Annett Lust, *From the Greek Mimes to Marcel Marceau and Beyond* (Lanham, MD, 2000), p. 210.

25 Karal Ann Marling, 'Clowns with Bad Attitudes', *Images from the World Between: The Circus in 20th Century America* (Cambridge, MA, 2007), pp. 142, 143.

26 David Lewis Hammerstrom, *Inside the Changing Circus* (Duncan, OK, 2012), p. 140.
27 Ernest Albrecht, *The New American Circus* (Gainesville, FL, 1995), p. 165.
28 Lillian Ross, 'Popov', *New Yorker* (30 December 1972), p. 25.
29 Wall, *The Ordinary Acrobat*, p. 234.
30 Stephens, 'Rethinking the Political', p. 260.
31 Marcel Marceau quoted in Lust, *From the Greek Mimes to Marcel Marceau*, p. 93.
32 Towsen quoted ibid., pp. 204–5.
33 Mel Gussow, 'Miminalist Circus Loaded with Maximum Punch', *New York Times* (5 June 1988), p. H5.
34 Little, 'Pitu's Doubt', p. 55.
35 Wallace Fowlie, *Clowns and Angels* (New York, 1973), pp. 128–9.

EIGHT
FEATS

1 Dora Albert, 'Cannon into Ploughshares', *New Yorker* (20 April 1929), p. 15.
2 James Stevenson, 'Cannon Fodder', *New Yorker* (17 July 1965), p. 26.
3 Thomas Frost, *Circus Life and Circus Celebrities* (London, 1881), p. 189.
4 Wieland quoted in Peta Tait, *Circus Bodies: Cultural Identity in Aerial Performance* (London, 2005), p. 52.
5 Ibid., p. 50.
6 Edward Hoagland, 'Circus Music', in *Sex and the River Styx* (White River Junction, VT, 2011), p. 88.
7 Marilyn R. Brown, '"Miss LaLa's" Teeth: Reflections on Degas and Race', *Art Bulletin*, LXXXIX/4 (December 2007), p. 745, quotes article in *Era* (2 Feb 1879).
8 Antony Hippisley Coxe, *A Seat at the Circus* (Hamden, CT, 1980), pp. 62–3.
9 Duncan Wall, *The Ordinary Acrobat* (New York, 2013), p. 88.
10 Arthur Chandler, 'On the Symbolism of Juggling: The Moral and Aesthetic Implications of the Mastery of Falling Objects', *Journal of Popular Culture*, XXV/3 (Winter 1991), p. 116.
11 Gilligan quoted in Wall, *The Ordinary Acrobat*, pp. 68–9.
12 Pisoni quoted in Terry Lorant and Jon Carroll, *The Pickle Family Circus* (San Francisco, 1986), p. 75.
13 Chandler, 'On the Symbolism of Juggling', p. 121.

14 George Speaight, *A History of the Circus* (London, 1980), p. 63.

15 Thomas Dwight, 'The Anatomy of the Contortionist', *Scribner's Magazine* (April 1889), p. 493.

16 George Van Hare, *Fifty Years of a Showman's Life* (London, 1888), p. 79.

17 Frost, *Circus Life and Circus Celebrities*, p. 136.

18 Letter from Titus to Kattenberg, 17 April 1936, quoted in Karl Toepfer, 'Twisted Bodies: Aspects of Female Contortionism in the Letters of a Connoisseur', *Drama Review*, XLIII/1 (Spring 1999), pp. 118–19.

19 Letter from Titus to Kattenberg, 3 December 1936, Burns M. Kattenberg Collection, Harvard Theatre Collection, Houghton Library, Harvard University, MSThr648.

20 Letitia Preston Osborne, *Through Purple Glass* (Philadelphia, PA, 1946), p. 18; Jeanet Philips, 'Double-Jointed Romeo', *American Weekly* (12 April 1953), pp. 8–9.

21 Wall, *The Ordinary Acrobat*, pp. 213–14.

NINE

PRODIGIES

1 Various sources give different spellings for names in the girls' biography: their mother is sometimes referred to as Monemia, their owner as Jabez or Alexander McKay, and the girls themselves as Millie-Christina. I chose spellings as given in their memoir and circus publicity materials.

2 Millie-Christine, *History and Medical Description of the Two-Headed Girl* (Buffalo, NY, 1869), p. 6.

3 Ibid., pp. 11, 15, 17.

4 David A. Gerber, 'The "Careers" of People Exhibited in Freak Shows: The Problem of Volition and Validation', in *Freakery: Cultural Spectacle of the Extraordinary Body*, ed. Rosemary Garland Thomson (New York, 1996), pp. 40, 47.

5 'Wages of the Circus People', *Washington Post* (19 January 1908), p. M4.

6 Alva Johnston, 'Sideshow People – III', *New Yorker* (28 April 1934), p. 90.

7 Joseph Mitchell, 'Lady Olga', *New Yorker* (3 August 1940), pp. 23, 28.

8 'Royalties Go to the Circus', *New York Times* (27 February 1898), p. 7.

9 'Jo-Jo Before the Physicians', *New York Times* (27 March 1885), p. 8.

10 'The "Freaks" of the Circus', *Washington Post* (12 May 1907), p. MS2.

11 Chang Woo Gow, *The Autobiography of Chang, the Tall Man of Fychow* (London, 1866), pp. 13, 17, 18.

12 'Prodigies in Conference', *New York Times* (13 April 1903), p. 6; 'Human Prodigies Society', *New York Times* (28 January 1907), p. 4.

13 Nadja Burbach, *Spectacles of Deformity: Freak Shows and Modern British Culture* (Berkeley, CA, 2010), p. 17.

14 Route Book, Billy Rose Performing Arts Library, New York Public Library.

15 'The Circus Freak Seen Off Guard as a Human Being', *New York Times* (6 April 1913), p. SM11.

16 Clifton Crais and Pamela Scully, *Sara Baartman and the Hottentot Venus: A Ghost Story and a Biography* (Princeton, NJ, 2009), p. 50.

17 *The Times*, London (26 November 1810), p. 3.

18 George Sanger, *Seventy Years a Showman* (New York, 1926), pp. 195–6.

19 Circular letter from P. T. Barnum, 9 August 1882, in *Selected Letters of P. T. Barnum*, ed. A. H. Saxon (New York, 1983).

20 Eric Ames, *Carl Hagenbeck's Empire of Entertainments* (Seattle, WA, 2009), pp. 70–71.

21 Ibid., pp. 95, 97.

22 Robert Lewis Taylor, *Center Ring: The People of the Circus* (New York, 1956), pp. 98–9.

23 Ibid., pp. 100–192; *Washington Post* (31 May 1933), p. 3.

24 Gerber, 'The "Careers" of People', p. 4.

25 *The Nation* (11 March 1931), p. 271.

26 Edward Hoagland, 'Circus Music', *Sex and the River Styx* (White River Junction, VT, 2011), p. 78.

27 Donald Platt, 'Congress of Freaks with Ringling Brothers and Barnum & Bailey (Combined) Circus, Season – 1929', *Southern Review*, XL/3 (Summer 2004), pp. 470–74.

28 Thomson, ed. 'Introduction', in *Freakery*, pp. 12, 11.

TEN

TRANSFORMATIONS

1 Interview with author, 2 May 2013, Berkeley, California.

2 Quoted in Ernest Albrecht, *The New American Circus* (Gainesville, FL, 1995), p. 225.

3 Quoted in Terry Lorant and Jon Carroll, *The Pickle Family Circus* (San Francisco, 1986), p. 122.

4 Quoted ibid., p. 132.

5 Quoted ibid., p. 72.

6 Interview with author, 14 February 2013, Berkeley, California.

7 Albrecht, *The New American Circus*, p. 43.

8 Quoted in John Culhane, *The American Circus* (New York, 1990), p. 376.

9 Mel Gussow, 'Minimalist Circus Loaded with Maximum Punch', *New York Times* (5 June 1988), p. H5.

10 See websites for these new circuses: www.royal-de-luxe.com; www.cirque-baroque.com; www.cirqueplume.com.

11 Bartabas quoted in John Rockwell, 'France's Summer Hit is a Circus. Sort of.', *New York Times* (8 August 1994), p. C9.

12 Mel Gussow, 'Cirque Imaginaire', *New York Times* (20 November 1986), p. C25.

13 Jennifer Dunning, 'Serene Simplicity and Fleeting Magic of the Small Circus', *New York Times* (28 November 1986), p. C1.

SELECT BIBLIOGRAPHY

Adams, Bluford, *E Pluribus Barnum: The Great Showman and the Making of U.S. Popular Culture* (Minneapolis, 1997)

Adams, Rachel, *Sideshow USA: Freaks and the American Cultural Imagination* (Chicago, IL, 2001)

Anteleker, Kristopher, *Ringmaster!* (New York, 1989)

Assael, Brenda, *The Circus and Victorian Society* (Charlottesville, VA, 2005)

Beatty, Clyde, and Edward Anthony, *Facing the Big Cats* (New York, 1964)

Bogdon, Robert, *Freak Show: Presenting Human Oddities for Amusement and Profit* (Chicago, IL, 1988)

Bouissac, Paul, *Circus and Culture: A Semiotic Approach* (Bloomington, IN, 1976)

Bratton, Jacky, and Ann Featherstone, *The Victorian Clown* (Cambridge, 2006)

Chindahl, George L., *A History of the Circus in America* (Caldwell, ID, 1959)

Circopedia, The Free Encyclopedia of the International Circus, www.circopedia.org

Circus Historical Society, www.circushistory.org

Clair, Jean, ed., *The Great Parade: Portrait of the Artist as Clown* (New Haven, CT, 2004)

Cook, James W., ed., *The Colossal P. T. Barnum Reader* (Urbana, IL, 2005)

Coxe, Antony Hippisley, *A Seat at the Circus* [1951] (Hamden, CT, 1980)

Croft-Cooke, Rupert, and Peter Cotes, *Circus: A World History* (New York, 1975)

Culhane, John, *The American Circus* (New York, 1990)

Daniel, Noel, Dominique Jando et al., *The Circus: 1870–1950* (London, 2008)

Davis, Janet M., *The Circus Age: Culture and Society Under the Big Top* (Charlotte, NC, 2002)

Disher, Maurice. *Fairs, Circuses and Music Halls* (London, 1942)

Durbach, Nadja, *Spectacle of Deformity: Freak Shows and Modern British Culture* (Berkeley, CA, 2010)

Earenfight, Phillip, ed., *Picasso and the Circus* (Carlisle, PA, 2011)

Eckley, Wilton, *The American Circus* (Boston, MA, 1984)

Feiler, Bruce, *Under the Big Top: A Season with the Circus* (New York, 2003)

Fenner, Mildred S., and Wolcott Fenner, eds, *The Circus: Lure and Legend* (Englewood Cliffs, NJ, 1970)

Gustafson, Donna, ed., *Images from the World Between: The Circus in 20th Century America* (Cambridge, MA, 2007)

Halttunen, Karen, *Confidence Men and Painted Women: A Study of Middle-class Culture in America, 1830–1870* (New Haven, CT, 1982)

Hammarstrom, David Lewis, *Behind the Big Top* (South Brunswick, NJ, 1980)

Harper, Paula, *Daumier's Clowns, les saltimbanques, et les parades* (New York, 1981)

Harris, Neil, *Humbug: The Art of P. T. Barnum* (Chicago, IL, 1973)

Hartzman, Marc, *American Sideshow* (New York, 2006)

Jando, Dominique, *The Circus Book, 1870–1950* (London, 2010)

Jensen, Dean, ed., *Center Ring: The Artist, Two Centuries of Circus Art* (Milwaukee, WI, 1981)

Jones, Louisa E., *Sad Clowns and Pale Pierrots: Literature and the Popular Comic Arts in Nineteenth-century France* (Lexington, KY, 1984)

Joys, Joanne, *The Wild Animal Trainer in America* (Boulder, CO, 1983)

Keen, Sam, *Learning to Fly: Trapeze* (New York, 1999)

Kelly, Emmett, *Clown* (Englewood Cliffs, NJ, 1954)

Kline, Tiny, *Circus Queen and Tinker Bell: The Memoir of Tiny Kline* (Champaign, IL, 2008)

Knaebel, Nathaniel, ed., *Step Right Up: Stories of Carnivals, Sideshows, and the Circus* (New York, 2004)

Lax, Robert, *Circus Days and Nights* (Woodstock, NY, 2000)

Lewis, Robert, ed., *From Traveling Show to Vaudeville: Theatrical Spectacle in America, 1830–1910* (Baltimore, MD, 2003)

Lipman, Jean, ed., *Calder's Circus* (New York, 1972)

Lorant, Terry, and Jon Carroll, *The Pickle Family Circus* (San Francisco, 1986)

Manning-Sanders, Ruth, *The English Circus* (London, 1952)

May, Earl Chapin, *The Circus from Rome to Ringling* [1932] (New York, 1963)

Murray, Marian, *Circus from Rome to Ringling* (New York, 1956)

North, Henry Ringling, and Alden Hatch, *The Circus Kings* (Garden City, NY, 1960)

Ogden, Tom, *Two Hundred Years of the American Circus* (New York, 1993)

Rearick, Charles, *Pleasures of the Belle-epoque: Entertainment and Festivity in Turn-of-the-century France* (New Haven, CT, 1985)

Richards, Kenneth, and Lara Richards, *The Commedia dell'Arte* (Oxford, 1990)

Ritter, Naomi, *Art as Spectacle: Images of the Entertainer since Romanticism* (Columbia, MO, 1989)

Saxon, A. H., *Enter Foot and Horse: A History of the Hippodrama in England and France* (New Haven, CT, 1968)

——, *The Life and Art of Andrew Ducrow and the Romantic Age of the English Circus* (Hamden, CT, 1978)

——, ed., *Selected Letters of P. T. Barnum* (New York, 1983)

Shapiro, Barbara Stern, *Pleasures of Paris: Daumier to Picasso* (Boston, MA, 1991)

Smith, Sharon L. and Stephen J. Fletcher, *Life in a Three-ring Circus: Posters and Interviews* (Indianapolis, IN 2001)

Speaight, George, *A History of the Circus* (London, 1980)

Stoddart, Helen, *Rings of Desire* (Manchester, 2001)

Tait, Peta, *Circus Bodies: Cultural Identity in Aerial Performance* (London, 2005)

——, *Wild and Dangerous Performances: Animals, Emotions, Circus* (London, 2012)

Taylor, Robert Lewis, *Center Ring: The People of the Circus* (Garden City, NY, 1956)

Thomson, Rosemarie Garland, *Freakery: Cultural Spectacles of the Extraordinary Body* (New York, 1996)

Towsen, John H., *Clowns* (New York, 1976)

Wall, Duncan, *The Ordinary Acrobat* (New York, 2013)

Weber, Susan, Kenneth Ames and Matthew Wittmann, eds, *The American Circus* (New Haven, CT, 2012)

Wilkins, Charles, *Circus at the Edge of the Earth: Travels with the Great Wallenda Circus* (Toronto, 1998)

ACKNOWLEDGEMENTS

Thanks to my editor Vivian Constantinopoulos and her colleagues at Reaktion Books for their interest and support. I am grateful to the performers and circus directors who took time to talk with me: Randall Booker, who grew up in his father's California circus; Shana Carroll, Founding Member and Artistic Director, Les 7 doigts de la main; acrobat and literary scholar Ralph Ciancio; Tim Cunningham, of Clowns Without Borders; Mike Finch, Artistic Director of Circus Oz; and the incomparable gadfly, social activist and clown Wavy Gravy. I appreciate the generosity of the San Francisco School for Circus Arts for allowing me to sit in on a trapeze class. Skidmore College supported my research with a Faculty Development Grant; Scribner Library Interlibrary Loan Supervisor Amy Syrell provided instant gratification for my many requests. I am extraordinarily grateful to my perceptive and patient readers Susannah Mintz and Mason Stokes. Thilo Ullmann read every chapter with enthusiasm that kept my spirits high; to Thilo, my son Aaron, and daughter-in-law Alison I offer this book.

PHOTO ACKNOWLEDGEMENTS

The author and publishers wish to express their thanks to the below sources of illustrative material and/or permission to reproduce it.

Big Apple Circus: pp. 256, 257, 258; Cirque Invisible: pp. 268, 269; Cirque Plume: pp. 262, 263, 264, 265; Hans van Dijk/Anefo: p. 197; Freekee: p. 119; Hannes Grobe: p. 193; James G. Howes 1992: p. 83; Les 7 doigts de la main: pp. 248, 252; Library of Congress, Washington, DC: pp. 17, 21, 24, 25, 34, 37, 42, 43, 44, 46, 49, 60, 68, 72, 82, 84, 88, 89, 90, 92, 93, 95, 100, 104, 105, 106, 107, 109, 110, 118, 120, 129, 130, 131, 133, 134, 135, 136, 139, 150, 154, 155, 156, 160, 163, 164, 168, 169, 170, 174, 175, 178, 203, 205, 208, 209, 211, 212, 214, 217, 218, 219, 220, 221, 228, 230, 231 bottom, 233, 234, 240; © Succession Picasso/DACS, London 2014: p. 58; Victoria & Albert Museum, London: pp. 30, 182, 183; Yale Center for British Art, New Haven, CT: p. 158; Zingaro: pp. 266, 267.

INDEX